NIAGARA COLLEGE

LEARNING RESOURCE CENTRE

Glendale Campus

OVERDUE CHARGES
$.25 PER DAY

APR 1 7 2008	

Praise for *The Special Events Advisor*

The special events industry attracts creative geniuses, but they can benefit immensely from this guide to running a profitable business. When put to use, the collection of sample forms alone will make up for the cost of the book!

—Robert Sivek, CSEP, CERP,
The Meetinghouse Companies, Inc.

Finally—an event industry book that's all business! David Sorin has masterfully addressed all the tough issues an event professional faces. Even after nearly twenty years of owning a business, I learned something new in every chapter. This is a must-read for anyone who understands that the special event industry is serious business.

—Mary Tribble, CSEP President,
Tribble Creative Group

I L-O-V-E THIS BOOK! It is fresh . . . it is real . . . AND, having been in this industry 15 years, it is just the jolt I needed to renew my energy and enthusiasm! I only wish I'd had this resource when I started my business. Well done, David Sorin!

—Chris Buerger, CEO of CEO, Inc.
(Corporate Event Organization, Inc.)

David's experience shines through this comprehensive and well-written work! After all my years in the business, I still need this Advisor at my desk to support my success and help me navigate the issues of the challenging event business. A must-read for every planner!

—Betsy Wiersma, CSEP,
Wiersma Experience Marketing

THE
SPECIAL EVENTS ADVISOR

THE BUSINESS AND LEGAL GUIDE FOR EVENT PROFESSIONALS

DAVID SORIN, J.D., C.S.E.P.

WILEY

John Wiley & Sons, Inc.

Contents

THE
SPECIAL EVENTS ADVISOR

Introduction

Experience is the hardest kind of teacher. It gives you the
test first and the lesson afterward. —Anonymous

Sometimes, the seat with the best view is not in the first row. After being in the events industry as a business owner for 16 years, this is abundantly clear. We all tend to think that nobody knows our business like we do, and therefore there is no good reason to take advice from people who in our opinion must know less. We mistakenly believe that our view from the trenches provides us with the most and the best information.

The special events industry is all about fun and excitement, creativity and rising to the challenge. It is about meeting crazy deadlines and impossible budgets and coming up with breathtaking results that the clients love and that give the providers satisfaction and compensation. The industry attracts people who have flair and ideas and artistic and technical abilities, people who love to use their talents on event after event. The last thing these creators want to be worried about is legal boilerplate, insurance and financial statements, the stuff out of which nightmares are made. They want to create, be applauded, get paid, and do it all again. And sometimes they want to be owners.

It is common knowledge that being a great floral decorator isn't the same thing as being a great owner of a floral decorating company. Being a wonderful, creative chef is not sufficient qualification to manage the variety of personalities and functions required in a top-notch catering company.

Yet many companies in special events are started, managed, and grown by individuals who exhibit a talent learned or enhanced working elsewhere who decide to go out on their own. There is nothing wrong with this in theory—it is the American way. But these talents need to recognize that there is much about running a business that they do not know. Some have the inherent common sense and business sense to fill out their company's knowledge and experience base by bringing others into the company. Others, unfortunately, do not. Accordingly, many companies have business problems that the owners do not even know about yet—and may not know about until it is too late.

As the artist becomes more and more successful, the unthinkable begins to happen: An organization forms around him or her—

employees, a warehouse, big insurance policies, trucks, shipping and receiving, and all manner of bureaucratic and administrative apparatus. Soon, the visionary is knee-deep in details never previously thought about, requiring decisions that do not depend on creativity but rather on business sense, with some legal, accounting, or logical basis. Each area of a business adds innumerable situations for the owner to review, and if the right knowledge base is not present, and it usually isn't, the situations become problems.

One of the theoretical benefits of being an owner is the right to choose how you wish to spend your time within the business. Most prefer to spend time doing what they like to do the most. Typically, this coincides with what they do best. Unfortunately, this can lead an owner to delegate many key business tasks to others. If these others are well intended but not well suited to handling the situations, it creates a void in the management of key business issues.

As Michael Gerber puts it in the Foreword to his fabulously successful book, *The E Myth*, "Despite common belief, the people who succeed in business don't do so because of what they know, *but because of their insatiable need to know more.* Conversely, the problem with most failing businesses is that . . . *they (the owners) think they know enough.* And so they spend time defending what they know, rather than discovering what they don't."

I came into the special events industry after having been a practicing lawyer for a number of years as well as a business owner. In my practice, I advised many young start-up companies and individuals buying businesses. It is easy to do as an outsider. It is amazing how different the playing field looks when the viewer is not emotionally wrapped up in the view. It was amazing for me to see how quickly passion and emotion can cloud the objectivity when the objective outsider becomes the excited insider.

We learn lessons every day. They don't *all* have to be learned the hard way. Many of the lessons I learned came at great expense, even though I relied quite a bit on my lawyer, my accountant, and, in many situations, outside consultants.

I wish I'd had a volume like this when I was a company owner. I would have avoided some big traps. Hopefully, this book can serve that purpose for you, helping you learn some of the things you don't know or, for that matter, don't even know you need to know. This book is not intended to take the place of lawyers or accountants or consultants of any kind. It is intended to help special event business owners and managers have smoother sailing, to help create a bit of order out of their chaotic world. It is intended to point you in the right direction when you are grappling with issues and to open your eyes to issues of which you may not be aware.

I hope it works for you. You don't need to read it cover to cover to derive benefit from it. Certain chapters will have relevance to your particular business, while others may not. Different information will be of use to you at different times in your company's growth process. Some of it should be applicable on an ongoing basis.

Information in some chapters could just as easily be raised in others. It is separated into topics to make it more easily digestible. This book raises issues, points out pitfalls, and may offer potential solutions. However, the ultimate solution for your company will be based on the facts of your situation, on the good work of your management, and perhaps on your outside professional advisors. The event world could be viewed as one big, chaotic mélange of creative people who are creating, but looking deeper it is clearly a group of businesses performing their functions together for the greater good. In order for these companies to be able to create for years and years to come, they must act like businesses, deal with business issues, and behave professionally and responsibly. This volume will not help anyone arrange flowers better or create more exciting menus. But it should be able to assist the owners and managers of companies that can perform those functions to run their businesses in a smarter and more informed manner.

Planners should want their suppliers to survive and flourish, and vice versa. In order for that to happen, they have to educate each other, understand each other's businesses, and understand and interact with the larger event world, the business world, and the world at large. Professional companies have insurance, get business licenses, pay taxes, put employees on payroll rather than trying to pass them off as independent contractors, and generally function as real businesses. The industry should support companies that function in that manner and try to educate those that don't. The more professional each individual company acts, the more professional the industry as a whole becomes.

The appendix contains a number of forms that are provided as examples of documents mentioned in the text. Feel free to copy these forms in whole or in part. Certain clauses may have to be adjusted for use in your state or province. They have not been researched to determine the enforceability of every clause of every agreement in every state in the United States and every province in Canada. But again, the forms are generic, included here to give you ideas on how matters can be handled. There is never only one way to solve a problem, and once you see how to arrive at a conclusion or a solution, you may come up with some creative answers that will work well for you.

The special events industry is viewed by those outside the profession as exciting and fun. People often express jealousy that event folk have so much fun at what they do. It is fun, but special events companies are still businesses that must be run *as businesses* to succeed. Business and fun can go together, and in striving to reach that ideal life, finding a profession that is enjoyable, challenging, and fulfilling does make special events professionals very lucky people. They are luckier still if they have the talent or hire the talent to help them find business solutions to potential problems. Addressing the issues presented herein before they become problems will help keep the fun in the business.

Chapter

1

Starting an Event Business

*Small opportunities are often the beginning of
great enterprise. —Demosthenes*

So, you have decided to make the leap from talented amateur to full-time professional events person. For years, everybody has said you throw the best parties, and now you want to do it for a living. Friends have promised that their companies will give you all of their events. You have events on the books before you have books. Where do you begin? How do you start a business?

First and foremost, you must decide on the form of the business. Realistically, the options have narrowed somewhat over the years. Whereas in the past, sole proprietorships and partnerships were somewhat popular, mostly due to the fact that there were no separate corporate and individual taxes, just individual, today they are fairly rare. The big reason for this is that both leave the owner(s) open to personal liability. This means that any debts of the business become debts of the owners personally, and any liabilities of the business can become personal liabilities.

■ CORPORATIONS

Most businesses are corporations. A corporation is a legal business entity established under the corporate laws of the state in which it is formed. It is formed for a particular business purpose and is governed by rules called *bylaws*. The corporation is a legal entity separate from the individual shareholders. It keeps its own books and records and finances separate from those of the individual shareholders. Its big advantage is that a shareholder's liability is limited to the amount invested in the business itself. A corporation is normally formed by filing Articles of Incorporation or a similarly titled document with the state. Therein, the corporation will have a fictitious name, and a document registering that name is also usually filed.

Thereafter, a form must be filed with the Internal Revenue Service to obtain an Employer Identification Number. This will be the number under which all tax filings and returns will be submitted to the IRS. Once the EIN is in hand, the business can open its bank accounts and begin its business activities.

➤ C Corporation

The C corporation is the most common form of business. A C corporation is one in which taxes are paid pursuant to Subchapter C of the Internal Revenue Code. As a taxpaying entity, the C corporation is required to pay federal taxes on its taxable income at the corporate level prior to making any distributions to shareholders. Many states also have a state tax on corporate income for which the corporation is responsible. Distributions to shareholders are taxed again.

C corporations are allowed to issue more than one type of stock (*common* and *preferred*) with different voting rights and dividend rights. There is no limit on the number of shareholders.

Certain legal formalities are required of the corporation, such as holding annual board meetings and annual shareholder meetings and keeping books and records according to state corporate law. Separate corporate bank accounts should be maintained. Likewise, federal and state tax returns must be filed.

As long as the required corporate steps are followed and corporate assets are kept separate and not commingled with personal assets (i.e., the corporation is not just a device or alter ego of the shareholders), corporate shareholders are protected by the *corporate veil*. The veil is a concept that separates the corporation as a legal entity from the individual shareholders. If the corporation is sued for any reason, the individual shareholders should be protected from any personal liability for the actions or omissions of the company. Liability is limited to each shareholder's capital investment in the corporation.

Because shareholders do not directly pay taxes on undistributed corporate profits, they do not need an additional dividend to cover the tax. Therefore, additional capital can be left in the business for expansion.

Susan has started an event planning business and has set it up as a C corporation. In her first year, the company loses $15,000. The loss stays in the company, and none of it is attributable to Susan's personal tax situation. The next year her company earns $25,000 in profit. She keeps it in the company to cover the cost of a bigger office space, and the company pays corporate tax on the profit. This has no impact on Susan's personal income.

➤ S Corporation

An S corporation requires the filing of a Subchapter S election with the IRS. By so filing, S corporations elect to be taxed under Subchapter S of the Internal Revenue Code. S corporations have limitations regarding number of shareholders and business purpose, but they are popular because all income passes through to the shareholders and there is no separate federal corporation tax. In the earliest stages of the business (and sometimes later on, although hopefully not) they have the additional advantage of allowing all losses to pass through to the shareholders. That may not hold true for state taxes, though.

Say Tom opens a party rental business, which he sets up as a Subchapter S corporation. In the first year of business, the company loses $75,000. Tom is able to apply the loss against any personal income he may have, thus lowering his personal tax liability (federal). In year 2, Tom's company makes $75,000, which Tom wants to leave in the business to purchase new tables and chairs. Under Subchapter S, he has to personally pay taxes on the $75,000, even if it is not distributed to him. This can be personally burdensome, and therefore the company can distribute the amount of the tax to him as a dividend to cover his tax liability.

Tom should now determine whether he wants to maintain the Subchapter S status. If his company is making money every year but needs to keep that profit in the company to grow the business, he will need to take a dividend every year to pay tax on the income attributed to him that he doesn't receive. He may want to speak with his accountant about dropping the S election and becoming a C corporation.

Just like a C corporation, an S corporation has a distinct legal identity, and all records must be kept separate and apart from those of the shareholders. All other corporate formalities must be followed to maintain the corporate shield from personal liability. Even if followed carefully, the possibility of personal liability exists if financial institutions require personal guarantees for financing. In such cases, any shareholders giving the guarantee are personally liable to the financial institution only.

➤ Limited Liability Company (LLC)

The most recent business form to gain approval under federal and state law is the limited liability company. It is a totally new form—not corporation, not sole proprietorship, not partnership. The owners are called *members,* not shareholders. It is now authorized in all 50 states and by the Internal Revenue Service. An LLC is created by filing a form with the appropriate department within state government.

LLCs are gaining popularity because they combine some of the best advantages of corporations and sole proprietorships and the benefits of a Subchapter S corporation, but without some of the restrictions. (See Table 1.1.) They offer the limited liability protection of a corporation, meaning the owners are not personally responsible for the debts and liabilities of the business. They are also pass-through tax entities, meaning that their income or losses pass through to the owners.

The philosophy behind the LLC is that the members should be free to *contract,* to agree among themselves, how the company is to be managed and to have that agreement stand up in court. This business form also offers substantially less red tape. Corporations require meetings of the board, meetings of the shareholders, corporate resolutions, corporate minutes, and other record keeping. LLCs have no such requirements. The operating agreement can contain any procedures and rules that the parties desire. The LLC offers simplicity of operation and very little ongoing maintenance.

At the same time, an LLC can have an unlimited number of owners, as opposed to the restrictions on a Subchapter S corporation. It can be owned by foreigners or by C corporations, other S corporations, many trusts, partnerships, or another LLC.

Decisions about the form of the business should be based on discussions with both an attorney and a certified public accountant. While many attorneys do have some tax knowledge, they do not always view matters from the same perspective as an accountant. Further, the accountant may have a better sense of personal financial considerations.

An individual starting a business will probably want the attorney to draft the necessary paperwork, just to make certain that all filings are taken care of according to law. Attorneys will often maintain the company books and records, making certain that all legal requirements are met year in and year out. Shareholder and board meeting minutes, corporate resolutions, and other important documents need to be created and regularly updated. Many companies can handle this on their own if they so choose. One way or the other, the records must be kept current.

Once the company form is determined, the accountant needs to be involved to set up the company's books and to set up the requisite accounts with the taxing authorities. Both the Internal Revenue Service and the state government require that filings be made, some quarterly and some annually.

Table 1.1 Comparison of Entities

Characteristics	Sole Proprietorship Partnership	Limited Liability Company	S Corporation	C Corporation
Formation	Agreement of parties involved	File with state for permission	File with state for permission	File with state for permission
Duration	Dissolved by death or bankruptcy	Typically limited to a fixed amount of time	Perpetual	Perpetual
Liability	Unlimited liability	No liability for members	Limited to capital invested in the corporation	Limited to capital invested in the corporation
Number of owners	1, 2 or more	1 or more	1 to 75	1 or more
Simplicity of operation	Few requirements	Relatively few formal requirements	Many formalities of record keeping and filing	Many formalities of record keeping and filing
Restrictions on ownership	None	None	Several	None
Management	Typically, each partner has equal voice	Members have operating agreement outlining management	Management by board of directors appointed by shareholders	Management by board of directors appointed by shareholders
Taxation	Each partner shares income or loss on his or her percentage ownership	Should be no tax at entity level—income or loss passed through to members	No tax at entity level—income and loss passed through to shareholders	Corporation is a taxable entity
Double taxation	No	No	No	Yes
Pass through income/loss	Yes	Yes	Yes	No

The outside professionals can train internal personnel to perform many of the necessary tasks, which will minimize the expense of legal and accounting hours. However, the professionals should be kept involved in the life of the company, reviewing its status periodically to make sure all is well. Further, over time, conditions change and the outside professionals can make recommendations to alter the structure based on those changes. A subchapter S election may be dropped, or a line of business may be organized into a separate entity.

So, while setting the company up is important, it is not necessarily final. It is important to remember that a company is a living, breathing entity, one that may change many times and in many ways over the course of its existence. Change can be good and healthy for the organization. Although many naturally resist change, it should be welcomed as progress.

■ SUMMARY

➤ Business forms vary, so careful thought should go into the choice.

➤ The key issues are legal liability and tax liability.

➤ Corporations (both S and C) and LLCs are the best combinations.

➤ You don't need a lawyer to file the papers, but legal and accounting advice in choosing a business form are important. Don't be penny-wise and pound-foolish. Doing it right from the beginning will save time and money.

➤ Once formed, the company needs to be maintained—books and records and yearly filings need to be kept up.

Chapter 2

Buying an Event Business

*Confidence is what you feel before you comprehend
the situation. —Proverb*

Another way to get into the events industry besides starting a company is to buy an existing business. Event companies are bought and sold all the time. Sometimes, employees of a company find a way to buy the company and retire the boss; other times, it is purchased by outsiders.

The decision to buy a business as opposed to starting one can make a lot of sense. In a relatively mature marketplace, there may not be any demand or room for an additional company within a given niche. Thus, starting a new business may make no sense and may end up being a losing proposition. Likewise, finding the talent to stock a new business may be difficult, whereas buying a company with good employees avoids such a situation. Further, individuals getting into the events business without any experience could be much better off purchasing a company with a proven track record than trying to start one from scratch without really knowing what they're doing and what it will take to be a success.

The steps in purchasing an existing business should be the same whether the purchaser is an insider or an outsider. An insider may already have a lot of knowledge about the business, but should still use due diligence in making a decision to purchase. Insiders may have an advantage in that the process has been ongoing, that they've worked with the owner on his or her exit strategy, and that clients have become accustomed to dealing with the new ownership prior to the transfer.

For instance, Sarah is a salesperson for the XYZ Limousine Company owned by Betty. Betty wants to retire by the time she is 55. Sarah is ambitious and has expressed interest in being an owner. Sarah and Betty begin talking about Sarah buying the company at some point in the future, and when Betty reaches her fifty-second birthday, the two of them come up with a plan to transfer ownership when Betty hits 55. Betty promotes Sarah to senior vice president of the company, overseeing not just sales but finance and administration, too. Sarah already knows most of the clients, but she makes sure to meet the others, as well as getting to know the vendors, the subcontractors, and the workings of the whole business. When she takes over in three years, she will know all aspects of the business and be known by almost everyone with whom the company deals.

If inside purchasers are given access to the company's finances, they can also work with their advisors to come up with a reasonable way to finance the purchase. Maybe they can get the owner to take a note agreeing to be paid out of cash flow. They may be aware of the hidden strengths and weaknesses of the business, which can be used advantageously to strike a deal with the owner. Existing owners would probably feel more comfortable backing someone they know well as an employee.

■ DUE DILIGENCE

Typically, a prospective purchaser will hear of a business being for sale through the grapevine or from contact with lawyers, accountants, or business brokers. The Internet has also become a factor, with interested parties learning about companies for sale through a variety of web sites. If a company is represented by a broker or investment banker, a marketing package is normally put together to describe the business and provide pertinent data on it.

What does a prospective purchaser need to know before buying a business? First and foremost, buyers must have a clear idea of what they are looking to accomplish. Special events is a diverse profession. Wanting to get into the industry is not a clear enough vision. A desire to be involved with lighting or catering, floral decor or trade show management, for instance, narrows it down somewhat.

Some buyers have expertise or a knowledge base in one of the event disciplines, and that gives them a leg up. Others may be entering the industry blind, but may have vast business experience, and reading a company's marketing package may cause them to see things that excite them, steps that have not been taken that could be, ways to make money that have not been explored, or ways to cut expenses to improve the bottom line. Thus it can be said that there is more than one way to approach entry into the events industry.

Whatever the approach, it is important to get as much information as possible on (1) the company's mission; (2) the services provided by the company; (3) the potential market for those services; (4) the competition; (5) the client base and their satisfaction level with the company; (6) the marketing plan; (7) the sales plan; (8) the quantity and quality of the employees and the role each plays in helping the company achieve its goals; (9) the satisfaction level of the employees (are they happy or are they one bad day away from walking out?); (10) the skill level of the company relative to its competition; (11) the reputation of the company within the marketplace; (12) the pay scale and benefits of the company relative to others in the marketplace; (13) what the owner's leaving will mean to employees and to clients; (14) the financial condition of the company; (15) the quantity and quality of the inventory and equipment; (16) the age of the inventory and equipment; (17) existing contractual obligations of the company, such as employment contracts, union contracts, real estate leases, equipment leases, truck leases, bank loans, and prepaid obligations to clients for services; (18) intellectual property of the company, including copyrights, trademarks, patents, and licenses; (19) pending litigation and claims; (20) insurance coverage of all types; (21) necessary licenses and permits; and (22) software licenses.

Current and historical financial statements are critical. A prospective purchaser should review them carefully with an accountant to get a sense of profitability, cash flow, and current financial condition. Are accounts current with vendors? Are receivables being collected in a timely fashion, or are some so old that they're uncollectible? A review of a few years' worth of statements will help determine whether the company is in a growth mode, stagnant, or in decline.

Ideally, prospective purchasers can come in and openly examine whatever they want and speak to all of the employees. If the owner does not want the employees to know that the business is for sale, purchasers are put in an uncomfortable and perhaps untenable situation. If they respect the wishes of the seller, they may be unable to obtain the information needed to make a decision about buying the company.

Another situation that may arise is that owners of competing companies in the marketplace may wish to look into the purchase of the company for sale. Sellers may feel squeamish about letting competitors inside their business. They need to determine whether competitors are just using a ploy to find out all they can or whether they are serious buyers. At the very least, sellers should require competitors to sign a confidentiality agreement to not discuss or use the information derived from their due diligence in any way deleterious to the company. Sellers can also demand to see competitors' books to determine whether in fact they are in a financial position to buy or to finance the purchase of the business. Competitors who fight this too strongly may just be window-shopping.

A competing or complementary company may actually be an ideal purchaser. If a lighting company wishes to get into audio or video to broaden its services to its existing clients and to attract new clients, buying an audio or video company could be the best way to do it. If this is a purchaser's motivation, there are other items that should be looked into as part of due diligence. The most obvious is the cost savings that could be effected by moving two businesses into one warehouse and by consolidating workforces, if not totally, at least partially. Marketing expense can be consolidated, as can sales forces.

After due diligence is completed, prospective purchasers should have a good understanding of the business and a good sense of whether they want to move forward and structure a transaction. Here are some examples of what due diligence can uncover:

➤ The current owner is integral to the business and needs to stay on for at least one year to help make the transition.

➤ The workforce is underpaid and at the point of rebellion. The raises they require will make the business unprofitable.

➤ The business is marginally profitable but has never been marketed; with proper marketing it has a great chance to be a huge success.

➤ The business is overstaffed and there is overspending. Expense cuts will add a substantial amount to the bottom line.

➤ The company's trucks are old and falling apart and will need to be replaced. This could kill the transaction.

Perhaps the biggest issues to take a hard look at revolve around ownership: What will the exit of the old owner mean to the present clients and future prospects of the business? What will the entrance of the new owner mean to the company's old clients? Sellers may have developed a personal following based on a flamboyant style or great public relations. Either their personalities or unique talents are the reason why the clients come to the company in droves. Even if they have built a strong supporting staff that actually produces much of the fine work of the company, if sellers have marketed themselves rather than the company, their departure could cause clients to look for the next superstar. Purchasers must make this determination before plunking down good money. They may need to structure a deal that calls for the seller to stay on for a year, assisting in the transition, familiarizing clients with the talented staff, and depersonalizing the public relations.

Likewise, if the purchaser is already in the industry, he or she has to be concerned that some of the company's old clients will be turned off by the purchase and take their business elsewhere. For instance, suppose a caterer decided to buy a linen company. The linen company's client base was 60 percent caterers. How would they feel about putting dollars into the pocket of a competitor by renting linens from it? What happens to the linen company if all of the caterers find a new vendor? Is the purchase still worthwhile?

Another example is a company looking to buy a similar business in another geographic area. Would the new company's style, pricing, or quality of service be a shock to the old clients? Would it cause them to leave, forcing the new owner to build a whole new client base?

All sorts of insights can be gained and conclusions drawn from the due diligence. Two prospective purchasers could look at the same information and draw totally different conclusions based on their mind-sets (glass half full or half empty?), their situations, and their goals. A transaction that might be a loser for one would be an outright winner for another. This points out that there is no hard-and-fast formula that will provide a definitive answer to the question of whether a transaction should be done.

Some additional, less general areas of due diligence may apply to specific situations. One is looking into environmental concerns ranging from asbestos to radon, from hazardous waste disposal to soil contamination. Another involves looking into ERISA issues and other pension and profit-sharing plan questions. If other regulatory agencies come into play in a given business, it is important to know the status of the company with them. For instance, laser and pyrotechnic companies are subject to federal regulation for safety reasons. If manufacturing of a product is involved, have product liability issues been addressed? Are there plant-closing laws that need to be reviewed if that might be part of the plan? Are there antitrust implications?

■ ASSET OR STOCK PURCHASE

Once due diligence has been completed and a decision to move forward has been made, the purchaser has to decide how to structure the purchase offer. The biggest decision is whether it will be an asset or a stock purchase.

Simply put, an asset purchase involves purchasing the assets of the business only, not the liabilities and not the stock. Any payables or debts of the company will stay with the seller. All of this is set forth very carefully and very explicitly in the purchase agreement. State law varies on how asset purchases are construed by the courts. While they may be generally accepted, there can be exceptions to the rule, and the purchaser must be aware of the exceptions and how they might affect the transaction at hand.

Exceptions include situations where the purchaser expressly agrees (or implies) to assume the obligations of the seller; situations where the purchasing entity is merely a continuation of the selling entity; situations where the transaction is fraudulently entered into in order to escape liability; or the transfer is without legally adequate consideration and without adequate provision for the creditors. There may be other exceptions that exist under the law of individual states, and they should be explored and understood before an asset purchase is structured. If an asset purchase falls within one of the exceptions, the purchasing company can find itself in a very uncomfortable situation of being held liable for the debts of the seller, the seller's negligent acts, or even criminal charges based on the acts of the seller.

In an asset purchase, the purchasing company should clearly differentiate itself from the seller. This probably means that the purchaser will be changing the name of the business, as the old corporate name will remain with the seller, who maintains ownership of the corporation. It definitely means that the purchaser will have to either move the assets to a new location or negotiate a new lease with the seller's landlord. The purchaser will want to make it clear to the vendors and clients of the seller that this is a new business. The purchaser would also be wise to have the asset purchase agreement cover the payment of the vendors and the old company's liabilities so that the new company won't be negatively impacted. In some transactions, the sale price of the assets will not cover the liabilities of the seller, leaving the purchaser in a situation where vendors may harbor residual bad feelings.

Liabilities the purchaser is assuming, if any, should be clearly spelled out in the agreement (e.g., payroll liabilities, tax liabilities, contractual liabilities). The agreement should also unequivocally state that the seller will remain legally responsible for discharging any liabilities and contractual obligations not specifically assumed by the purchaser.

In a stock purchase, the purchaser buys the company, lock, stock, and barrel. The seller walks away without any further obligations or responsibilities, knowing that the purchaser has taken over all aspects of the business. The purchaser is entitled to full disclosure of all corporate liabilities that are known to the seller, and the seller should be required to give covenants warranting that it has disclosed all liabilities.

A variety of state and federal laws may come into play in the sale and purchase of a business. Both sides should be represented by competent counsel familiar with the law in this area. Both parties should be fully apprised of their postclosing obligations.

If a purchaser already owns a company and desires to merge the purchased company into its existing business, other issues may come into play. Again, both counsel and an accountant should be consulted, as there are issues of liability and tax consequences to consider.

If not treated as a merger, the purchaser may decide to treat the new purchase as a separate company or as a wholly owned subsidiary of its existing company. There are pros and cons for every business decision, and the right answer can be determined only by looking at the facts peculiar to the particular situation. Whatever options exist in a given jurisdiction should be explored fully with the company's professional advisors. Keeping the companies separate to protect one company from the liabilities of the other is an important consideration. On the other hand, tax benefits may be found in a different view of things.

There is no pat, easy answer to the question of whether an asset purchase or stock purchase is a wiser course of action. Each can have its distinct advantages under different factual situations. After a review of the facts and the applicable state and federal laws, the purchaser and seller, with advice from their lawyers and accountants, will be able to determine the best alternative.

■ SUMMARY

➤ Before buying a business, purchasers must do their homework. Due diligence is critical to gain an understanding of the business and of all the pluses and minuses that make it what it is.

➤ Even company insiders who think they know the business well need to investigate every aspect of the company.

➤ Determine what the owner's leaving will mean to the business.

➤ Determine if your purchasing the company will have a negative or positive impact.

➤ The decision to buy the assets or the stock is an important one.

➤ An asset purchase means creating a new trade name and establishing new relationships with clients and vendors—it diminishes some of the benefits of buying an existing business.

➤ On the other hand, an asset purchase can substantially limit potential liability of the new owner.

➤ A stock purchase puts the purchaser in the shoes of the seller, for good and for bad. It must be structured so the purchaser knows what liabilities he or she is buying.

➤ Tax and personal considerations must be added to the mix.

Chapter

3

Partners and Shareholders

*In business partnerships and marriage partnerships, oh the cheating
that goes on. —American proverb*

It is not at all unusual for two or more individuals to start a business
together, each bringing different skills into the mix. Each of these
individuals will have ideas about their value to the business and how
it translates into percentage of ownership. These individuals will work
out the percentages among themselves, based on contribution of capital, experience, clients, talents, or sweat equity.

Nor is it a rarity to at some time offer employees a piece of the
action after years of loyal service or to bring a talented individual into
the business with the offer of ownership as an incentive. In the special
events industry, as in many others, being successful is directly related
to the quality of people working for the company. To hire good people
and to retain them long term often requires more than a decent salary
and benefits package.

It seems that nearly everyone aspires to an ownership position,
thinking it means garnering a percentage of the company's profits
and not understanding that it also means assuming a percentage of
the responsibility. For some reason, a profit-sharing plan is not nearly
as attractive to employees as ownership. Owners may give in to this
mind-set in order to keep their employees happy. They may do so
without sufficient thought because of all of the other issues with
which they are dealing at the time. But giving up shares in the company, no matter how small a percentage, requires thought and planning and meetings with the company's lawyers and accountants.

Very few true partnerships remain in existence. As a legal entity, the
partnership is outdated. Much like a sole proprietorship, it leaves the
owners subject to personal liability, and virtually everyone views that as
the big no-no. Consequently, most firms are set up as corporations of

some sort, where liability is limited. Partners are really shareholders, even if they continue to refer to their associates as their partners.

It is absolutely essential that every corporation with more than one shareholder have a shareholder agreement, setting forth the relative rights and responsibilities of the individual shareholders. Failure to establish this agreement will lead to nothing but trouble. Shareholder agreements are often alternatively called *buy-sell agreements*.

Limited liability companies are corporations. They are governed by operating agreements, and the shareholder agreement clauses should be made a part of the operating agreement rather than a separate document.

It should be noted that shareholder agreements will have federal and state tax consequences and therefore should be reviewed carefully by a CPA or other tax professional.

■ KEY CLAUSES

Small, closely held companies are typically made up of people who like each other and who work well together and whose skills complement each other. They are in business together because they choose to be, not because they are forced to be. First and foremost, *it is important for a shareholder agreement to restrict the transfer of shares by any shareholder,* so that the remaining shareholders are not stuck doing business with people they do not like, trust, or value.

This is critical when there are only a few shareholders. Picture a situation where two people, Max and Pierre, own a catering business. They have known each other for years and have worked together closely to build a company. Their goals are similar and their business philosophies compatible. At some point, Pierre decides to retire early and "find himself" at an ashram in California. He sells his shares to a third party, Louie, who always wanted to be in the catering business but who knows nothing about it. Louie turns out to be a bit of a flake, and before long he and Max are at each other's throats on a regular basis. The business slides downhill.

Even when there is one primary owner/shareholder and many small minority shareholders, it is important to the majority shareholder that the shares in the company be restricted. Primary shareholders do not want to see employees leave and sell their shares to just anyone. Nor do they want to see company shares go to spouses or significant others in divorce or palimony suits, forcing partnerships with people they don't know, people that don't work for the company, people that don't have the company's interest at heart.

The shareholder agreement should have a very detailed clause stating that no shares shall be sold, transferred, or passed by will or other testamentary device, through divorce or property settlement, or by any other means, except for the means set forth in the agreement. Likewise, if a shareholder is terminated, quits, becomes disabled or incompetent, or if any assignment is made for the benefit of a creditor or transferred involuntarily via bankruptcy or attachment, the agreement should step in—that is, the terms of the agreement then become the only mechanism by which shares pass.

Some situations may be looked at differently than others. A company may feel very differently about employees who quit or are terminated than those who die or are disabled. Accordingly, contractual clauses may differentiate among the scenarios and treat them differently. There should be some language in the agreement indicating that the minority shareholders received their shares as an incentive to remain with the company long term and to work diligently on the company's behalf at all times. If, for any reason, their employment does not work out, the reason for having the employees as owners no longer exists. Noncompete and confidentiality clauses are often inserted in shareholder agreements for situations in which employees leave the fold.

Most often, shareholder agreements state that any shareholder desiring to sell his or her shares must first offer them to the corporation to buy for a fixed period of time. Thereafter, if the corporation does not exercise its right to purchase, then the right is typically offered to the other individual shareholders for an additional period of time. If there is insufficient interest, the selling shareholder may then offer the shares to others, although any purchaser will be bound by the terms of the shareholder agreement. This way, at the very least, any new shareholders will have to comply with the terms that govern the others.

When a minority shareholder desires to sell, the company or the shareholders can usually manage to purchase the shares. When there are two fifty-fifty shareholders, it may be more difficult for the company or the other shareholder to come up with payment, particularly if the business is very valuable. The shareholders should recognize this potential difficulty and plan for it by putting payment terms and schedules into the agreement or by creating a funding mechanism within the company. The major shareholders can plan for death much more easily by having sufficient life insurance on each other to cover the stock's value. There are even first-to-die policies for such instances. One last item in this area relates to spouses of shareholders. It is a good idea to have them sign an attachment agreeing to the terms and waiving any rights to the shares.

Going along with the stock restriction clause is the portion of the agreement that places a value on the stock. The *valuation formula* is extremely important. It has to be thought through carefully, because it can cut both ways. At the time it is drafted, none of the shareholders will have a sense of which one will be seeking to dispose of shares first and therefore which ones will have to buy according to the formula. Therefore, the formula will need to be drafted in an evenhanded manner acceptable to all.

For instance, if a company founder has brought three of his key employees into the ownership fold in the hope that they will buy him out in the future, he would ideally like the buyout formula to give him the largest possible return. If he writes the valuation formula to his own advantage down the road, there is no guarantee that one of the employees won't want to sell first. If that is the case, he will have to come up with money to purchase the shares, probably at a time when he would rather be reducing his holdings to cash. Suppose Company X does $5 million in sales with net income of $250,000. Joe, who owns 100 percent of the shares, decides to give Tom, Bob, and Barb each 3 percent of the company as a bonus. He creates a shareholder agreement, and the valuation formula says that the shares shall be valued by multiplying the net income by a factor of six multiplied by the percentage of shares owned. His shares are worth $1.5 million times 90 percent, or $1.35 million. He likes that.

But what if the three employee shareholders wish to leave and start another company? Joe has to come up with $150,000 to pay them for stock he basically gave them. He doesn't like that.

Because Joe is the founder and the heart and soul of the business, he needs to get input from his accountant on valuation and on tax consequences and from his lawyer on other facets of the agreement. They need to remind him of the possibility that the employees may decide to sell first, and he should take that into account. They also need to remind him that if he really wants to use the agreement as an exit strategy, he has to be reasonable enough to enable the employees to handle the buyout.

Buyout formulas are not exactly scientific. They definitely fall more into the art column. There is no single recommended approach to the question of how shares should be valued. Accounting terms such as *book value* and *EBIDTA* (Earnings Before Interest, Taxes, Depreciation, and Amortization) are often used in the valuation, but not always in the same manner. The bottom line is that a business is worth what a buyer is willing to pay for it, and that will vary based on market conditions, how badly the buyer wants the business, what similar businesses are selling for, and any unusual attributes the particular business has.

Buyouts are based on a price-per-share formulation. This price could evolve from net income, book value, appraised value, capitalization of earnings, gross sales, or the averaging of one or the other over a number of years. It could take into account the amount of debt the business is carrying. It could simply subtract current debt from current assets on the balance sheet. Any of these formulations could have a multiple applied to it, ranging any where from 3 to 15. An example would be six times net income as a sales price.

What is a business really worth? Take a set-building business as an example. Buyer Bart finds two such businesses for sale at the same time. One specializes in corporate events and maintains an inventory of rental sets, so it has hard assets to sell. The other designs sets for rock-and-roll tours that are disposed of after the tour is over, so it has no inventory of any value. Both have good clients that provide regular business, and sales numbers for each company are close. So which is worth more? To someone anxious to get into the music business, the latter is exciting, a great opportunity, and probably worth more than the former. To someone looking for steady business and reusable sources of income, the corporate client–based business might be more valuable.

When it comes to establishing the value of a company, sometimes luck and timing come into play. Remember, a company is worth what someone is willing to pay for it. There may be four businesses with very similar financials, employees, and inventory. The first three sell for very similar prices. The fourth sells for twice that amount. That is not because it is better, but because it is the only one left on the market, or perhaps a wealthy person wants a business like that and is willing to offer enough to ensure that. Sometimes, when a company goes on an acquisition binge, the earliest purchases are at steeper prices to ensure that the company gets its most sought-after acquisitions first. Later purchases then involve lower prices. There is no fixed, immutable rule. Timing is everything. Supply and demand applies, and luck doesn't hurt.

An employee inside a business should have a good sense of how well the company is doing. He or she should also have some thoughts about what could be done to make the company operate even better. Before an employee jumps at the chance to purchase, his or her accountant should look at the numbers and determine whether the purchase price can be justified based on the valuation formula. The corporate business may have looked great in a strong economy, and the valuation may have been very fair at that time. But if the economy is in a downward spiral at the time a shareholder wishes to divest, the valuation of the shares may be unrealistically high.

If the company or the shareholders decline to purchase at the formula price, the shareholder can check the marketplace to see if anyone is willing to purchase at that price. If there is, then that person can buy the shares subject to the terms of the agreement. But the agreement can specify that the company and/or the shareholders have the right of first refusal after an outside buyer's offer is made, giving them the "last look."

Minority shareholder rights need to be considered at all times. While in most states the majority shareholders do have control as long as they act in a businesslike manner, they cannot act in a manner that is illegal, fraudulent, or oppressive. The majority has a fiduciary duty to the minority that includes loyalty, good faith, and fair dealing. In structuring the agreement, the majority shareholder(s) must be careful to act appropriately and within the bounds of state law while pursuing their interests.

Dispute resolution is another area that should be covered by the agreement. If a transaction should become unfriendly, there should be a mechanism in place to resolve the dispute. The shareholders do not want a free-for-all or a time-consuming lawsuit that can paralyze the business and polarize the employees. Some sort of arbitration can be specified in the agreement, as can an alternative valuation handled by an outside, unrelated valuation expert.

In the event that any type of lawsuit arises out of the agreement, it is important to include a *choice of law provision.* Such a clause specifies which jurisdiction's law should be applied to the issues under discussion. This is not a trivial issue. State laws differ greatly, and if shareholders reside in different states, it is important to understand which law is the most advantageous to a majority shareholder or for prompt and fair resolution.

Further, there should be a *venue provision,* which specifies in which state any action must be brought. This can be a deterrent to shareholder suits. If the majority shareholder resides on the East Coast where headquarters is established, a West Coast shareholder will be at a disadvantage having to bring suit there rather than in the state in which his or her branch is located.

In conclusion, it is imperative that any corporation or limited liability company with more than a single shareholder have a shareholder agreement. It is important for business management and succession, for tax planning, and for general business reasons. It is not a difficult document for an attorney to draft. The valuation formula and tax aspects should be prepared by a tax professional in conjunction with counsel. Every shareholder, whether original or coming later, should be added to the agreement under the same terms as all shareholders. Such an agreement will serve shareholders well.

■ SUMMARY

➤ Every business having shareholders should have a shareholder agreement.

➤ The agreement should restrict the transfer of shares.

➤ A formula for valuing the shares should be specified in the agreement.

➤ Majority shareholders who set the value high in order to be paid a lot when selling need to remember that the formula cuts both ways: They will have to pay off any minority shareholders who want to sell using the same formula.

➤ Majority shareholders may want to look for ways other than share transfer to keep employees happy, unless the transfers are part of an overall exit strategy.

Financing: Working with Banks and Leasing Companies

A banker: The person who lends you his umbrella when the sun is shining and wants it back the minute it rains. —Mark Twain

There comes a time in the life of each business owner when growth cannot be sustained simply by bootstrapping. It would be ideal if a company's cash flow could cover all of its growth needs indefinitely, but that is highly unlikely. The cost of new vehicles, new technical equipment, office expansion or construction, and virtually every other growth move probably requires more cash than is available. Thus financing is needed to complete the transaction.

One of the natural results of business success is an increase in business, which usually necessitates an increase in staff, materials, equipment, and work space. When planning the scope of these increases, the farsighted owner is going to look to the needs of the business several years down the road. Cash flow may not generate enough capital to fulfill those needs. So the owner looks to a bank, leasing company, or a similar business that is set up to provide expansion funds for growing businesses. If the numbers are right, it can be the ideal solution. There is nothing wrong with this. It is a normal part of doing business, and it makes the business world go around. Financing enables a business to have the benefit of the assets immediately while paying for them over time.

Obviously, financing is a numbers game. How large a monthly payment over a period of how many months at what interest rate makes sense for the company? What is the effect on cash flow? These are not really the types of questions that special events professionals like to consider, but they are critical enough for someone to consider seriously. Signing of loan or lease documents is not something that should be done in a cavalier fashion. There are too many ways that these documents can come back and bite you in the end!

■ DUE DILIGENCE

A business owner sees an opportunity or feels a need to make purchases or add assets. Even if the company has an internal accountant or controller, it makes sense to use the outside accounting firm to crunch numbers for the company. The accountants can also put the company's data in order so that it is submitted to the financial institution organized and complete.

Assuming the company's finances are good, the best source for a business loan is a bank. If there is already an established relationship with a financial institution, start there. If a bank already knows the company and is familiar with management and the company's cash flow, then there will be a built-in comfort level. That, however, does not mean that the bank is going to come back with the best loan terms. A business owner should be aware of what the current prime rate is and should have a sense of what interest rates the bank's best customers are being offered.

If the bank's offer does not seem to be ideal, which is likely, it pays to comparison shop with one or two other local banks. This may provide leverage with the company's existing bank to improve its offer. If another bank comes in with better terms and the company accepts its proposal, the company will probably transfer all of its business to that bank. Therefore, the due diligence on the new bank is not just about the loan terms, but about all of the terms that fall within the company's banking relationship. Checking account fees, overdraft protection, and other business terms need to be considered seriously. Also, the location of the new bank's branches is an underrated factor. Making daily deposits and having a convenient location for employees to cash or deposit their checks is extremely important.

Regarding the loan itself, the borrower needs to understand what the money is costing, and this means more than just the rate of interest. Loan terms that are important are the dollar amount of the loan, the length of the loan, the interest rate, whether there is a balloon payment at the end, whether the bank is charging any points for writing the loan, what the bank fees will be, and what the bank covenants will be in the agreement. The company's reporting requirements can also be a factor. For instance, if a bank requires audited financial statements rather than reviewed, the cost to the company will be several thousand dollars per year higher. Even internal reporting can be time-consuming and expensive if the bank wants monthly receivables reports, cash flow statements, and profit and loss statements.

Numerous fees are tacked onto the interest payment, and they can add up. Late fees and other penalties, collection fees, legal fees, administrative fees, filing fees, and other fees can add to the transaction cost. The way a deal is structured is also important for tax purposes.

Another area to explore is the customer base of the offering bank. The question is one of the company's compatibility with the bank's customer base. If a bank writes a lot of business with companies of similar size or has an expertise in the industry of the company, that can be helpful. But if the company writes mostly larger loans for bigger companies, this loan may not really fit into the mix, and at some point, a bank may decide to jettison the loan for no other reason than its incompatibility.

Another area of inquiry, to be discussed in greater detail later, is whether a personal guarantee is required of the company's principals.

The final question in this area is one of personal feelings. Is the company management comfortable with the bank's loan officer and account manager? Thinking of the bank as a business partner, how does it feel to have its representatives ask probing questions about company actions or decisions? How will they handle bad news? How much slack is there in the relationship?

■ REVIEW BY COUNSEL

Once all of the preceding issues have been addressed and a decision has been made to move ahead, it is time to bring in corporate counsel to review the documents. Any business owner or shareholder asked to sign the myriad documents that accompany any transaction with a bank or leasing company needs to read them all carefully and have them reviewed by counsel. These documents are all drafted in favor of the company providing the funds, and many of the provisions are by nature heinous for the business owners.

This book does not go into all of the various issues that might arise from review of loan documents. Each state has different banking laws, and the contractual boilerplate may vary from state to state. It should be enough to know that every clause in every bank document will be drafted in favor of the bank. The bank will not knowingly allow any loophole that might leave it unprotected in any instance. The issue becomes one of the bank's willingness to compromise on any of the clauses. Typically, such willingness is not to be found when it comes to the form language. The actual terms of the loan will be slightly more negotiable. A loan is a product and, like any other product is therefore subject to the laws of supply and demand. In a buyer's market, loan terms may be more negotiable than if money is tight and credit is not readily available.

Bank loans are subject to the rules of the marketplace. Their pricing can be based on the cost of money to the bank, the marketing plan of the bank in terms of its desire to pursue a certain type of business, its reading of the security of the loan, and other factors. Accordingly, terms such as interest rate, length of the loan, and collateral may be somewhat negotiable. But when it comes to the bank protecting itself against the possibility of default, it rarely gives any quarter.

Knowing that, it is imperative for a business owner to have counsel review the documents to fully understand them. Counsel should let the owner know what conditions must be met during the loan term and should clearly delineate what acts or failures to act constitute loan default. Business owners enter each new credit arrangement with optimism and a total belief that they will easily meet all loan requirements. Somehow, they must be made to hear what could wait for them in the future. Most entrepreneurs want their attorneys to make deals happen, not to find reasons to kill them, so counsel may gloss over the negative side of things. But a smart and savvy business owner will be aware that he or she is always on thin ice with the bank and that default may be just around the corner.

Terms of default should be reviewed with great care. Bank covenants normally express ratios or financial levels that a company must maintain in order to avoid default. It is important to understand the true nature of banks. They love you the most when you need them the least. When times are great, when cash flow is positive and the business seems highly successful, the bank can be your best friend. When sales slow and the economy reverses a bit, when margins shrink and cash flow disappears, the bank at first expresses concern, which can then turn to worry, to insecurity, to workout, and to default. If you want to think of the bank as your partner, think of it as a fair-weather partner. Banks can find ways to call in loans as soon as they no longer want them in their portfolios. Be aware of this. Constantly be on the lookout to establish other possible relationships so that if trouble arises with your bank, other options may exist.

■ THE DOCUMENTS

A bank loan normally involves more than one document. There is, of course, the loan document itself. This is often called the *commercial loan agreement.* Then there are the *promissory note,* the *security agreement,* the *UCC documents,* and possibly the *personal guarantee.*

The *loan agreement* sets forth the terms of the loan and all of the loan covenants. It states the responsibilities of the borrower and the rights of the lender. It is mostly boilerplate, with some blank spaces to individualize the agreement to the particular transaction. The boilerplate, or small-print form language, is rarely open to discussion, but that does not mean that counsel shouldn't try.

The *promissory note* is the IOU, the promise to repay.

The *security agreement* is used to establish and secure the lender's interest in the loan collateral until such time as the obligations contained within the loan are fulfilled. It grants to the bank a security interest in whatever the collateral happens to be—typically inventory, equipment, furnishing and fixtures, accounts receivable, and even bank accounts. The security agreement normally describes the collateral and states where it will be kept. This is important in the event of foreclosure. Banks sometimes have problems in dealing with event companies because the collateral is always on the move, whereas machinery bought for a factory will stay in one place. Intelligent lighting instruments, tents, or catering equipment typical of event planning businesses may rarely stay in the warehouse—or even in the same state.

Companies should try to keep the collateral limited to the value of the loan. Banks will normally try to secure themselves with everything, even if that far exceeds the amount of the loan. Negotiation should be employed. Perhaps collateral can be limited to accounts receivable. If hard assets are included, it limits the company's ability to do anything with those assets without first getting permission from the bank. For instance, if a tent company normally sells off used equipment every year, it cannot do so if there is a security interest in that equipment.

Lenders normally have debtors sign another document called a *UCC-1 financing statement,* which is a form that a lender files in every state where collateral may be located. It is designed pursuant to the Uniform Commercial Code, a federal law, and it gives the lender a recorded security interest in the collateral. This is critical, because in the event of default it gives the lender priority in the disposition of the debtor's assets.

Whether a lender has perfected security interests in equipment, and which equipment, is quite important. Placement as a secured creditor puts the lender ahead of any and all unsecured creditors. If a business gets into financial trouble, secured creditors have priority over unsecured creditors. This means that a bank with a perfected security interest of $10,000 will be able to collect ahead of an unsecured vendor owed $50 or $500,000.

Vendors are often hung out to dry when a business finds itself in dire financial straits. Whereas they may be the good guys, giving the company extra time to pay and extending additional credit to a formerly good customer, they will find that the company's bank won't be as understanding, and it may swoop in and shut down the business, recouping its own money but leaving unsecured vendors fighting over the scraps.

In the events industry, most companies are relatively small, and most have only a small (or perhaps no) credit department. They are usually unaware of their customers' ongoing financial situation until they realize that a balance has become overly large. By then, the realization should hit that they are one of several or many vendors in the same situation. It is a tough place to be.

Security agreements and loan documents need to be understood to see if there are cross-collateralization and cross-default provisions. This means that a company with more than one loan may find that the bank has covered itself by collateralizing loan number two with the collateral from loan number one (and vice versa) for extra protection. Further, the bank may cross-default the loans, so that defaulting on one automatically defaults the other. Borrowers need to watch out for this very carefully.

Perhaps most important, one must consider whether it is prudent to sign a *personal guarantee*. The bank will often request this of the borrower's primary shareholders. This step should not be taken lightly. While lenders use the reasoning that a personal guaranty shows the commitment of the borrower to the company, what it really shows them is that they have an additional source for repayment if the company goes bad. The lender will use every tool at its command to exact repayment from a borrower. This one is definitely more the stick than the carrot. If there is sufficient collateral in the business for the loan, the shareholders of the borrowing company should fight against the guaranty, even to the point of the bank refusing to do the transaction without it.

Every business owner has faith in his or her company and a belief in its glorious future. Most business owners wear the proverbial rose-colored glasses. The outside advisors need to be objective in their view of the business and its ability to repay the loan. If they have doubts, they should voice them loud and clear so that their clients do not commit to a dangerous course of action.

If the guarantor is married, the bank will also seek the guaranty of the spouse, thus giving it access to the jointly owned family home. Borrowers can lose their houses and anything else in their names. Avoid guaranties if at all possible! If it's not possible, then try to limit the scope by keeping your spouse off of the guarantee, excluding the primary residence, or limiting the guarantee to a certain dollar amount. Banks will not shy away from taking personal assets. Do not innocently believe they will always stop short of that.

One other point worth mentioning is that the bank can seek redress from the guarantors even before they go after the assets of the company. Remember, the bank will look for the easiest way to be made whole. This is a simple business transaction for the bank and it does not have the same emotion attached to it that it does for the borrowing company and its guarantors.

When the bank begins to get a sense that things are not going as well financially for the company as it had hoped, it may begin to apply pressure to repay the loan quickly or to refinance. Remember, the bank is getting financial information from the borrower on a regular basis, so it can see when receivables are slow coming in or when sales have fallen off. The bank may begin seeking regular meetings, trying to maintain a handle on the financial situation. If the company's status does not improve, the bank may then place the loan in *workout.*

The workout department is responsible for bringing the relationship with the borrower to a conclusion as quickly and painlessly as possible. The painless part means that the bank should be made whole, or as close to whole as possible. Once in workout, the company is dealing with all new bank representatives. The friendly relationship is gone, and the air becomes tension-filled.

The bank will forbear from taking any formal default action during this time, but usually wants something in return. The bank will request a *forbearance agreement,* under which it will forbear from taking action if the company pays something additional or gives up whatever few rights it might have left. The bank may assume control of company accounts, deciding which checks to honor and which not to honor.

If workout does not lead to a finalization of the relationship, the last step is default and seizure of the assets under Article 9 of the Uniform Commercial Code. This is the end, the turning over the keys to the bank, which will auction the assets to get its money back. If there is something left over, the company will retain it to cover unsecured creditors, taxing authorities, and anyone else who might be owed.

■ LEASING COMPANIES

As stated previously, the first place to seek financing is a bank. Interest tends to be at the going market rate, and the loans are part of an overall ongoing relationship. If a company has difficulty getting a bank loan, it must look elsewhere. Often, the next type of loan to investigate is an equipment loan from an equipment leasing company. Sometimes, manufacturers have a relationship with a leasing company, or may even own their own, and they will offer financing even before it's requested. They try to make it easy for the company to go for the big purchase.

If a video company wants to purchase a new video wall system with plasma screens, it can easily cost upward of $250,000, which might scare off the more fainthearted company. But if the manufacturer offers to finance the purchase over five or seven years, the transaction all of a sudden looks more doable. The hope is that the company will say yes right away.

However, the company needs to look at the interest rate being charged. Equipment leases typically have fairly high interest rates, sometimes usuriously high rates. With regard to equipment leases, caveat emptor. There are huge differences in interest rates throughout the marketplace. The more you need the lease, the higher the rate, typically. It is advisable to shop leases very carefully. It is not only the initial rate that needs to be negotiated. Another important clause is the buyout, or early payment clause. Many leases penalize the borrower for paying off early, and at a very high rate. It is surprising how often this comes into play. When interest rates are falling in the market, it is an ideal time to refinance a lease or buy it out and include it in a bank financing, but only if there is no penalty (or a small one).

It is also important to know the payoff figure at the end of the lease. Everyone assumes the equipment just becomes theirs at the end, but there is often a substantial buyout waiting for the unsuspecting.

■ OTHER OPTIONS

Even when the preceding financing options are not viable, there still remain some possibilities. All sorts of commercial finance companies exist in every marketplace. Many charge high interest rates because of the high-risk nature of the loans they accept. Others, called *factors,* will basically buy a company's receivables at a fixed percentage rate, giving needed cash flow.

Even though company owners are on the lookout for the best possible loan terms, they have to be aware that there are times when circumstances do not warrant them. When banks and the better commercial finance options are not available to a company, exploration of the other options must be made. Perhaps short-term money, even at an exorbitant interest rate, can get a company over the hump. Outside advisors should be employed to examine the offers made by these sources as carefully as any other. Financial companies specializing in hard-to-place high-risk loans know their business and therefore know that they will have to foreclose on a high percentage of their loans. They know when to do it and they know how to do it. So getting involved with them means making sure the financial and cash flow projections are done carefully and conservatively.

■ CONCLUSION

Numerous financing options are available to companies looking to grow or companies that need additional cash for other reasons. They vary greatly and, accordingly, need to be looked at carefully. The company's outside advisors need to be included in the decision-making process. Care should be taken to make sure that the cost of the money is affordable and that the accompanying conditions are acceptable.

A conservative growth plan has a good chance of success if financed within the company's means. A high-risk growth plan has the potential of high reward, but also the risk of dramatic failure. Business owners should match their styles with advisors who can paint a reasonable picture of the future and with a financial institution that can share the same vision.

■ SUMMARY

➤ Bank loans are a good traditional way to fund growth of your business, but the money comes at a cost—make sure you know what that cost is.

➤ Avoid personal guaranties whenever possible.

➤ If one bank won't finance you, try others. They do not all use the same criteria and do not all seek the same type of client.

➤ If banks are not the right answer for your equipment purchase, try leasing companies.

➤ Take a hard look at interest rates, points, and early payment penalties.

Chapter 5

Planning

*Planning without action is futile, action without planning
is fatal. —Unknown*

Once the owner has started or purchased a business, it is time to establish operating principles and procedures. Just because many individuals in the events industry are free-spirited and creative does not mean they should abandon good business sense and avoid rules and structure. If anything, those who have a tendency to be unstructured in their own behavior and style need structure in the corporate environment.

Many event people have an idealistic view of the world as a whole and of their part of it in particular. Those who feel that they want to avoid a so-called corporate approach to business often find themselves going too far in the other direction. Then they learn that as much as they hate to admit it, their employees feel the need for structure to understand the direction in which the company is headed and what is expected of them to be in sync with it.

There is a telling example that some business consultants use to help their loosey-goosey business-owner clients understand how their style negatively impacts their companies. In it, the owner is driving in a car by himself, having a general sense of where he is going but not quite sure how to get there. The employees are following behind in another car, trying to keep up and to follow their leader, but without having a clue about where he is headed, without knowing whether each turn is in the right direction or not. No turn signals are used, no warning when the owner does a complete U-turn, no lights on when it gets dark to make it easier for the employees to follow. They become frustrated, stressed, and ultimately disenchanted.

This example shows that it is no picnic working for someone who keeps the entire plan for the company in his or her head. If anything, it is dangerous and counterproductive. Rebellion against structure is fine when you are a teenager trying to establish your individuality, but not when you are trying to run and build a business. An owner who cherishes core values can certainly make them the values of his or her company, but there is no reason for there to be a conflict between core values and basic business common sense. How many times have we described a friend in the events industry as being smart but not really having common sense? This can be a dangerous combination.

If company owners recognize a personal inability to do the actual planning and to focus on the direction of the company, they should find someone within or outside of the organization who can spearhead the planning process. It is critical to plan, to choose direction, and to gain the knowledge necessary to be a successful organization.

■ THE BUSINESS PLAN

Concurrent with dealing with the question of business form, the start-up company should be creating a *business plan.* Many entrepreneurs know this term from being asked to produce one when seeking financing. Finance companies want to know whether the company seeking the capital has its act together and whether it has thought through how the funds will be used and what will be gained. Many view the creation of a business plan only as a chore required to satisfy potential sources of funds. However, a business plan is much more than that. It is a blueprint for the business, a written thought process showing the step-by-step approach to building a successful business. Numerous books have been published on how to write a business plan, and computer software exists that allows the author to just fill in the blanks. So there is certainly no shortage of good information on the subject.

Who can forget the high school coach screaming at the athletes, "No pain no gain"? Creating a business plan falls on the pain side of the equation. It is not fun. But it is valuable, and there is gain.

Very briefly, basic elements of a business plan include a statement of purpose; an executive summary (a short and sweet description of the contents of the plan); a table of contents; a description of the business, which includes information on what the business does, what makes it unique, background of the management team, management structure, and key employees; description of the basic operating procedures; a discussion of the physical plant and whether it suits the business and will support the growth of the business; information on the quantity and quality of inventory and equipment; a discussion of the types and amounts of insurance coverage; and a description of the company's banking relationships.

Taking a hard look at the abilities of the *management team* is critical. Managing a business requires more than just desire. It requires dedication, persistence, the ability to make decisions, and the ability to manage both employees and finances. It should be no secret that it is the rare person who somehow exhibits all of the personality and intellectual traits necessary to successfully manage all facets of a company. Numerous studies of personality types have been done, and each study divides personality types into different categories. Despite all of the nomenclature, the differences are quite clear. There are sales personalities and technocrats, the former being good with people and aiming to please, and the latter being better with machines, technology, and process. There are creative free thinkers and detail-conscious number crunchers. Some people see the big picture; others can cope only with small parts of it.

It is important to ascertain the requisite skills needed throughout the business organization and to make sure that all are present among the management team. It does no good to have great salespeople if there are no financial talents to manage the funds and guide the growth of the company. It is almost counterproductive to have a great staff if there are no managers capable of overseeing people and getting the best from them. There should be a staffing plan so that the owner knows which positions need to be created and filled next.

It is often helpful to create an *organizational chart* for the business as a start-up, showing the positions that will be added as the company grows. (See Figure 5.1.) It is quite likely that many of the boxes will contain the name of the founder(s). If possible, it would help for the chart to show the skills required for each of the positions as well. As the company grows, the founder's name should be removed from

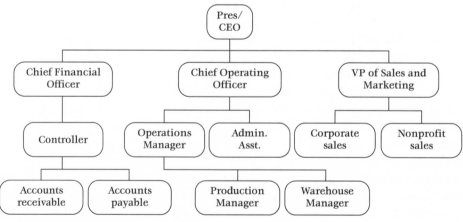

Figure 5.1 Sample organizational chart.

many of the boxes, substituting the names of employees hired specifically because of their particular skills and the skills required of their position. Typically, owners should end up handling the tasks that they enjoy and at which they can succeed.

The organizational chart is a useful document in showing who in the organization holds what position. It is also important to show lines of authority. Employee complaints need to be addressed, and for this to occur in an organized fashion there must be an understanding of the chain of authority—who reports to whom. Decisions need to be made, and there must be a shared knowledge of who deals with issues.

The business plan should also have a detailed *financial section,* containing both current and historical financial data, including profit and loss statements if the business has a history, pro forma projections for three years if it does not, balance sheet, cash flow projections, break-even analysis, assumptions on which the projections are based, loan applications or agreements, and possibly personal financial statements of the primary shareholders. There should be a start-up budget and a projected operating budget.

To effectively manage finances, a sound, realistic budget must be planned by determining the actual amount of money needed to open the business (*start-up costs*) and the amount needed to keep it open (*operating costs*). The first step to building a sound financial plan is to devise a start-up budget, which includes such one-time-only costs as major equipment, utility deposits, and down payments. The operating budget is prepared when the company is actually ready to open for business. It will reflect priorities in terms of how money will be spent, the expenses that will be incurred, and how they will be met. The operating budget also should include the funds needed to cover the first three to six months of operation.

This book does not delve into all the details of the various documents and reports needed to provide a complete financial picture of the company. An accountant or a chief financial officer will be involved in their creation and tweaking, so such discussions are best left to the experts.

Next, the financial plan should discuss the type of accounting system that will be employed, including the software. Most businesses put their books on a computer system. Manual management is time-consuming, mistake-prone, and a waste of employee time. Besides the general ledger, the checking accounts, the cash flow statements, and the payables, receivables, and billing, the accounting software should keep track of capital assets, handle depreciation, and be able to generate all types of reports that will enable a variety of employees to do their jobs better. Balance sheets and income statements can be generated internally with the right software, thus cutting back on expensive outside account time.

Accounting software is an important decision because of its useful life. Buying a cheap, low-level package may seem like the way to go initially, but the company may soon outgrow it. There may be a very limited number of users who can access the program at a given time, and the program may crash easily if too much is asked of it. Data can be lost and the company can fall behind by having to locate and reenter past transactions.

On the other hand, some programs may be too much program for a young company. It makes no sense to invest in a $200,000 package from the get-go to serve the company's growth for 15 years. There must be a balancing of expense versus current needs versus future needs. The outside accounting firm may have some strong advice, and software consultants who specialize in this type of software can be very helpful.

Finally, the financial portion of the plan should discuss the inventory control system, including software, and, if the business is a rental operation, whatever software is required to manage it. The software is a major part of the financial operation, as it keeps track of the inventory or the equipment the company relies on for profit. If equipment is lost, left behind at a client's, or not returned promptly by someone renting it, the company loses profit on that gear. Multiply that loss of profit by 100 (which could represent a small percentage of overall transactions the company enters into in a year), and the loss of profit can be staggering. The inventory control or rental management software should ideally have an interface with the accounting software.

The next portion of the business plan should set forth the *marketing plan*. Marketing plays a vital role in successful business ventures. How well a company is marketed will ultimately be one of the determining factors in its level of success. Marketing plans are discussed in detail later in this chapter.

When completed, the business plan should be able to give its readers all they might want or need to know about the company. It should be kept as a constant reference source for the key managers of the business. And it should be viewed as a living, breathing document that will be amended in many ways over time as the market changes, as the knowledge and understanding of the management team broaden, and as factors not previously known or seen become evident.

■ MISSION STATEMENT

If a business plan is not in the cards, it might be worthwhile to focus the company initially by creating a *mission statement,* which is a broad statement of what an organization wants to achieve over a period of time. It provides an overall sense of direction for decisions and actions. *It is a reminder of what the company is, what it does, and what it is trying to achieve.* The exercise of creating a mission statement is a positive one in that it requires everyone involved to give serious thought to why the company exists and what it should accomplish. It also gives every employee a reference point at all times, and it should serve to keep everyone's eye on the ball. Management should keep the mission statement in front of the employees as much as possible so they will always be cognizant of what is important.

> **Example:** *The Philadelphia Catering Company's mission statement reads as follows: "Our mission is to be a profitable, professional catering company, providing high-quality services to corporate, nonprofit, and association clients within a 50-mile radius of Philadelphia."*
>
> *Of what should this mission statement remind the employees of Philadelphia Catering Company?*
>
> 1. *We want to be profitable. Therefore we must price carefully, know what it costs us to do business, and so forth. We are not only culinary artists, we are in this to make money as well.*
>
> 2. *We want to be professional, so we better decide what that means to us and to our clients and act accordingly. We must have ethics and a company culture that tells our employees how to act in given situations.*
>
> 3. *We are a catering company, not a coordinator, not a planner, not a decorator.*
>
> 4. *We know who we want our clients to be, and we don't want to handle social business.*
>
> 5. *We know we do not want to travel far to handle events and that we are set up to be a local company, handling business within a defined radius of Philadelphia.*

Once the mission is established the company then needs to be a bit more specific and create its goals and objectives. *Objectives* are relatively general statements of what an organization wants to achieve in given areas. *Goals* are specific measurable things that the organization wants to attain by a specified time in order to achieve its objectives. *Action plans* specify the particular steps that must be taken, by whom and by what date, in order to achieve goals and thus meet objectives.

Example: *In order to be profitable, the Philadelphia Catering Company's first objective is to avoid extreme seasonality in its business.*

The goals set to meet this objective include the following:

1. *By the end of the first quarter, have a plan for a corporate picnic program for July and August.*

2. *By the end of the second quarter, have a plan together offering incentives to clients for certain services during first quarter next year.*

3. *Make sure each plan has the marketing tools to be used, with a budget for each, complete menus priced out, and so on.*

The action plan becomes a matter of assigning each goal to someone:

- *Have X research picnic sites in our region and prepare a complete list, with all pertinent facts about the facilities included, including fees, amenities, and backup literature. Have this done by February 15.*

- *Have Y begin talking to other vendors to put together a package, including tents, lighting, rentals, and so on. Have this done by February 15.*

- *Have Z put together menu options at various price points. Have this done by February 15.*

- *Have A review the client database and prepare a target list of potential picnic clients. Have this done by February 15.*

- *Devote February 15 to sharing data and researching and structuring the plan.*

- *Have menu with prices, cover letter, and a fax-back form prepared by March 1.*

- *Have mailing out by March 15.*

- *Have follow-up schedule for March and April.*

Business owners will always be faced with opportunities that, if pursued, will cause them to stray from their expressed mission. Continuing with the preceding example of the Philadelphia Catering Company (PCC), suppose that the following three opportunities present themselves.

1. PCC is offered an exclusive at a facility that does nothing but weddings, mostly in May to June and September to December.
2. A client with an office in Baltimore, 100 miles away, would like PCC to handle all of their catered luncheons there.
3. PCC is asked to bid on a city festival, providing for food for 3,000 in August.

Each one of these three opportunities conflicts with the mission statement of the company in some way. It should be clear that the mission statement is not and should not be carved in stone. Sometimes change is called for, circumstances dictating that changes be made for the continued success of the company. However, if the company strays from its mission statement, it should be done for a strategic purpose, not just to snap up an exciting piece of business.

When it comes to steps in the action plan, there will be any number of reasons to go off task. Urgent client needs, from proposals to events, may get in the way of planned steps, but after all, those needs are why the company is in business. Short-term priorities, such as writing proposals clients need immediately, can cause us to stray. Once the emergency is handled, get back to the plan. Don't stray further.

The longer a company waits to create its mission statement, the more difficult it will be, as the group will have to try and make sense of a jumble of activities that may be inconsistent with each other. Each will have its proponents, which means people will have a vested interest in hanging onto their activities and somehow forcing them into the mission statement, even if they do not make sense. The process is easiest when the company is young, when no disparate paths are already being followed.

Once the mission is clear, the next step is to create the marketing plan that will allow the company to pursue the types of business it desires.

■ MARKETING PLAN

Marketing is the performance of those activities that seek to accomplish an organization's objectives by anticipating client needs, by creating goods or services to satisfy those needs, by providing clients with information about those goods and services, and then by directing a flow of need-satisfying goods and services from producer to client.

To be successful, a company's mission has to be compatible with a need in the marketplace *or* the company has to be willing to go out in the marketplace and create that need. Without a mission statement, a marketing plan has little value, because the company does not have a sense of who it is and where it should be directing its energies on a daily basis.

Creating a marketing plan is not brain surgery. Consider it a long homework assignment that may be somewhat tiresome, but once the research is done it offers a compilation of valuable information. It can also show companies how much or how little they actually know about their geographic and product/service marketplaces and give them a renewed sense of direction. On the other hand, if a company has never actually marketed, but has relied on word of mouth to get its clients, the task of creating and following a marketing plan may be quite daunting.

There is absolutely nothing wrong with growth by word of mouth. It is obviously a tribute to the company to have clients speak of it positively to friends and business associates, who may then become clients themselves. Many companies proudly state that they do not have time to market because they are too busy handling the work coming in the door. However, company owners should view this as a mixed blessing. As long as the telephone rings, all is well. But what happens if it stops ringing? The company is left with no other viable means of bringing in business.

A *marketing plan* is an organized comprehensive document that crystallizes the marketing situation, spells out strategies, and relates them to business goals and to the needs of those markets in which the company wants to be a factor. Reduced to its very simplest, the marketing plan should answer these questions: Who is the company's best client? What makes it the best? How should the company go about finding more just like it? The answers should provide all of the information a company needs to market effectively. Take the information, insert it into the following categories, and voilà, a marketing plan.

The main sections of a comprehensive marketing plan include (1) the company and its business (a summary of the business, describing its products and services; a discussion of the company's market, including geographic area, product niches, and distribution channels; the company's objectives for market position, sales revenue, client mix, product/service mix); (2) *market research* (which includes a description of the overall market; a look at trends, present and future; an assessment of the competition; a listing of important clients and why they are so; a projection of key present and future opportunities; an appraisal of risks and the resources needed to combat them); (3) *marketing strategy* (a statement of the company's unique attributes; a list of specific marketing goals; a discussion of overall positioning strategy, including pricing, quality, and customer service policies; a description of the company's position on charity discounts, freebies, commissions, etc.; a plan to target the most desirable potential clients and determining the right approach to them; a plan to target allied companies; a review of industry organizations for benefit to the business; a strategy for client retention through communications, etc.); (4) *marketing tools* (a large number of marketing tools are available to incorporate into the marketing plan; the right mix is more an art than a science; if one tool doesn't work, it should be removed from the list and something else should be substituted for it).

Before making the decision about which marketing tools should be employed in the company's marketing mix, the company should know how much it wants to spend on marketing and then create a marketing budget. Items like business cards, letterhead, and envelopes are marketing tools and thus should be part of the budget. Client discounts and even freebies should be factored into the budget. They may not involve dollars spent, but they definitely involve revenue given up. Companies should not fall prey to the pleas from nonprofits, and even some corporate clients, that they have no money and need a deep discount, but it will be worth it to the vendor because important people will see their work. Instead, companies should have a plan setting forth how many nonprofits they will offer discounts to or choosing which causes they wish to support. The amount of these discounts should be budgeted and tracked.

Even demonstrations for clients, which take worker-hours, equipment usage, and possible expenditure, should be factored into the budget. Some companies will set up elaborate demonstrations in their warehouses and invite clients to come in one or two times per year. Some bands will run showcases on Sunday afternoons to bring in brides-to-be and other potential clients. Florists do samples and caterers do tastings. All have a cost attached to them. That cost should be reflected in the budget.

Along with the budget, the company should also create a marketing calendar. The former will set forth the monthly spending on marketing, and the latter will specify when during the year each marketing task will take place. It is helpful to look at a full year to see when ads will run, when direct mail campaigns will go out, and when videos will be shot and distributed.

It wasn't long ago that marketing meant direct mail, advertising, and press releases. Then event companies used their creativity to come up with splashy literature mailed to a targeted list or left behind after sales calls. With changes in technology, there have been numerous new ways to get a company's name out in the marketplace. Event photographs were once common to showcase a company's work. Then short videotapes were created to show the services in action. Now, CDs are sent to clients, or even e-mailed to them. All event companies have web sites, ranging from very simple to very elaborate. Streaming video can make a site very exciting. It won't be long before custom DVDs will be used, and new technologies continue to evolve. New forms of messaging do not necessarily eliminate the predecessors. There are tools for every budget.

Event photographs can still be effective as a marketing tool. When enlarged and artfully hung throughout the company's office, they can make a bold statement. When photo blowups of a client's event are sent as a thank-you, they can serve as a constant reminder of the successful working relationship.

Part of marketing is *branding*, establishing a name that becomes well known and easily recognized. Companies brand themselves with the quality of their logo. This should be consistent and evident throughout all materials on which it appears. This includes business cards, letterhead, signage, and anything else that has the company's name and logo on it. It can include thank-you notes to clients after events, holiday cards, and company newsletters sent by mail or electronically. Another marketing tool is to offer promotional items—paperweights, clipboards, mugs—anything that may remain on clients' desks for a long time. Part of marketing is keeping the company's name before the clients and potential clients. That means getting something into their hands at least four times per year.

Some companies in the event industry justify their fancy offices and large conference rooms as marketing tools. This theory should be monitored, as office space is expensive, and if the company is not bringing clients in for meetings and demonstrations, it might make sense to scale back the size and expense of the offices.

Networking is a form of marketing, albeit a potentially expensive one. Sure, Chamber of Commerce cocktail events are relatively cheap. But industry organizations have yearly dues, monthly meetings, and yearly conventions. When all is said and done, belonging to an organization for marketing reasons means really working the meetings, getting together and networking with as many people as possible every month. This can easily cost $2,000 to $3,000 per person per year. If a typical company is working on a 10 percent net profit, then it needs to derive $20,000 to $30,000 per year in sales from each person's networking just to break even on the expense.

The marketing plan should set forth the means by which leads will be generated and the manner in which leads will be followed up. Lead generation comes from networking, from research, from allied companies in the industry, and by referral. Once the leads are generated, the company must have a process for turning them into business. There may be an initial telephone call or e-mail followed by something in writing. Hopefully, this process will lead to the pitch, which must then be followed up with additional contact.

Marketing is an important activity, and one that should be handled in a very planned-out and professional manner. Of course, the company must come through for the client once the marketing process has brought the client in. Company behavior and individual behavior are critical. It is a business maxim that it is easier to retain an existing client than to go out and bring in a new one. So client retention steps are as much a part of marketing as anything else and should be taken seriously.

■ SALES PLAN

The marketing plan lays out all of the steps to locate the right potential clients for the company. The sales plan picks up where it leaves off, dealing with how the company's sales team is going to bring the clients into the fold. Sales plans can be written by a sales manager or vice president of sales, or they can be a group function, with each salesperson contributing something to the effort. In that salespeople are responsible for executing the plan, it makes sense to have them involved in the drafting, which gives them a sense of ownership. Sales plans set forth territories for each salesperson based on geography or client type. One salesperson may be assigned only corporate clients, another only nonprofits. One salesperson may be assigned the city, another the suburbs.

The *sales plan* is a document that gives the salespeople a fairly detailed road map. It can cover the prioritization of the most ideal prospective clients as developed through the implementation of the marketing plan. If the marketing plan indicates that the most profitable events are those produced for corporate clients within one hour of the company's headquarters, then the salespeople must put together a plan to approach and land such clients. If there are 100 companies in a salesperson's geographic territory, he or she still needs to figure out which to approach first and what the approach is going to be for each company on the list. Research is very important, and it has become so easy to do on the Internet that there is almost no excuse for walking into a meeting ignorant of the client's history and present way of doing business.

At the same time that salespeople are pitching new business, they must be following a *plan for client retention*. They must also allow time to write proposals and handle their ongoing event responsibilities. Some sales managers find it helpful to have their salespeople create a monthly sales calendar. If it can be generally stated that the typical month has four weeks, or 20 office days, then the calendar can be used to set aside sufficient time for all necessary activities. If the directive from the boss is for the salesperson to spend 50 percent of the time developing new business, 25 percent on client retention, and 25 percent on proposals and paperwork, the math is fairly simple. Ten days of the month should be spent on new business, five days on client retention, and five days on paperwork and proposals. Of course, that can be broken down further into half days or even hours.

Client retention can involve a variety of steps. Some companies analyze their client list carefully and put their clients into several different categories, which can be based on loyalty and years of doing business together, on how many events per year they have, on potential, or on the profitability of their events. Once the clients are categorized, the sales team can decide what efforts need to be made for the retention of each category. One category may require a phone call every two weeks and a personal visit once per quarter, regardless of event activity. Another may require only a weekly e-mail. Some clients may require a lunch or dinner every few weeks and a lot of personal attention. A chart can be made and kept up-to-date so that it can be submitted to the sales manager at the end of every month.

Some companies really go all out to hang onto their clients. They wine and dine them; they give them photographs of their events together; they send thank-you notes after each event; small gifts go out periodically. They do all they can to build the client's loyalty to them.

It must also be recognized that business runs hot and cold. When it is hot, more proposals need to be written in a timely manner, which means cutting back on one of the other areas. When it is cold, more time may need to be spent on bringing in new business or calling on old clients who have not been active lately. The plans have to be flexible, but not abandoned.

Going after new business requires a distinct thought process. Some event salespeople chase events, setting up meetings with those in charge of them. Others look to develop client relationships and let the events fall where they may. The following example shows the difference.

An article in the local newspaper indicates that USA America Corporation is building a new hotel, and there will be a grand opening in nine months. Company A's salesperson sees the article, makes a few telephone calls, and ends up with an appointment to discuss the opening. He goes in and pitches hard, showing his company's qualifications and pushing to land a piece of business. The corpo-

rate marketing person thanks him for his interest and tells him she will get back to him as the plans develop a bit further. She puts his material in a file full of brochures that is marked "potential vendors."

The salesperson for Company B, equally aggressive, calls and requests an appointment for two weeks down the road. She then gets on the Internet and finds everything she can about the USA America Corporation, its history, its corporate culture, its way of doing business, and its growth plans. When she gets in to see the corporate planner, she is armed with lots of knowledge and lots of questions about the company's needs. She phrases everything in terms of benefits to the client. She also makes it clear that she is more interested in developing a long-term relationship than in just landing a single event, even if it's a large one. When she leaves, the planner creates a new folder for her literature marked "potential strategic partner."

Neither approach is right or wrong. Both salespeople aggressively followed up on a lead and pitched their companies well. They employed two different approaches, one an immediate, short-term view, the other a long-term, big-picture approach. Either approach can reflect the culture of the salesperson's company. Some companies go so far as to have a separate *sales manual* that lays out for the sales staff procedures covering all aspects of their demeanor with clients, with facilities, and with all others. That culture will dictate how salespeople dress and act (for instance, calling clients Mr. or Ms. until told by the client not to), how they structure their pitch, and how they relate to clients. It will dictate the ethics that salespeople must cling to at all times. For instance, a company that uses negative selling, putting down the competition, either truthfully or otherwise, rather than selling on its own merits, has a poor sales ethic. Even the manner for dealing with client complaints should be addressed in the sales plan or sales manual. This is a critical area, because how a company deals with an unhappy client may well determine their future dealings. There should be procedures in place for the eventuality of a mistake or a problem on an event. The salesperson, as the point of contact throughout the event process, should be out front on this. Sales should call the client the day after each event to find out the client's level of satisfaction. If there is a problem, it is better to defuse it immediately by handling it promptly. Notes should be made of the conversations and kept in a folder where they can be easily retrieved if necessary. If investigation is required to get to the bottom of the complaint, it should be handled at once.

Many times, the client complaint will be valid. The client should be advised of this, and then, of course, comes the issue of redress. Obviously, this depends on the severity of the problem, and hopefully, the two sides can agree on the amount of the discount. If not, a practical consideration comes into play: Is this a client worth hanging on to? If so, don't jeopardize a potential long-term relationship by nickel-and-diming. If the client is more of a problem than anything else, the company may want to stick to its guns, knowing that losing such a client is not a tragedy.

If, after investigation, the client complaint appears to be exaggerated or wrongly placed on the company, the salesperson needs to objectively state the facts and let the client know that the company fulfilled the terms of its agreement and did nothing wrong. This may or may not sit well with the client, and the same type of analysis as should be employed. Should you discount to keep the client, or is he or she not worth it? Sales personalities like to be liked by other people and therefore prefer to avoid conflict with their clients. This trait might make them poor negotiators in these situations; therefore, once the salesperson has reported the facts to the client, any negotiation should be handled by the sales manager or the accounting department.

The final portion of the sales plan should deal clearly with sales compensation, always a hot topic. Some companies keep their sales staff on straight salary, while some unlucky souls are on straight commission. Most fall somewhere in between, with some combination of salary plus commission. However simple the commission system seems, there will always be all sorts of issues that need to be addressed. It is difficult to do on a case-by-case basis, as some people will always feel unfairly dealt with compared to their associates. Be ready for aggravation.

Commission can be based on gross sales, on net sales (however defined by the company), on profit, or on whether the client represents new business. Simple percentages are the best. But of what? What if the client doesn't pay at all? What if the client goes bankrupt? What if a job must be discounted due to a mistake by the production crew? What if the client pays, but 60 days late? What if the production went over budget because the salesperson did not estimate well? What if it went over budget because the shop mispacked the truck? What if the client was a house account that the salesperson was required to handle? What if, what if . . . ?

Tracking the sales of individual salespeople is time-consuming and can be confusing. Who should do it? Either the salespeople or the accounting department can handle this chore, and there will be inevitable disagreements. If a solid system is in place and is managed objectively, the disagreements will be resolved and the commission system will motivate the sales staff to sell.

■ SUMMARY

➤ Every business requires structure.

➤ Becoming *corporate* should not have a bad connotation. To employer and employees it should mean being organized, having a plan, and heading in the desired direction at all times.

➤ A *business plan* is more than an exercise—it is a road map to the future in a thought-out, well-planned direction. It should also be an objective assessment of the business at a given time relative to its competitors and relative to where it wants to be in the future. It provides goals and objectives for every aspect of the business.

➤ A *mission statement* is a reminder of what the company is, what it does, and why it is in business. It should be a constant reference source and a theme that drives the employees in their day-to-day activities.

➤ A *marketing plan* is an organized, comprehensive document that crystallizes the marketing situation, spells out strategies, and relates them to business goals and to the needs of those markets in which the company wants to be a factor.

➤ A *sales plan* directs the sales team toward clients in the order of their priority to the company and sets forth guidelines for bringing in new business and retaining existing clients. It should also address client and salesperson satisfaction.

Chapter

Operating a Business

For the things we have to learn before we can do them,
we learn by doing them. —Aristotle

The operation of the business encompasses a wide range of activities. Operational issues really relate to all of the activities required to keep the company running efficiently. Many business owners feel that their business is very simple and therefore there is little in the way of operations on which to focus. Yet every business is a lot more complicated than it might appear.

Even a small company will have numerous decisions to make concerning who in the company needs what information in order to do their jobs well. That, of course, begs the question of where the paperwork is going to come from. Processes and procedures need to be set up specifying what the information is, what form it should take, who should generate it, for whom it should be generated, how it is to be transmitted, and when it will be transmitted.

> **Example:** *An event producer has working for him a creative director, a technical director, an operations/production director, an office manager, and a bookkeeper. This is a six-person company—by all measures, a small business. But communication is bad. Although everyone knows what their job is, they have not figured out how to interface with their co-workers to become an efficient team.*
>
> *The event producer comes up with the event concept and sells it to the client. The client wants to know what it will cost to produce this event. The producer goes to his creative director and technical director and asks them to come up with some rough designs and pricing. They, in turn, ask the operations/production manager to*

source materials and subcontractors and to figure out the cost of labor and all other production expenses. This seems pretty simple, but it is only the beginning.

Let's just look at the questions that are raised:

1. *Did the event producer generate a written proposal?*

2. *Did it have a file number assigned to it for the computer system?*

3. *Was the proposal shared with others in the company? Who?*

4. *What paperwork did the creative director generate? Where did it go? Was it on a company-created form?*

5. *What about the technical director's estimates?*

6. *What information did the production manager receive to enable him to price the job?*

7. *What paperwork did he create?*

8. *Was a job-costing form used?*

9. *How was profit figured?*

10. *Was the bookkeeper brought into the mix?*

11. *Did all paperwork have the same job number?*

12. *How did the paperwork make its way back up the chain?*

13. *What did the producer ultimately receive?*

14. *What did the client ultimately receive?*

15. *Who else got copies of what the client received?*

16. *Once the contract was signed, where did it go?*

17. *How was accounting informed?*

18. *How were the designers informed to finalize their designs?*

19. *How did the production manager hire subcontractors?*

20. *Who approved the contracts?*

21. *How did they get from him to accounting for payment of deposits?*

22. *How were they entered into the accounting system?*

23. *Who paid the vendors, and who was informed of the payments? What about purchase orders, vendor contracts, and shipping arrangements?*

24. *What about travel arrangements, booking flights, and hotels?*

25. *What about petty cash needs?*

26. *When is the client invoiced?*

27. *Who does it?*

28. *Who is informed when the client pays or doesn't pay on time?*

29. *What was stored on the computer? Where?*

The preceding example is only a beginning to the questions that can be asked in a discussion regarding the procedures needed to efficiently process each event. Now imagine a slightly larger company that has hundreds of events to cope with over the course of a year. Think of how problems can magnify and how standard methods for approaching situations are a must to keep from being buried under lost paperwork, unpaid vendors, missing equipment, drawn-out receivables payments, and all sorts of other problems. A recent discussion with the owner of a $10 million per year technical company is telling. He said that when meeting with consultants about choosing new accounting software, they charted out close to 300 individual steps in the information flow among the various parts of the company!

A similar issue is how much information owners desire their employees to have access to. There are different philosophies about this. Some business owners feel that the less the employees know, the better off they are. If employees know the company is making a lot of money, they will all ask for raises. If they know the company is doing poorly, some may bail. Therefore, tell them nothing.

Other owners believe that knowledge is power, and in order to be successful they must empower their key employees. Therefore, they allow them to have all of the information they need to do their jobs effectively. They advise them of the confidentiality of what they are being given and the importance of not blabbing about it to everyone in the company.

It is really the personal style of the owner that will determine how much and by what means information is shared. Ideally, key managers will have all of the information they need to effectively perform all the functions of their position. In Chapter 5, many of the planning issues were discussed. Just as important is working out the policies and procedures under which the company and its employees will operate.

■ CONTROLS

Every business needs controls in place to make certain that its financial information and inventory figures are accurate. Management must have accurate and reliable accounting information to make intelligent business decisions and to meet the goals and objectives of the business.

Part of this is to establish control over cash to avoid misspending, overspending, fraud, and outright larceny. *Control activities* are defined as those specific policies and procedures put into place for the purpose of minimizing the risk of such detrimental activities. In order to create these policies and procedures, the particular risks need to be identified. Control activities are designed to address issues such as adequately separating duties so that one employee does not have sole responsibility for handling cash, placing orders, writing checks, and so on; following authorization procedures for purchasing; providing adequate documentation and record keeping; maintaining actual physical control over the assets of the business and the records pertaining to them; independently checking on all activities; and properly training new hires.

Management should be a part of the control process. It should be interposed into key areas such as signing checks and reviewing supporting documentation; doing the first review of all bank statements and canceled checks prior to the accounting department review; reviewing bank reconciliations; and having the person responsible for opening the mail prepare a daily list of deposits and checks received so it can be compared to daily deposit slips. All of these responsibilities should be reflected on the company's organizational chart. It should also be reviewed periodically to determine whether the procedures used are effective or whether they need to be amended, expanded, or deleted.

Controls will normally touch the sales department in a variety of ways. Sales projections by salespeople are made on a monthly basis. A sales manager has to compare actual sales with projections. If commission needs to be figured, the sales manager has to figure it, or double check the computations of the salesperson. Sales reports have to be reconciled to monthly financials as well.

The production department of an event company needs to have controls imposed on it as well. Job costings must be prepared on each job. Preliminary costings need to be compared to actuals. Rental reports have to be prepared and reconciled. Inventory reports must be reconciled. Production worker-hours claimed must be compared to time cards and compiled to be compared to payroll reports. Production supplies and subcontractors engaged for events must be logged on purchase orders, and the amounts on the purchase orders must be compared to the actual bills that arrive and checks that are cut.

The accounting department must make certain that the amount of each event contract is the amount billed to the client and determine the reason for any variance. The amount of every check cut should comport with the purchase order and the vendor's invoice. No check should be written unless all are compared and reconciled. All invoices must be entered onto the accounting system in a timely manner. All company billing must be completed and entered onto the system in a timely manner.

Cash control is critical. Petty cash should be controlled by one individual, and a system for petty cash requests, distributions, and reconciliations needs to be very tight. If the company does a volume of cash business, there should be strict controls in place to make certain that all cash is accounted for.

There are many more areas of control that each individual business should be overseeing. Tight control is critical in so many areas. Inventory control is as important as cash control. Controls can be established over Internet use by reviewing logs on company servers. Long-distance telephone or cell phone use can be controlled by requiring codes or attribution of each call to a particular client or account. In every area a company may be bleeding expense, controls can and should be established.

■ JOB COSTING

Figuring out the appropriate way to cost event productions is a major step toward the ultimate success of the business. Having prices that are too high will eliminate a company from the competitive mix. Having prices that are too low will push the company toward failure. There is a safe middle ground. At least there should be.

The actual costs of producing the individual event are called *direct costs.* They include labor, cost of materials, transportation cost, and whatever else goes into directly taking the production from conception to creation. Some in the industry would take that number, add 20 percent to it, and feel as though they made a 20 percent profit on the job.

But what about the cost of the warehouse, the power tools, the electricity, the insurance, the office equipment, the employee benefits—all those items that go into making the company what it is? These are *indirect costs,* and they have to be allocated to the individual jobs, too.

Example: *Floral Artistes do 10 big events in the course of a year. They average $50,000 per job with a 20 percent gross profit. The* *company does $500,000 in revenue and has $100,000 in gross profit. The company has $80,000 in overhead cost, leaving a net income of $20,000, representing 4 percent of gross.*

Now let's assume same company, same numbers, except that overhead is $150,000. In this case, the company loses $50,000.

In the preceding example, indirect costs are not factored into the pricing equation, and they clearly have to be. In the first case, overhead represents 16 percent of gross revenues ($80,000 out of $500,000). In the second, overhead represents 30 percent. Somehow, these percentages have to be allocated into each proposal the company issues to clients to make sure that their overhead is covered by the events they produce.

Cost accounting is a tricky area. Overhead as a percentage of sales can change from year to year, so any formula may need to be adjusted. Some companies work out their formulas internally, using simple spreadsheet formulas. Others develop complicated software tied into their accounting and general software packages. As scientific as the formulas may seem, a lot of tweaking will be required that may make the costing process as much an art as a science.

In a tight economy or a competitive market, the temptation (or even the need) to cut prices to land business may be persuasive. This should not be done randomly or without thought, because the more prices are cut, the less overhead is covered by the events being produced. Direct costs may be covered, but at the end of the day, there are a lot of bills to pay.

Even in a rental operation, all costs need to be factored in. The equipment cost is one thing, but the cost of the workers who are taking the phone calls, writing up the orders, prepping the equipment, loading the trucks, delivering the equipment, and then doing it all again in reverse must be taken into account. The truck usage and expense is there. All of that is direct cost, and if the company were to do that rental at cost, the price would have to include all of those cost items. How profit is to be computed is another issue. Is any amount over direct cost to be considered profit? Or does profit come in only after indirect cost is accounted for?

Example: *Company A produces a $250,000 event. Of that amount, $100,000 is direct cost. Another $75,000 in indirect cost is attributed to that event. The balance of $75,000 is indisputably profit.*

Some companies would say that their break-even point was $100,000 where direct costs were covered. Others would say breakeven occurs at $175,000. That is a big difference. When an event company is looking to give a discount to a good client or to a nonprofit organization, it should know what its break-even point is.

Job costing in the event industry can be a major topic in itself. There is much to discuss and analyze in each individual business, and it is a process well worth following.

■ COMPANY POLICY MANUAL

Just as common as underestimating the complexity of the processes used to operate a business is the underestimation of the need for a company policy manual. The latter, however, carries some serious repercussions. Whether it's called an employee manual, an employee handbook, or a policy and procedures manual, the name is irrelevant. The document, however, is not.

Why does a company need one? It is a primary line of defense in many types of lawsuits that can be brought by employees or third parties against the company. It will also serve to avoid lawsuits. It will increase employee awareness of the company's position on issues, thus improving employee-management relations, and it should help to decrease turnover and therefore increase productivity.

The policy manual provides the employees with the ground rules under which the company operates, rules that will be applied objectively and across the board without bias or discrimination. It provides employees with a code of conduct and a set of standards that they are expected to uphold. Importantly, it lets the employees know what the consequences will be when they fail to follow the prescribed rules and regulations.

Depending on the nature of the business, there may be a need for a general employee manual and additional, more specific, procedure manuals, dealing, for instance, with production issues, technical or otherwise, or sales issues.

The discussion to follow is general in nature and should not be relied on as a substitute for consulting with an employment attorney. Every manual should have an *initial disclaimer* regarding its content. An example follows.

> *It is our hope that each employee will find the company to be a fulfilling place to work and that the description of benefits and policies contained in this manual will be of assistance to you. However, it should be clear that nothing contained in this manual or any other manual or policy or work rule of the company represents promises, nor does it constitute a contract of employment.*

The employment relationship of each employee is, remains, and always shall be as it has always been at will, meaning that it may be terminated at the company's option or the employee's option at any time for any reason or for no reason, with or without prior notice.

The benefits and policies contained herein set forth guidelines that are subject to change by the company at its discretion, without prior notice and without approval or consent by the employees. This policy statement supersedes and replaces all prior statements and other prior rules, procedures, and benefits.

This policy is subject to change solely by the president of the company when done in writing and signed.

■ CIVIL RIGHTS CONCERNS

The manual should then deal with the basic issues of importance in the day-to-day operation of the business. Those of constitutional and federal importance should be addressed up front. They include a general statement that the company is an *equal opportunity employer* in its recruiting, interviewing, hiring, training, transferring, promotion, and administration with regard to race, citizenship, color, religion, age, sex, marital status, national origin, ancestry, disability, handicap, veteran's status, and any other bias protected by federal, state, and local law, regulation, or ordinance.

Equally important is a detailed and clear-cut *sexual harassment policy.* This policy should define and give examples of forbidden sexual harassment and prohibited conduct, ranging from unwelcome advances to creating an intimidating, hostile working environment. This policy should be given the sense of importance that it merits.

It should also be unlawful to retaliate against anyone who has complained in good faith. All complaints should be reported to a designated manager. All complaints should be immediately investigated, and on completion of the investigation the results should be communicated to all parties with a finding. If sexual harassment is found, appropriate discipline should be imposed.

Other federal laws that should be mentioned are the *Americans with Disabilities Act* (ADA) and the *Immigration Reform and Control Act of 1986.* The former is relevant to companies employing 15 or more employees. The act prohibits employers from discriminating against "qualified individuals with disabilities" in job application procedures, hiring, firing, advancement, compensation, and other terms, conditions, and privileges of employment. A "qualified employee or applicant with a disability" is a person who has a physical or mental impairment limiting one or more major life activities but, who, with or without reasonable accommodation, can perform the essential functions of the job. "Reasonable accommodation" includes making existing facilities used by the employees accessible and usable by persons with disabilities, job restructuring, and/or modifying work schedules. An employer must make reasonable accommodation so long as it would not impose "undue hardship" on the operation of the business. *Undue hardship* is defined as an action that requires significant expense or difficulty based on the size and resources of the business. Employers may not ask job applicants whether they have a disability. Applicants and employees engaged in the use of illegal drugs are not covered by the ADA.

The ADA also impacts businesses that deal with the public and sets certain design and access requirements, which become relevant in some of the event services provided (ramps leading up to stages, etc.).

The Immigration Reform and Control Act (IRCA) prohibits employers from knowingly hiring or recruiting an alien who is not authorized to work in the United States. It requires that all employers verify both the identity and employment eligibility of all regular, temporary, and casual workers and retain an I-9 form so documenting. Failure to comply can lead to the assessment of substantial fees.

Other important policies that should be set forth at the outset relate to *workplace violence* and *drug and alcohol policy*. It is important for the company to take a stand on both issues. A zero tolerance policy on violence will discourage any sort of unwelcome contact and will provide the employer with ability to terminate for cause anyone who acts inappropriately. In the event industry, the drug and alcohol policy is very important, because many individuals operate vehicles or heavy equipment, operate at height, or work with power tools.

Many companies like to put their *mission statements* and *core values* in their manuals to reinforce them with their employees. If particular *ethical considerations* are important to the company and the industry, they should be reiterated. The more often they are stated and the more often they are discussed among the employees, the more they become a part of the *corporate culture* of the company.

■ SAFETY CONSIDERATIONS

Safety considerations should be near the beginning of the manual as well, again showing the priority they are given by the company. Mention should be made of OSHA and the company's concurrence with its standards. Specific rules should be stated regarding safe use of tools, ladders, lifts, paint booths, and chemicals. Safe lifting standards should be described. The company should establish a safety committee and should discuss it with the workers' compensation insurance carrier.

If company management feels strongly about smoking, a smoking policy should be laid out. This should include where smoking is and is not allowed, in the company's offices and warehouse, in company vehicles, and on event sites. It should also specify how smoking breaks are to be handled and how many are allowed.

Procedures regarding accidents on the job and reporting them should be laid out clearly for the employees. The policies should include whom to inform, time frame for notification, writings required, how to handle police reports, and what to do if someone has to go the hospital. Sample accident report forms should be included, and employees should know where to find them when needed.

Information should be provided on workers' compensation insurance and procedures for applying for it. All necessary forms should be readily available to employees.

■ HIRING PROCEDURES

Hiring is a lot trickier than just asking a few questions, then offering someone a job. Interviewing policy should set forth the type of questions that are forbidden and what to do if the applicant volunteers forbidden information. Policies for hiring relatives, rehiring former employees, and other hiring issues should be set forth.

All paperwork required of the employee upon hiring should be listed. This can include a signed confidentiality/noncompetition agreement, all necessary payroll tax forms, a copy of the employee's driver's license, agreement to undergo drug testing, and a letter discussing the introductory or probationary period.

■ OPERATING PROCEDURES

Absenteeism and *tardiness* policies should be made clear. If tardiness is an issue, disciplinary action should be specified. In companies where production work is done, an entire crew can be sitting around waiting for one late employee before they can leave for an event site, thus negatively impacting the productivity of a number of people.

Hours of operation should be specified. What to do in case of *inclement weather* should be set forth. Policy regarding lunch breaks, rest breaks, and other aspects of work scheduling should be covered. How to record time should be clearly described, with copies of any pertinent forms attached. The workweek and the company's overtime policy should be explained. Disciplinary steps the company can take for breach of procedures should be listed.

Company time spent on personal telephone calls, personal e-mail, and writing and receiving personal mail at work should be a part of the policy. It should be made perfectly clear to employees that there is no right of privacy, nor should there be any expectation of privacy with regard to telephone calls and e-mails. The company has the right and may exercise the right to monitor all communications. Further, the computer system of the company remains the property of the company, and the management can, at any time, access any files on the system. All passwords should be registered with a manager so that the company has access at any time. The company will want to maintain a variety of security levels for its system and will expect its employees to keep confidential information confidential.

Employee conduct and work rules should be set forth, along with examples of infractions that may result in disciplinary action—up to and including termination. It should be clear that the list of infractions is not totally inclusive, because it is not possible to list all forms of behavior that might be considered unacceptable.

Discipline should be laid out with an emphasis on the desire for administering equitable and consistent consequences for unsatisfactory conduct in the workplace. If discipline is to be progressive, the various steps should be specified (e.g., verbal warning, written warning, suspension, and termination). Depending on the severity of the problem and/or the frequency of the occurrences, there may be circumstances when one or more steps may be bypassed.

An employee appeal process should be available to employees. If termination is the discipline, the company should make certain that it gets back all items that have been issued to the employee, including client lists and other databases, Rolodexes, credit cards, calling cards, photo albums, tools, equipment, keys, manuals, written materials, laptop computers, cellular telephones, pagers, computer passwords, CDs or disks containing company information, security codes for alarm systems, and any other company property, intellectual property, or third-party property entrusted to that an employee.

Seemingly simple areas like personal appearance and dress code are important to the company and should be addressed in the policies. The maintenance and appearance of company vehicles and employee work areas can be discussed as well.

Employee care of company equipment, tools, office equipment, and vehicles should be made clear. The attitude toward care and avoiding damage may be a function of how strong the policy is. The policy involving employee use of company equipment and vehicles should be explicit as well, as this is a common situation. For instance, employee A, a model employee and a driver with a clean record, wants to borrow a truck to move some personal things on a Sunday. The manager agrees. Employee B, who is careless and less than trustworthy, wants the same privilege and the manager says no. Lawsuit? Dissatisfaction? Without a specific policy, there could be major unhappiness. But a policy stating that no employee can use company vehicles except as approved by a manager, based on employee history of responsibility and care, offers the company some backing for its actions.

In the event industry, the concept of freelance work is one with which everyone is familiar. Many workers spend their careers accepting short-term assignments from a variety of companies, thus maintaining their independence and freedom of movement. At some point in their maturity process, some of them may seek the security and continuity of full-time employment. However, even then they may wish to retain the ability to work an occasional gig with someone else. There should be a policy dealing with this subject, stating clearly whether full-time employees may work part-time for others in the industry, particularly with competitors. In the lighting and audio businesses, it is not uncommon for an employee to want to go out on a particular music tour for a few months and then have the ability to come back to their job. This can be very disruptive to a company trying to stabilize its workforce.

Likewise, smart employees may see an opportunity to create a small business on their own, selling products to other companies on the side. Say an employee of a floral decorator discovers an unbelievable source for unique clay pots and decides to create a small business on the side to sell them to other companies. Who does this hurt? The employer may have an answer to that! A clear policy against employees having such other interests in the industry can nip the problem in the bud.

■ HUMAN RESOURCE POLICIES

There should be a job description for each and every position within the company. Each employee should have one, and there should be a signed copy in each employee's file. An employee's performance should be measured against the job description. Some interesting twists can take place in this regard. Suppose a production worker, Ralph, has it in his job description that driving trucks to and from event sites is a major part of his job. Therefore, he must at all times have a valid driver's license. What happens if he is found guilty of driving under the influence and has his license suspended for one year? What should management do? What *can* management do? What happens if the employee loses his license, doesn't tell management, and continues to drive, and management doesn't find out until after his license is returned?

Every employee wants to advance in life, make more money, have a higher position, maybe even accept more responsibility. How to achieve advancement should be a part of the company manual. *Employee evaluations* should be dealt with in detail. Objective standards for evaluation should be created to allow comparison among workers to determine how they rate among each other based on a number of discernable factors. Evaluations should show employees where they need to improve in order to be promoted or to receive a salary increase. Deficiencies should be noted carefully. Employees should be given copies of their written evaluations.

Building a good staff has its very definite pluses. However, one of the oft ignored negatives is that when it comes time to promote someone, others may be left behind and may develop negative attitudes or may seek promotion outside the organization. In a fast-growing, ever-expanding company, this may not be much of an issue, but in smaller, more stable environments it can cause major upset. A raise and high evaluation may suffice with some, while others will take the failure to promote very negatively.

There should be a policy about whether employees have access to their personnel files and, if so, under what conditions. There will always be one employee who wants a copy of his or her file. The company needs to have a policy on this issue. All disciplinary action should be documented in the file, as well as any other material that might help provide a basis for disciplinary action, up to and including termination at some future point in time. Positive statements should be maintained as well, for future reference, including client letters or notes from client telephone calls.

If the company has a bonus plan, it should be described in detail, with full and easy-to-understand explanations of how bonuses can be earned. Many employees view a bonus plan as a carrot that ultimately provides no sustenance, and therefore they treat it skeptically. There are numerous views regarding whether bonuses should be individual, companywide, by department, or whatever. There is no pat answer, no categorical right or wrong.

Example: *The company bonus plan states that 10 percent of company net profit will be allocated as a bonus to the employees equally. The company's net profit is $100,000. Therefore the total bonus allotment is $10,000. With 10 employees, each gets $1,000.*

Example: *The company bonus plan states that if the company has net income in excess of $200,000, each employee will earn a bonus equivalent to 2 percent of his or her annual income.*

Example: *The company bonus plan states that all sales people who exceed their sales quotas will receive a bonus of 10 percent of the dollar value of that excess.*

Example: *If the production department finishes the year having completed all projects within projected cost, each production worker will receive a bonus.*

■ BENEFITS

The benefits section of the employee manual may be the most important. Within it should be a detailed account of the benefits available to employees and at what point they become available. In many companies, benefits do not kick in until an employee has completed a probationary period. Some health plans accept new members only at given times of year, so those dates have to be laid out in boldface type and repeated a few times.

Health insurance, dental insurance and disability insurance are three of the most common benefits. If the company is paying the full premium, the policy manual should so state. If it is paying a fixed amount or a percentage, with the balance coming from payroll deduction, it should be stated even more clearly. Very often, single employees get a better deal than married or married-with-children employees. If they are treated differently, the policy should so state.

Other benefits, like 401(k) plans or other pension or profit-sharing plans, can be very confusing. The policy should be kept as simple as possible while still providing as much information as it can.

While most employees do not view them as such, vacation days, personal days, and sick days are a benefit. They are not mandated by any federal law, so an employer is not under any statutory obligation to provide them. Most employees view them as a right, and they may also view them as interchangeable. Sick days are taken as vacation days, and personal days are taken as vacation days. Employers need to delineate what is acceptable and what is not. Some have merged sick and vacation days into a single category. Whatever the policy, it should be spelled out clearly and without gray areas. Employees are incredibly adept at finding loopholes.

Some companies give more vacation to workers with longer seniority. That policy should be made clear. How a year is calculated should also be made clear. Is it a calendar year or a year beginning on the date of hire and subsequent anniversary dates?

Paid holidays are also a benefit. This should be simple, right? What about Christmas Eve? New Year's Eve? What if a holiday falls on a Saturday? A Sunday? What if an employee works on the holiday? If some employees are paid by the hour and others are on salary, differences may arise.

Other issues that arise involve jury duty, military duty, bereavement leave, and family and medical leave. All of these need to be addressed in a policy. Long-term illness or disability needs to be addressed also, with a specified amount of time stated before the employee can be terminated.

■ EMPLOYEE PAY

Payroll procedure is important. An explanation of what the pay week is and when payment for that week will be made is valuable information to employees. The procedure for submitting hours for payroll should also be stated and restated, along with the due dates. How to submit hours when employees are out of town on events should be set forth, as traveling is such a big part of the event business.

Reimbursement for expenses is a key area of frustration for both employers and employees. Employers want records, receipts, documentation. If they don't, they should. Employees want reimbursement. Forms, procedures, expense approvals, and whatever other controls a given company needs should be laid out in the policy.

Similar procedures should be in place if the employee has been advanced cash by the company. Receipts should be turned in, along with change, totaling the original amount. Company credit card use should have similar controls.

The question of per diem expenses for employees on the road also needs to be addressed. There are tax issues involved in this area, so discussion with the company accountant is important. If handled improperly, the per diem money could be treated as income to the employee. Depending on how the company handles it, the responsibility can fall on the company to collect receipts from the employees;

or the company can give the money directly to the employees, making it their responsibility to collect and submit the receipts.

■ OUTSIDE PROFESSIONALS

Every event company has to learn to rely on outside professionals to provide services and advice required to keep the company within the law and acting in a wise, prudent, and cost-effective manner. Sometimes they use the professionals only on an as-needed basis. Other companies keep them very involved—in fact, encourage them to be involved. Some even set up an outside board of advisors and urge their professionals to be a part of it.

Most companies have used the services of an attorney to set up the company. While this is not 100 percent necessary, it is a good idea. Counsel fees for helping to establish a company should not be excessive, and getting matters taken care of properly initially gets the business off to a good start. Thereafter, maintenance of company books and records can theoretically be done by the company, after counsel has advised of the requisite steps.

A company may determine that it is the easiest and best course of action to have its attorney draft all of its agreements initially—client agreements, rental agreements, subcontractor agreements, and other contracts. Thereafter, an attorney may not be needed again for some time. Certainly, if the company requires bank financing or any other type of financing, an attorney should be involved in at least review, if not drafting, of the agreements. If any acquisitions are made or sale of the company is contemplated, the attorney should be consulted to discuss the nature of the transactions and the drafting of documents.

Some businesses desire to keep their counsel involved in their business and to review all issues annually. Some owners use counsel as a sounding board for business as well as legal decisions.

The second valuable member of the professional team is the accountant. The accountant should assist the business in setting up the initial books of the company, preferably on the computer system. Helping the company choose the right accounting software is a useful service. Establishing a working relationship with the inside person handling the books is quite important, as the two will interact quite a bit. The outside accountant will review the internal documentation of the company and will do quarterly, semiannual, or annual financial statements. The statements can range from the most basic, *compiled* statements, to either *reviewed* or *audited* statements. The latter may be required only by a lender or if the company decides to go public.

Before any loans are taken out or large purchases made, the accountant should be consulted to determine whether the company can truly afford the course of action. The accountant can help with projections for a new line of business, new acquisition, even decide how much expansion the company can afford. The accountant should have an ongoing relationship with the company that is probably more involved than that of the attorney.

The third member of the team should be the company insurance agent(s). Although we have been trained as a society to avoid contact with insurance agents whenever possible, insurance is so important to event companies that a close relationship is critical. The agent will be the one to explain what each type of policy covers, advise which is worth having, and discuss which may not be cost-effective. Insurance agents will help find the right coverage from the right company, and they will be available to answer questions and to advise a company on an ongoing basis. A good agent will advise what steps should be taken to reduce premiums, be it the establishment of a safety committee, a larger deductible, or whatever.

Valuable agents will take the time to get to know your business and the issues with which it struggles. They will keep the company advised on insurance developments and will find and offer new products that are worthy of consideration. They will not come across as salespeople, but as trusted advisors.

The fourth advisor is the benefits provider, the individual who handles the company's 401(k) or pension plan. Workers value this benefit highly, and it is important for the individual to be trustworthy, available, and willing to spend time with each individual, if required, to keep them happy.

Some companies outsource their payroll services and preparation of their W-2 reports and forms. This payroll company is not an advisor per se, but an important aspect of the business operation. It takes a huge amount of pressure off of the internal staff, and, taking staff time saved into consideration, the cost is relatively inexpensive.

Sometimes, business consultants are brought in to help a company deal with a particular situation. Once that situation has been addressed, the consultants may have earned their spurs and may become regular problem solvers for the company. Such consultants can range from psychologists to turnaround specialists.

Some companies succeed on their own without a lot of outside help. Others require the assistance of their advisors on an ongoing basis. There is no right or wrong. Every company has to find the right advisors, ones it trusts and relates well to, and use them to the degree that is comfortable. Special event company owners will benefit from these relationships and will hopefully flourish as a result of what they learn from them.

■ SUMMARY

➤ Information flow and information sharing are extremely important issues in the efficient operation of a business.

➤ Understanding job costing is critical, and every company should have a system in place that takes into account both direct and indirect costs to arrive at the true cost of the production.

➤ Reasonable pricing, not too high and not too low, is critical to a company's survival, and it can be arrived at only by keeping the actual cost of producing the event in mind.

➤ Each company should have a policy and procedures manual clearly setting forth company policy in every area in which the company desires to regulate employee behavior and clearly stating the company's stance on important issues like sexual harassment, equal opportunity, workplace violence, and so forth.

➤ Outside professionals should play a role in helping the company determine the most efficient and most effective ways to operate, as well as the policies that protect the company and its employees from legal liabilities.

Chapter 7

Client Service

If you mean to profit, learn to please. —Winston Churchill

A book called *The Service Edge* by Ron Zemke with Dick Schaaf, speaking about the importance of service in business success, characterizes our economy as a *service economy*. The author states that service leaders charge, on average, 9 to 10 percent more than their competitors, yet grow twice as fast and improve market share and profitability. According to Zemke, "Quality control of a service entails watching a process unfold and evaluating it against the customer's judgment. The only completely valid standard of comparison is the customer's level of satisfaction. That's a perception—something appreciably more slippery to measure than the physical dimensions of a product. . . . The intangibility of the service means you must persuade customers that what you can do is something they want and need done and that you do it well . . . it is important to recognize that the receiver's expectations— and perceptions—of the service are integral to his or her satisfaction . . . what we, as consumers, think we are going to receive, compared and contrasted with what we perceive is being received, and the process we go through receiving it, determine our level of satisfaction. It is an all or nothing three-factor formula based on the assumption that the level of our satisfaction with the entire process is the critical link to repeat business." So, both the perception of the service and the process of receiving it are important—meaning that the client looks at how the event company pulls it off, not just that it did.

Now, skip ahead 10 years. In his book, *The Entertainment Economy*, Michael Wolf says that in today's fast-paced world, service is not enough. He states, "The two-word answer is the 'E-Factor', that is, entertainment content and experiences. . . . Given the pervasive impact of entertainment in our economy today, companies must exceed the efforts of the competitors to amuse, arouse and inform customers. In other words, companies need to provide entertainment experiences that engage consumers."

Well, sure, that's what we hope that our clients are thinking when it comes to entertaining their customers, because that means more work for us. But we need to think about what that means for us in selling and producing for our clients. Joseph Pine II and James Gilmore take this thought process further in their book, *The Experience Economy*. They say that theater is not a metaphor for work, but a *model.* "In the emerging experience economy, companies must realize that they make *memories,* not goods, and create the *stage* for generating greater economic value, not deliver services. It is time to get your act together, for goods and services are no longer enough. Customers now want experiences, and they're willing to pay admission for them. There's new work to do, and only those who perform that work so as to truly engage their guests will succeed in this new economy." They go on to say, "In the emerging experience economy, any work observed directly by a customer must be recognized as an act of theater."

Event companies have to take that to mean that every act that they perform with and for a client, from the sale to the production is part of a theatrical performance that is part of the experience of working with their company. How the workers dress, how their trucks look, how professional they act is part of the overall impression they need to make—and it must be a positive one. In the company's own theater, they want top-notch performances; they want standing ovations from their clients/audience.

Yes, just when event companies thought that good service was enough, they are faced with a new challenge of making the experience pleasurable and memorable. Perhaps the authors have overstated the obvious because the level of service that many companies aspire to does provide that experience. It is really more of an evolutionary stage that we have passed through than a revolutionary one. But whatever you call it, it is "show time."

Picture a situation where your furnace breaks down and you call Company A because of its ad in the telephone book. Someone shows up within one hour after the call in a shiny, waxed truck. A repairman wearing a clean, pressed uniform steps through the front door of your home, pulls out a pair of booties, and puts them on his feet so as not to track anything into the house. He immediately diagnoses the problem, pulls out the defective part and shows you where it had worn out. He pulls out a laptop, connects to his company's inventory program on a wireless network, sees that the part is in stock, and, on a portable printer, prints out a repair estimate on the spot. He advises that his schedule will allow him to return within three hours to make the repair, or, if time is really of the essence because of very cold weather, the parts department can deliver the part right away for an additional charge. On completion of the repair, the repairman pulls out a small vacuum and cleans up the area in which he was working. What a performance! Professional, quick, and clean, and if it cost a bit more than a competitor might have charged, the homeowner gladly paid it because of the exceptional service.

If the repairman had showed up the day after the emergency call, tracked in snow, made the same diagnosis, but said he had to go back to the shop to see if they had the part and then find out what it cost and when he could get back, the performance would not have been nearly as impressive. Even if the ultimate price had been less, the homeowner might not have found value in the process. The performance would have gotten mediocre reviews.

The same may hold true for event companies and their performance. Showing up on time or early, looking professional, acting like a professional, and doing the work in a professional manner say a lot about the company, regardless of the price charged. Does any client want cheap but sloppy work? Equipment that is poorly maintained? Of course not. Every client wants good quality, good service, and a low price.

But guess what? Many wise business consultants have said that the three main elements to what a vendor provides a client are quality, service, and price, but they say that it is impossible to be the best at all three. The company offering the best service and the best quality cannot stay in business if it also offers the lowest price. The consultants say the most a client can hope for is two out of the three. How would that work?

If clients value quality and service highly, then they should expect to pay for both of them. The peace of mind that comes from using vendors who can be counted upon to do it right the first time every time is worth a lot to some clients. They budget for the best vendors because the best vendors make the client look the best.

Other clients stubbornly insist on the lowest price. That basically means eliminating either the best service or the best quality. Perhaps a high level of service is not the most important element to a client. The vendor could be a rental company that has great inventory but terrible service. If the client arranges for delivery far enough in advance of when the goods are actually needed so that lateness will not compromise the event and leaves a time window for a second or third trip to get the order right, then things may work out fine. The client may not value piece of mind as highly, or may figure that for the lowest price, "almost right" is good enough. Perhaps the same client would not feel the same way about a vendor that has to produce good work in a narrow time window (e.g., an audio company that has to load in a sound system for a major press conference in a very short time span). For this event, quality and service are both important and therefore price may have to give way.

Take a situation where a planner needs a tent company to put up 40 small tents for a carnival to raise funds for a hospital. Company A has brand-new tents and top-notch installers who can install any complicated tent job. The cost is X. Company B has old inventory and a crew that can install small tents well, but it would be lost on a complicated installation. The cost is X less 25 percent. Company C has old gear, a spotty service record, and a price that is X less 30 percent. In this instance, the quality of the gear is the least important factor. Low price and reasonable service are of more value to the client. Company B would win the contract for this event.

The combination of the three factors (quality, service, and price) produces a client's definition of value for a given service on a given event. All clients want value from what they purchase, yet there is no objective way to put a value on a given event service. It is not like a commodity that has a suggested retail price. Some people find value in a $5,000 wristwatch, others in a $50 timepiece. If the individual finds value only in knowing what time it is, then the $50 watch is probably the answer. If the value is in owning an exquisite piece of jewelry, then the former is the better value. If an event service offered by a vendor is not needed by the client, then the client will not want to pay extra for it and there is no value in it. However, if two companies offer the same quality and the same price, but one offers an additional service that is of use, then that company offers the better value.

When all three areas are fairly equivalent in competing companies, what is going to be the deciding factor? Going back to the theorists who espouse the "experience economy" or the "entertainment economy," the value-added factor may be a bit of that performance magic. Beginning with the person who answers the phone at the office and the person who greets visitors at the door of the office, the "show" must carry through the sales process, the creative process, the event production process, and all the way through invoicing, payment, and beyond. The event company is selling pizzazz, and the client ought to see it.

The pizzazz adds a new element, perhaps a decisive element, to satisfy the client. An event company that sees customer satisfaction as an investment rather than a cost probably understands the big picture. As Jay Conrad Levinson says in *Guerrilla Marketing Attack,*

> *Companies that enjoy remarkably high profits as a result of customer service have certain characteristics in common: They are*

obsessed with knowing what the customer wants. They know cus-
tomer expectations must be understood and managed before they
can be met and exceeded. They design their products and their
services to maximize customer satisfaction. They knock them-
selves out trying to be an easy company to do business with. They
know the money they invest in customer service will pay off in
satisfaction for the customers, profits for them. They repeat and
repeat again that customer service is the responsibility of every-
one in the organization.

Meeting expectations is enough for some companies: Give the client what is promised and call it a day. But in a competitive market, it may not be. Levinson goes on to say that clients don't really buy products or services, but rather, they buy expectations, and the measure of success is how well their confidence in the vendor is rewarded. Therefore, surpassing expectations would inspire the most confidence, thus resulting in an ongoing relationship and no need to sample other vendors.

Where do all of these different theorists come together in harmonious agreement? They all agree that service is critical. They all seem to agree that, at bare minimum, surpassing client expectations to some degree is almost an expected level of service. And to add one last spin, it seems that all of this needs to be done with a bit of flair and panache. The sizzle may be an investment on the part of the provider, but a good part of that investment should be in time and in training employees about what is important, what is expected, and what behavior is necessary every time. Having someone answer the phone the same way every time with a smile in their voice is not expensive. Training a salesperson to send a thank-you note every time does not cost much. Sending a client-satisfaction survey with each invoice can become a habit in no time. Telling clients their business is valued and repeating it at every step of the relationship can be ingrained without difficulty and is easier to teach employees than how to ride a two-wheeler. Giving clients shirts, sweatshirts, or jackets with their name on them is no less than what is done for every employee. Addressing client complaints in a positive and forthright manner and always looking to build a relationship rather than win a battle are learned traits—valuable for a company to teach as part of its definition of service.

In *Competing for the Future,* authors Gary Hamel and C. K. Prahalad make some very interesting points. First, they state, "Typically, the existing industry structure works to the disadvantage of everyone save the industry leader, and most especially to the disadvantage of aspiring aspirants. What is needed is a capacity to transform the structure of an industry." They then go on to add that "industries don't 'evolve.' Instead, firms eager to overturn the present industry order challenge 'accepted practice,' redraw segment boundaries, set new price-performance expectations, and reinvent the product or service concept." Perhaps that is what all the theatricality is about—an attempt to reinvent the service concept. Perhaps all of these theorists are actually in agreement.

Hamel and Prahalad's insights are fascinating and merit considerable study. If event company managers could take the time to read their book and digest their ideas, it would be well worth their while. If they could take the time to go on a retreat for a few days with a skilled leader, they could provoke thought and transformation in many companies. Consider the following from *Competing for the Future*. (Read it a few times until the words strike home.)

> *In our experience, strategic planning typically fails to provoke deeper debates about who we are as a company or who we want to be in ten years' time. It seldom escapes the boundaries of existing business units. It seldom illuminates new white space opportunities, provides any insight onto how to rewrite industry rules. It seldom stretches to encompass the threat from nontraditional competitors. It seldom forces managers to confront their potentially out-of-date conventions. Strategic planning almost always starts with "what is." It seldom starts with "what could be." . . . Strategic planning works well when the foundations of planning—assumptions about what is our "industry," what "business" are we in, who are our competitors, who are our customers, and what are their needs—remain unshaken. But in many industries these foundations are being shaken. They are being shaken by new competitors who have no stake in the past. They are being shaken by seismic shifts in technology, demographics and the regulatory environment. Strategic planning is well-suited to the challenge of extending leadership—adding a story or two atop the old foundation. It is not well-suited to the challenge of regenerating leadership—building new foundations. . . . To extend industry foresight and develop a supporting strategic architecture, companies need a new perspective on what it means to be strategic. They need to ask new strategy questions: not just how to maximize share and profit in today's businesses, but who do we want to be as a corporation in ten years' time, how can we reshape this industry to our advantage, what new functionalities do we want to create for customers and what new core competencies should we be building? . . . They need to apply new and different*

*resources to the task of strategy-making, relying on the creativity
of hundreds of managers and not just on the wisdom of a few
planners.*

Wow!

Hamel and Prahalad cite Wal-Mart, Southwest Airlines, and
Charles Schwab as examples of companies that have turned an industry on its head by using this thought process. They were small upstarts
in established industries, not market leaders, and look what they
became. It is a safe bet that there will never be a special event company that will become the size of Wal-Mart, but that does not mean the
same ideas can't apply. That does not mean that much smaller event
companies cannot awaken to the sheer ingenuity of these ideas and
apply them to their discipline and their industry. Some may fall into
it by luck. A few others will actually invoke the reasoning and come
up with ways to advance themselves to the top.

In summary, service is important. Even when clients more highly
value quality and price, service is important. *Minimal service* means
meeting client expectations. *Good service* exceeds client expectations.
Excellent service exceeds client expectations in a theatrical or entertaining manner. All event companies should be capable of each of
these levels without incurring outrageous effort or expense. Why more
aren't providing it is no mystery. They don't know, or they don't
understand, or they don't care. All three are poor excuses. The companies that reach the highest level of service should stay near the top of
their field as long as the shape of the field and the rules don't change.
But what if they do? Good service will still be important. It may just
look very different.

The companies that bridge the gap between what is and what could
be and find a way to market that as a benefit to their clients and to
markets full of potential clients will redefine service. Some of those
companies exist right now and are going through the process of creating a new vision for their companies that will make them competitive
leaders. Others will follow thereafter, again altering the landscape.
They have what Robert Kriegel and David Brandt, authors of *Sacred
Cows Make the Best Burgers,* call "change-ready thinking." Their three
rules for change-ready thinking are (1) "Tilt the playing field in your
direction. (2) Don't play by someone else's rules. Make your own. (3)
Head to head competition will give you a headache."

The last point to be made here is well stated by Pine and Gilmore
in *The Experience Economy.* They say "The strategy of business confers
meaning only if those called on to execute it understand—ideally, vis-
cerally—how the company plans to alter the very structure of the
world through its industry. Every activity of the company must be

performed *in order* to advance external change. The firm can then fulfill its specific strategic intention not by competing for the future but by actively attaining that future." This is a high-minded hard sell to all levels of employees, but if traditional service techniques can be made organizational gospel, there is every reason to push beyond that to new levels.

■ SUMMARY

➤ Service counts, and it will always count, even if the client doesn't see it as a priority.

➤ Client expectations must be met—and should be exceeded.

➤ How they are exceeded may be the most telling marketing the company does.

➤ Companies that play by existing rules need to focus on being leaders in service.

➤ Companies that change the rules, and thus redefine their business and their industry, will also redefine service.

Chapter 8

Contracts

*A verbal contract isn't worth the paper it's
written on. —Samuel Goldwyn*

The most basic reason for having a contract is to set forth clearly the
terms of the deal so each party knows its rights and responsibilities
and what the consequences are if responsibilities are not carried out,
no matter what the reason. Did the parties get what they bargained
for? If not, what happens? If there is a dispute about whether each got
what they were supposed to, then what? There was a day when a handshake was all that was needed to seal a deal for many people. But there
was also a day when contract disputes were settled by sword fights or
shootings.

Most engagements barely involve reference to the contract, because the parties are professional, the terms are clear, and performance occurs without a hitch. That is the most common experience,
but it is not one that should be relied on 100 percent. That is not a reason to bypass the contractual process. Remember, everyone in the special events industry has horror stories to share about disputes with
clients, vendors, or facilities. We all know about the vendor who didn't
provide what he was supposed to, or the client who changed her mind
three times while the event was being set up, or the facility that
promised to be available at 2:00 but was not available until 5:00. The
contract is the protective device to cover the instances when things do
not go as planned. It can also be a deterrent to an intentional breach.

When the contract must be relied on to enforce rights, numerous
clauses come into play, most of which nobody reads or cares about
when the deal is being struck, but which become highly relevant in
the event of a dispute. For that reason, they are critical to think about
in advance. Typically, such clauses are not even noticed or read carefully by the party to whom the contract is submitted. However, an
exception to the rule is the corporate client submitting the contract to

the legal department for review. An in-house lawyer reviews documents with an eye toward protecting the company, and any clause that works against the best interest of the company will be stricken. At this point, the vendor has the choice of either agreeing or refusing to accept the deletions (and perhaps risking the loss of the job). This is always a tough decision. It should be noted that subcontractors are faced with the same issue when presented with a contract by the party hiring them.

Vendors should be prepared for this eventuality and have a thought process worked out. Perhaps there is a backup plan with a compromise on terms, or perhaps it's a definite yes or no based on the vendor's probable exposure to risk. Just as problematic is the situation where the client has not stricken a clause, damage occurs, and the vendor is then faced with invoking the clause against a good client. If the client refuses to pay, then what? Sue a good client?

Instances occur when both parties have contracts they wish the other to sign. Obviously, it makes no sense to have two separate contracts governing the same transaction, especially if they contain different terms. This situation is one in which the principals have to be patient and take the time to work through each term in each contract, agree on what they can, and then see whether the result is acceptable to both sides. Typically, a salesperson or designer is not going to want to delve into contractual issues too much. That task will fall to the owner or chief operating officer, who may be busy with his or her own work and who does not have the interest in taking the time to deal with someone else's mess. Here is an opportunity for disaster. Someone in the company needs to act, no matter how painful it may be. Outside counsel is often not called because of the expense, but being penny-wise can be a costly exercise. Someone in the company must have the responsibility (set forth in a job description) to negotiate and decide these sticky contractual issues. In many cases, the nature of small companies dictates that this onerous task falls to the owner. Oh, it is lonely at the top. But, the owner needs to remember what might be at stake and who stands to lose.

■ WHAT CONSTITUTES A CONTRACT?

Again, I must reiterate that this is *not* a legal text, nor does it attempt to accurately state the specific law in any jurisdiction. This chapter offers readers insights into their situations, hopefully before they become a problem, and points out where legal advice might be warranted.

In its simplest form, a contract comprises an offer, an acceptance of that offer, and consideration, or something that passes between the parties to seal the deal. There must be enough specificity so that each party has a reasonable understanding of what each is getting, and this understanding should constitute a meeting of the minds.

> **Example:** *A party planner hires a florist to provide 25 center-pieces for an event on October 1 at a cost of $25 each, for a total of $625. The florist pulls out a standard order form, fills in the information, and the planner signs it. Contract? Offer, acceptance, and consideration are all present, so yes it is. What happens when the flowers are delivered at 3:00 P.M. on October 1, but the party was at 1:00 P.M.? What happens if the flowers are delivered and the planner doesn't like them or doesn't think they are worth $25 per centerpiece? What happens if the party is canceled and the planner won't pay for them even though the centerpieces are all made up?*

True, a contract exists, but it doesn't contain the provisions needed to ensure that both parties will get what they bargained for. That means that both parties needed to be more specific in their information and to include that information in the contract. The florist should have specified which flowers were going to be included in the centerpiece and what the container would look like. The planner should have made it clear that the flowers needed to be delivered no later than 11:00 A.M. on the date of the event. And both parties should have been concerned about cancellation charges. These terms could easily have been built into the florist's form, and thus any difficulty could have been avoided.

Interesting questions arise, some of which are practical or ethical in nature rather than purely legal, that can add further layers of difficulty. A vendor's particular situation and the importance of the relationship with the client may supersede the legal issues. A number of factors must be weighed, including (1) the importance of the client to the vendor in the bigger scheme of things, (2) the cost involved relative to the total amount of business generated by this client, (3) how much it will hurt the vendor to eat the loss. There is no right or wrong answer in this situation. The vendor can have the contract on its side, yet still, based on the answers to these questions, decide to not pursue matters.

> **Example:** *A planner hires a lighting contractor for a large event that requires a multiday installation. The vendor has a contractual clause making the planner responsible for any loss or damage to equipment while on site. On returning the second morning, the*

contractor finds $10,000 worth of equipment missing. Now what happens?

First and foremost, as everyone in the industry knows, the show must go on. The vendor needs to put the client on notice of the loss immediately and must then move ahead to have it replaced and install the show. A telephone call to the office should be made by the vendor requesting notification of the insurance company and that a letter immediately go out to the client's office formally advising of the loss and reminding the client of the clause in the contract making the client responsible. The vendor has then acted professionally in all ways. Theoretically, the client should also arrange to have its insurance company put on notice. On completion of the event, it should all be sorted out.

The vendor seems to be in a strong position here contractually, but what about practically? A number of questions can still arise. For instance, (1) what about consequential damages? What if the vendor had to go out and rent additional equipment to finish the job, with additional labor? Who pays for this? Even worse, what if the stolen gear had been rented from another company? (2) Does the planner have insurance to cover the losses? (3) Does the vendor's own insurance policy cover the situation? If so, what will invoking that policy ultimately cost the vendor? (4) Can the vendor afford to eat the loss? (3) Will the vendor's close relationship with the client prevent invoking the damage clause? (4) Will the fear of losing the client keep the vendor from invoking it?

If the vendor does invoke the loss clause and the client still refuses to pay, then what? Again, a practical question requires a practical answer. Suing the client undoubtedly means the end of that vendor-client relationship. What else does it mean? It could mean long hours and many dollars spent on litigation. Is it worth it? It could mean a degree of infamy in the local event community, causing others to steer clear of the vendor. It could mean an opening for the vendor's biggest competitor to snare that client's work. These are far-reaching ramifications. Some people see issues only in black and white, while others see many shades of gray. How these issues are viewed may depend on who is doing the viewing.

In the preceding scenario, one could also look into the contract between the planner and the event site to determine whether responsibility for security was the facility's. If so, that brings another party into the mix. If the equipment lost was, in fact, rental equipment, then the rental company becomes the fourth party involved in this situation. The contracts between (1) the rental company and the lighting company, (2) lighting company and planner, and (3) planner and facility all have to be examined to sort this out.

■ WHAT SHOULD BE IN A CONTRACT?

Special events companies are far from homogeneous. There are dozens of disciplines, each with unique issues relevant specifically to them. Beyond that, within different geographical regions other issues may present themselves that would be irrelevant elsewhere. It is difficult to create a comprehensive, specific list of clauses, but it is possible to spell out 9 broad concepts important to every contract.

1. *First and foremost, the contract should specify clearly who the parties are.* This may seem rudimentary, and in most cases it is, but there will be instances when a contracting party is merely acting as an agent for another. The names on the contract should include the names of the party responsible for providing the services and the party responsible for the payment for those services. If it comes down to a lawsuit, this is important. Too often, invoices are sent by a vendor to the name on the contract only to be told that a third party will actually be making the payment. The parties whose names and signature are on the contract are the ones with legal responsibility. If someone else has agreed to reimburse them, that is fine, but they are still responsible under the contract.

2. *Just as important, the expectations of the parties should be spelled out.* Services should be described in detail, and the payment terms should be laid out clearly. There should be no doubt about what is expected of either party. For example, if a deposit is required along with the signing of the contract, it should be made clear that no work will be done and no materials will be ordered until that deposit is received. It might help vendors to control the contractual process by not signing the contract until after the client has signed and returned it with the deposit. Without a deposit, there is no contract. If a *signed* contract is sent to a client who then signs and returns it without a deposit, a strong argument can be made that a contract exists, and the vendor may be obligated to order materials and begin work, even without payment.

If final payment is desired by the planner before the event actually starts, the contract should so state and should set forth the consequences for noncompliance. Some vendors are in a position to hold an event hostage (e.g., by not turning on the power for the lights, audio, and video or by refusing to bring out the food until payment is received). This will obviously create a tough situation for all, but if the client has had fair notice of the payment requirement and doesn't show up with the check, one can almost presume that the vendor has a good chance of successfully suing for payment down the road.

Likewise, the terms of delivery of the services should be covered. If something needs to be on-site at a given time, the contract should say so; and it should say that this is material to the contract. If a delivery needs to be at the loading dock between 11:00 and 11:30, the contract should so state. *The terms of the deal should be understandable by anyone who reads the contract.* Very often, contracts are sent out and signed before some of these details are actually known. Once the details are known, the contracts should be amended to reflect them, or a letter containing those details and indicating that it is part of the contract should be sent out by one party and signed by both parties.

3. *How additions or changes are to be handled needs to be made clear.* This should not be left to be sorted out after the event. Only a party responsible for payment should be allowed to sign for additions or changes. At the height of job-site stress, it is important to remember who the paying client is. If the client is not on-site to make the change order, then a new contract for the additional work should be signed by the party requesting the changes, with that party assuming financial responsibility for them.

4. *The contract should specify who pays which costs.* Event costs such as permits, licenses, facility fees, loading dock fees, and electrical charges need to be paid by someone. It is asking for trouble not to specify who. The vendor should make it clear what charges are included within its price and which ones are left for the client to pay. Likewise, if the client gives a vendor a budget that becomes the dollar amount of the contract, the contract should specify whether the amount includes the additional charges.

5. *In a union venue, spell out who is paying for the union labor and all related charges.* It should also be clear that the union labor estimate is just that, an *estimate*. If the union comes in higher, who is going to pay the overage? It is very often the case that vendors and clients unfamiliar with working in a union venue have no idea how charges are accrued. Both parties need to be educated about the workings of the various union contracts and what that means dollarwise.

6. *Define how contract termination or cancellation should be handled.* There are several factors to consider here. Termination of a contract may be requested before either party has been affected, but it can also occur after one party has been impacted (e.g., turned down work in reliance on a given piece of business filling the schedule, bought supplies, booked labor, or purchased expensive new gear).

Some vendors allow a contract to be terminated if they have not incurred out-of-pocket expenses or turned down work. Others expect full payment under any circumstances. It may be that a blanket rule cannot be set down for all cases. The parties need to give each set of circumstances some thought. What if the bride cancels out on the morning of the wedding? What does the planner do? What about her vendors? What about a last-minute cancellation due to weather? Conversely, what if the planner does not want to cancel for bad weather and the vendor won't send out a crew, fearing for their safety? There are no pat answers to these questions, nor is there a law that orders certain behaviors. It depends on what the parties agree to, and therefore it is mandatory that some thought be given to every situation.

> **Example:** *A client contracts with a tent company to put up a tent on Mount Snow in Vermont for a February sales incentive at the World Ski Championships. The tent company is hungry for that rare February piece of business and wants to go to contract immediately. Before doing so however, it should think through the possible negatives and cover them in its contract. What if the roads are blocked and the truck can't get there? What if it snows heavily during setup, causing major problems? What about snow buildup on the tent once it is up?*
>
> *The client should be concerned about weather preventing the guests from coming and causing a cancellation. Both sides need to think through their requested contractual clauses to best protect themselves.*

7. *The issue of insurance should be covered.* Planners and facilities like to make sure that vendors have insurance protecting them in the event of injury to persons or property or in the event of damage to the facility. Vendors like to know that if something happens to their gear, their client has insurance that will cover it. While everyone carries some insurance, most people prefer to use somebody else's rather than their own. This issue needs to be thought through carefully. If a lighting company takes 100 intelligent lights to a venue where it will be working for one week, it will want to make sure its equipment is as secure as possible and covered by as much insurance as possible. For $500,000 worth of equipment, the vendor will want to put a clause in the contract stating that the client will provide 24-hour security in the event space and will carry a minimum of $500,000 in property coverage.

The planner, and sometimes even the planner's client, will often want to have certificates of insurance from all vendors showing they have liability insurance and even property damage coverage. Beyond that, planners may want to be named as "additional insureds" on the vendor's certificate so that if they are sued as a result of a problem caused by the vendor, the vendor's insurance will cover them.

Example: *A guest at the event slips and falls on a greasy spot on the floor where one of the waiters has spilled salad dressing and neglected to clean it up. The guest sues the planner, the planner's client, the caterer, and everyone else who might be remotely responsible. If the planner and her client are named as additional insureds on the caterer's certificate of insurance, the caterer's insurance company ends up providing a defense for all three parties and pays any judgment against any of the three.*

8. *Be aware of standard clauses and understand what they mean.* If you use your attorney to draft your form contract, you will probably find loads of form language, affectionately referred to as *boilerplate*. It usually involves clauses that protect the drafting party in as many ways as possible. It provides the easiest way to bring a lawsuit, to get a judgment, to collect on a judgment. Typically, it is some of these clauses that are excised by corporate counsel. From a practical point of view, it is a good idea to have a sense of which clauses you are willing to compromise on.

Importantly, these clauses may also specify the state in which any lawsuit must be brought and which state's laws are to apply in the lawsuit. This can have far-reaching effects.

Example: *A planner from Pennsylvania is hired by a corporation headquartered in Illinois to handle an event in Maryland. When the event is over, the corporation refuses to pay the balance on the contract, believing that the planner did not perform under the terms of the contract. The planner decides to sue, and brings her case in Pennsylvania. The corporation refers to the contract, which states that all suits must be brought in Illinois. The suit in Pennsylvania is thrown out and the planner is forced to consider hiring an Illinois lawyer and bringing suit 800 miles away to pursue her fee.*

The fact that the contract specified where suit had to be brought made life easier for the corporation and miserable for the planner in this example. It pays to have such a clause in your contract when dealing with parties from another state.

Likewise, conflict of laws is an important issue when one party is dealing with a party from another state or when the work under the contract takes place in another state. Laws may vary from state to state on damages or liability. By stating in the contract which state's law applies, a party can protect itself from less advantageous laws of other states.

9. A good clause to have in the contract is one adding monthly finance charges for late payment. It should clearly specify when the charges commence (e.g., 30 days from the date of the event) and what the charges are. Contracts with finance charges of up to 2 percent per month have been upheld by courts. Additionally, a clause making the other party responsible for court costs and attorney fees is also a helpful deterrent to breach.

■ BREACH OF CONTRACT

To be successful in a breach-of-contract lawsuit, a party must be able to show that the terms of the contract are clear, that both parties agreed to them, that one party breached them, and that damages arose as a result of the breach. Those damages must be provable. Again, from a practical point of view, the damages need to be more than the cost of litigation or the case is clearly not worth pursuing. One point to remember—litigation is not fun. It is time-consuming; it unfolds very slowly over many months or years; and it is frustrating. Any time spent on a lawsuit is time away from business.

> **Example:** *A subvendor makes an awful mess of an event and the vendor takes the heat. The vendor had just signed an agreement to produce 20 events for the client, but the first one has so many problems that the client terminates the contract. The vendor refuses to pay the subvendor for services rendered.*
>
> *The subvendor may sue the vendor for breach of contract (non-payment). The vendor's defense is breach by the subvendor in not providing the quality of services contemplated by the contract. Even worse, the vendor may have a claim against the subvendor for all of the income lost from the remaining 19 events.*
>
> *The vendor may also have a claim against the client for termination, depending on how this is stated in the contract. There are several complicated issues in this situation, and a detailed understanding of the facts may help simplify them, but not necessarily to the point where a lawsuit's result is preordained.*

Very few breaches of contract are intentional. But it can be expected that there will be numerous instances where one party or another may take advantage of a gray area or may interpret a gray area in his or her favor. There may be technical breaches that are actually immaterial in nature and should be ignored. For instance, if a vendor contractually agrees to have all work completed one hour prior to the start of the event and actually finished 45 minutes prior to the event, there is a technical breach, but what are the damages? Usually, there would be no damages. But suppose the client wanted to photograph the finished event for a magazine cover prior to guests arriving, and further suppose that the photographer needed one hour to get the shots. An argument could be made that there are huge damages, as having the right cover photo could mean great publicity that would translate into many new clients. Contracts are an art, not a science, and so is the interpretation of them.

It is impossible to anticipate every single problem that may arise and to try to address it in an agreement. However, the common ones, which probably cover 80 percent or more of all situations, can be covered in several clauses in a form agreement.

> **Example:** *A vendor's contract with its client states that the contract price is contingent on getting the event space at the hour specified in the contract and on breakdown being able to take place at the time specified. The facility allows a prior event to run substantially over its allotted time, and in order to finish its work on time, the vendor must call in 10 additional staff to complete its work. To compound things, at the end of the evening, the event runs an hour and a half late, and the vendor's crew is sitting around earning overtime. The vendor certainly has the right to bill the client for additional labor charges. At the same time, if the client's contract with the facility gave a specific time for availability of the event space and it was not honored, the client may also have a claim against the facility.*

Obviously, the typical breach-of-contract argument is motivated by money and by one of the parties feeling aggrieved. A planning company may feel that it is being charged more than the contract called for or that it got less than it bargained for, and therefore it is going to pay less. On the flip side, a vendor may feel that the planner caused it to incur more event production expense than anticipated or added items of value that should be charged for.

Here are other common issues that arise with some regularity (and this is far from a comprehensive list):

➤ Payment issues—late payment, no payment, deductions from payment due to grievances

➤ Additional charges—additional work done, changes to the job, events running overtime, rentals returned late

➤ Equipment issues—some equipment not working properly, extra equipment requested at last minute

➤ Damage issues—damage to a vendor's equipment by client's guests, union labor, or unknown reason; stolen equipment, rentals, props; damage to a facility

■ TYPES OF CONTRACTUAL RELATIONSHIPS

Contractual relationships are limited only by the human imagination. Here we discuss those types most pertinent to the event planning industry.

➤ Contracts with Facilities

Working in a facility for the first time can be exciting, and finding the exact facility you want for an event can lead you to rush to sign the facility contract to lock up the space. Once signed, bargaining power goes out the window. It clearly pays to review the contract carefully before signing and committing an employer or a client to all of its terms.

Contracts arising between facilities and those renting the facilities for an event are normally form contracts presented by the facility and containing clauses totally favoring the facility. It is helpful to go over the contract clause by clause with the facility manager and to discuss and negotiate any clauses that the renting party might find questionable or unfavorable. It seems so simple and natural, but most people do not do it. They commit without knowing what they have committed to. And there can be some fairly serious consequences.

Many event people are under the mistaken belief that facilities really want them there. While this is true for facilities like hotels and conference centers that exist for that purpose, it is absolutely not true for museums, public buildings, and other edifices for which events are not a reason for their existence. What many of these facilities need, particularly museums or other public spaces, is the *revenue* from the rentals. They do not really want events, but their need has put them in the position where they must accept them. And they accept them very reluctantly. Typically, there may even be hostility toward events and the event department by the other departments, which tend to feel that events are nothing more than a giant inconvenience. In other words, their rules are not designed to make it easy for event people. They are designed more to protect the facility and bring in revenue.

For instance, some facilities may have a *loading-dock charge,* a fee for using their dock to get event items into the building. This is uncommon, but it does exist. Who in their right mind would agree to this if they were aware of it? So it's important to be aware. The same can be said for use of a facility's freight elevator, personnel lifts, and so forth.

Oftentimes a facility will charge an additional amount for electrical power consumed by the event. The charges are on a per-circuit basis, and they far exceed the actual cost—they are a profit center. Many times they are outrageous. These charges should be negotiated in advance, not after the contract is signed. A big show with much lighting, audio, or video could lead to thousands of dollars of additional expenses for the unwary. Likewise, there can be additional charges for use of water for laser shows.

Charges for extra personnel staying on-site during an event—for security, for overseeing electrical or other engineering services, or for cleanup—should be reviewed and discussed. Many times these charges are very high—again, a profit center for the facility.

There may be extra charges for setup and removal days that are not mentioned in the contract or disclosed verbally. The contract shows the event date as the rental date, but no mention is made of the time needed to set up beforehand and dismantle it afterward. The facility will then force the renter to incur additional charges for those days. Removal deadlines may be so short that they are impossible to reach without bringing in a tremendous crew at huge cost. Setup and removal should be part of the initial negotiations for the space. This means that planners have to understand the nature and complexity of their event and have a sense of the amount of time needed on either side of the event to accomplish everything.

Facilities often have contractual clauses requiring a renter to use certain facility services, such as catering, lighting, or audio. In many instances this is not a problem, but in some cases it may be. There may be a conflict with one of the exclusive vendors from past dealings, or the capabilities of those vendors and the quality of the available services may not be up to the standards of the renter. Exceptions to the exclusive-vendor clauses should be discussed before signing. If a renter has specific needs requiring an outside vendor to be brought in, that should be negotiated as a condition of the agreement. It may be that a fee will have to be paid to bring in another vendor, to break an exclusive, but the amount of the fee should be known up front.

Union issues may arise out of these agreements as well, and even though a renter may not be able to fight it, the clauses should be read carefully. Certain so-called union facilities do not disclose this in their contracts or verbal sales pitches. It is incumbent upon the potential renter to ask that question and to find out what the answer means to them. Any outdoor event in a public space in a typical union city has the potential of involving at least one or two unions—even if the space is not deemed a union space. The client needs to be aware of this and hopefully to get some sort of guarantee that the facility manager will deal with the unions for the renter.

The issue of responsibility for damages caused to the facility during an event is an important one. Clauses covering this subject are prominent in many facility contracts. These clauses should be reviewed carefully, because they leave the renter open to liability for damages that they (or their vendors or guests) may not have caused. In many contracts it is presumed that any damage that shows up after an event was caused by the event, and therefore the renting party is responsible. While a renter should undoubtedly be responsible for damages that it caused or that were caused by its vendors or guests, there should be some language requiring proof that the renter was, in fact, responsible.

A renter should do a walk-through of a facility with a facility representative before loading in, making note of any chipped columns, gouges in walls, and so on. This is basically the same thing you do with a rental car before accepting it. An end user who rents a facility may have a hard time disputing damages if a walk-through is not done prior to the event. If damage is noted immediately following the event, the facility will undoubtedly hold the event responsible. Because it is unlikely that the planner personally caused the damage, the planner should have a contractual clause with all vendors making them responsible for damage they cause.

The bill for repairs should be reviewed carefully, as it may not be itemized or may not represent the least expensive way of effecting the repair. It may even include additional repairs unrelated to the alleged damage. If the client looks to one or more of its vendors to pay the bill, there must be some proof of who is responsible. If a light being installed falls and breaks a display case, it is fairly obvious who is responsible. However, if a corner of a statue's base is chipped on an event where six vendors were wheeling hand trucks and dollies through the space, assigning responsibility may be difficult.

Finally, some facilities will make planners sign a clause stating that they are responsible for any costs billed to vendors that are not paid by the vendor. Thus, a planner could include within a vendor's budget all facility labor expenses. If the vendor does not pay the facility for those expenses, the planner could be responsible to the facility, effectively paying those expenses twice. Planners must watch out for this or include protective clauses in their agreements with their vendors.

➤ Contracts with Entertainers

Entertainment issues can also be a sticky contractual quagmire. Oftentimes, clients are so excited that the band they desire is available, they sign a contract without reading the small print or consulting with their key vendors first. Entertainment contracts can have outrageous riders under which a client is responsible for providing (and paying for) all of the lighting, special effects, audio, video, staging, catering, travel, and hotel rooms specified. Unknowing clients can agree to tens of thousands of dollars of additional expense, breaking their budget right out of the gate. First-class airfare or private jet, hotel suites, outrageous food and beverage demands, and other such "needs" are not uncommon. Many bands playing a corporate event in a ballroom will submit their arena or stadium technical specifications, which a planner may be bound to. It is much better to have the technical director or lighting or audio designer negotiate the rider down to a manageable size for the venue before the contract is signed.

Contracts with entertainers should clearly state that they are independent contractors, not employees for the show. This avoids many workers' compensation or tax issues. The contract should also clearly state the duration of the performance and the content. This can be critical with national acts and temperamental superstars who might walk off of the stage on a whim.

> **Example:** *A planner signs a contract with a famous comedian, calling for a 75-minute performance. The comedian is heckled 30 minutes into the show for a joke many thought was in bad taste. He gives the audience a rude gesture, walks off the stage, and leaves the premises. The client would have a cause of action against the performer for breach of a material clause in the contract.*

The final entertainment-related issue is the payment of the requisite fees to BMI and/or ASCAP to cover royalties on all music played as part of a meeting or event. It should be remembered that songs are copyrighted. These two organizations represent hundreds of thousands of songwriters, composers, and music publishers. The license fees they collect are distributed to the various copyright holders.

The license fees collected are for the public performance of copyrighted songs. This applies to events, conventions, and festivals where music is played either by live bands or via prerecorded songs. ASCAP defines *public performance* as "one that occurs in a place open to the public or at any place where a substantial number of persons outside of a normal circle of a family and its social acquaintances is gathered." This certainly covers most events we attend.

Many planners and producers totally ignore this area, out of either ignorance or a belief that they will not get caught. They may not get caught, but then again they just may. The royalty-collecting organizations have become much more thorough in their collection methods. Calls should be made to local offices to determine what is required of a client. Planners should put language in contracts with clients to protect themselves and to advise clients of their responsibilities in this area. Both BMI and ASCAP have multiple forms that are available for completion based on the type of situation involved. The fees are not high and the cost is fairly minimal, certainly less than the penalties if you are caught trying to avoid payment of fees altogether.

➤ Contracts with Subcontractors

At one time or another, every company in the special events industry has to hire a subcontractor to help fulfill a contract. Obviously, everyone wants their subcontractors to perform their services in a qualified, competent, and capable fashion, within budget and within time parameters. Beyond that, what could be desired from a sub?

Remembering that a subcontractor is a representative of the party bringing the sub into the event, it is important to remember priorities. If a company makes a point of maintaining a professional appearance and has rules of dress and comportment for employees, it may want those same rules to apply to the employees of the subcontractor. If so, this should be made a part of the contract with the subcontractor.

If the terms are not spelled out in the contract, there is no legal entitlement to have the subcontractor act a certain way. Typically, the areas covered by contractual terms are appearance and comportment. Rules regarding appearance may include such things as no shorts, no T-shirts with obscene or politically, religiously, or socially offensive words or slogans. Or perhaps employees of the sub must wear the T-shirt or uniform of the party hiring the sub. Comportment issues include rules about smoking, language, behavior in front of the end user client and/or guests, eating from the client's buffets, and so on.

Vendors certainly want to protect their relationships with their clients, and they do not want their subcontractors trying to establish a direct relationship, especially on the vendor's event. Accordingly, this should be addressed in the contract—no business cards being passed out, no business-related discussions with anyone on-site except the representative of the party hiring them, no discussion of prices, and so on.

Sometimes a project is of such complexity that the event company needs to work closely with its subcontractor on the creation of a proposal. The event company may become nervous about sharing so much information. This is particularly the case if the subcontractor is a popular one, or perhaps the leading company in its market. Knowing that other bidders on the project will probably contact the same subcontractor, the event company will want to protect against details of its proposal leaking out. Accordingly, event companies may require subcontractors to sign an agreement not to bid on a given project with anyone else. Even if they are not quite that stringent, event companies may still require a confidentiality agreement forbidding a subcontractor to reveal any details of their proposals.

These terms should be made material to the contract, emphasizing their importance and that breaching them will be treated as a serious matter. An example of a subcontractor agreement may be found in the appendix.

➤ Contracts between Clients and Vendors

Typically, the contract process between client and vendor is initiated when the client says, "Send me a proposal." The proposal is either accepted by the client, revised, or rejected. In the first two instances, it very often becomes the contract, and technically it *is* a contract. It describes what is being proposed and puts a price on the services. The client signs, indicating acceptance, and that is that. However, neither party is as fully protected as it could and should be.

Few people find paperwork to be fun. For most people, drafting detailed contracts probably ranks only a rung or two above having a root canal. But let there be no doubt—a root canal is preferable to litigation arising from a poorly written contract. Both sides should take the time to cover themselves.

If the vendor is the drafting party, it has the opportunity to frame the terms of the transaction in a manner favorable to it. First, it should clearly state the services being provided in as much detail as is practical. It is possible to keep stock phrases in the computer as templates and call them up as needed. Any renderings, photographs, or other descriptions that will ensure that the client understands clearly what it is getting should be attached and made part of the agreement.

An installation schedule should also be attached, making it clear how much time is required to do the installation and that this amount of time is material to the contract. If there is less time, the vendor cannot ensure completion of the installation. The same goes for removal. The client should be made responsible for making certain that the space is available when needed. This should include loading docks, because it makes no difference if the space is available if the vendor cannot get its trucks to the dock.

If the vendor needs access to an open floor space to the ceiling or some other area, it should be specified. If a video company needs dark time to focus projectors, it should be specified and included in the contract. If one vendor cannot do certain things until other vendors have completed their work, this should be specified as well, so that it is clear that the client must push vendors along to maintain the schedule.

If a vendor needs electrical power, water, or other venue services, it should so state in the contract and also state who is responsible for providing them. If the vendor is the provider, it should state their cost and make sure the client knows whether these costs are included in the price or in addition to the price.

The contract should state how additions and changes will be handled, particularly on the job site. The need for them, or, as the vendor sometimes sees it, the compulsive urge to tinker on the part of a planner or producer, makes the vendor vulnerable when time, equipment on hand, and allocation of available labor are sufficient to do the job originally contracted for but may not be sufficient to accommodate the requested additions or alterations. This invariably arises on complicated event productions, as producers or planners seek to fine-tune or adjust how their vision is taking shape. As a rule, vendors should complete the work specified in their contract before embarking on changes. This policy should be made clear to the client. Then, if there is time for additions or changes, they can be attempted. See the appendix for an example of a change order form.

Finally, the vendor should very clearly state the payment terms and that keeping to these terms is material to the contract. Some clients just do not take this issue seriously. If a planner is waiting for payment from her client, she may delay paying her vendors until she has been paid, even if that means going beyond their terms. Clients must understand that vendors must be paid whether they have been paid by their clients or not. If planners are on 60-day terms with their clients, and they need payment in full to pay the vendors, how can they agree to 30-day terms with vendors? Some assume they can pay late and it won't matter. Others give it no thought at all. Some require enough deposit money from their clients to pay vendors in full in a timely fashion. Fair dealing should require that the planner be honest with the vendor about when payment can be expected. If it is going to be 60 or 90 days, vendors should be apprised and should factor the cost of that time into their price.

Vendors should also specify which items may be taken by guests (centerpieces, tabletop props, etc.), which have to be returned, and the amount of charges if they are not returned. Guests at events have been known to take almost anything not nailed down, including trees, expensive vases, candlesticks, tablecloths, and props. Rental companies typically have breakage and missing item charges in their rental contracts. Their clients should be used to paying for missing forks and broken glassware. Caterers face this situation all the time. Do they put a clause in their contract with the planner saying that the planner will be charged for these items? Does the planner put such a clause in the contract with the end user? There should be consistency all of the way through the contracting process. The event giver should be responsible for the actions of their guests in breaking, losing, or taking rented items.

The client should make sure that all terms are acceptable to her before signing. She should be certain that the payment terms can be met and that the vendor is within budget, including any extra charges. She should look over the schedule carefully, comparing it to the facility contract and to other vendor contracts to make certain there are no time conflicts.

If the client has her own form contract, she will want to use it and incorporate the vendor's key terms into her contract. If the client is going to have a producer or production manager on-site during installation, she should specify that this person has the authority to order additions or changes and to financially bind her for the costs. If she has rules pertaining to conduct on her event site, she should include them in the contract.

Ultimately, the document should protect both sides in that it clearly sets forth responsibilities and obligations. Chances are, one party will be conceding or compromising on the boilerplate language. However, as long as both perform under the contract, it will be of no import.

➤ Contracts Covering Promotions, Trades, and Other Special Circumstances

At some time or other, everyone in the events industry is approached to provide services for free or at a deep discount. They are told "everyone who is anyone" will be there, or "it will be a great opportunity to showcase your services," or "you will get tons of work from this event." Of course, what they really mean is that they have no budget and they want you to do it for free. It is about them, not you. Nonetheless, everyone gives in once in a while and falls prey to the pitch.

Once that first mistake is made, it is important not to compound things. If vendors or planners are to derive any benefit from the donation, they must do a good and noticeable job. To skimp and do things cheaply showcases exactly the wrong image and gives the donor no chance of deriving benefit.

Services to be rendered should be shown in the same detail that they would be for a paying event. The vendor wants to make certain that the client knows what he is getting and that he gets what he expects. There is little incentive for the vendor to do the event except for client gratitude and some good publicity, that, at least, must be ensured.

Vendors should also make sure that the contract shows the value of the work being done. This will give clients a clear understanding of the extent of the favor they are receiving. Further, in every other way, the contract should have all of the vendor's regular contract language for the full protection of those clauses.

If the basis of the contract is a barter or trade of services, the vendor should again be certain to use his regular contract. What is most important in this instance is to specify clearly what the exact exchange of services entails.

> **Example:** *An advertising agency seeks help with an event but has no budget. Instead of money, the agency offers to create a brochure for the vendor. The value of both services must be established. If the trade is for equal value, then it may not be possible to accomplish one end of it. Say the vendor's services are worth $5,000, but the value of the agency services are $7,500. Will the agency produce the finished product or stop after $5,000 worth of work? Are the services valued at wholesale or retail? The contract needs to spell out these matters in great detail so that both parties understand what is being traded.*

➤ Contracts between End Users and Planners

The contract between a client, corporate or otherwise, and a planner should contain all of the typical event contract language. It should clearly set forth what the planner is expected to do, outlining the services as precisely as possible. Event planning can also overlap marketing, sponsorship, public relations, administrative work, and other areas. The planner will need to make certain that elements of those disciplines aren't slipped into the contract language without a price being attached to them. The planner will also want to be able to refer back to the contract when the client tries to add some of those tasks to the planner's work after the contract has been signed.

The contract should specify how the planner will be compensated—whether it is a project fee, an hourly rate, a percentage of the event budget, a markup on vendors, or any combination of these.

As in any instance when a contract is being drafted, the planner must think about what can possibly go wrong or be questioned by the client and then determine if there is a way to deal with that situation in advance via a contractual clause.

➤ Contracts with Consultants, Lawyers, Accountants

In dealing with professionals outside of the event industry, event professionals must still be alert and aware of what they are signing. They need to understand the services for which they are contracting, what is included, what is not included, and what the charges will be. Advertising and public relations agencies have their own language; lawyers and accountants use terms of art in their professions. It is important for event professionals to ask questions, request written clarifications, and make sure that when they ultimately sign an engagement letter, a retainer agreement, or whatever else it might be called, they agree with all the terms.

■ OTHER REMEDIES

There are situations that can conceivably arise that might be outside of the scope of a typical contract. These are instances where one party has performed its contractual obligations but has nonetheless caused damage to the other party or to a third party. For example, a rental company's employees, after taking down the tables, chairs, and other rentals after an event, might take a case of liquor. The prime vendor may be blamed for this and could lose the client as a result. How can the totality of the damages be weighed?

While the contract may protect against such behavior and the vendor may have a contractual remedy, it is unlikely, or the contractual remedy may not give the aggrieved party a full measure of damages. If such is the case, another basis for recovery would be to file a lawsuit for negligence or some other specific tortious behavior. While it was an intentional act to take the liquor, it could be argued that the rental company and its management were negligent in their hiring practices, their employee training and supervision, or in not having written policies against such behavior.

Take another situation, where a client to whom a creative proposal is submitted by a vendor declines the services of the vendor and then either produces the event as per the proposal or turns it over to another vendor to create. This is a common situation in the event industry, although rarely is anything done about it. In this instance, a much higher burden of proof exists, but it could be argued that the case involved theft of services, of intellectual property, or even a copyright violation.

■ CONCLUSION

Hopefully, this chapter has shed some light on the mystery of contracts and their importance to event professionals. All companies, whether end users, planners, vendors, or subvendors, should look to contracts for their own protection and financial well-being. They should know what clauses they need to incorporate in any document for their own protection.

For those who pride themselves on doing business with a handshake over the years, it is commendably trusting but realistically naive. No matter how long your lucky streak is, it will end, and it may end resoundingly in disaster. Potential problems aside, written contracts are crucial to every transaction. They establish the terms of the deal and the expectations of the parties. They cannot be so one-sided that they are a huge burden to the other party, but they should protect the rights of the drafting party as much and as fairly as possible.

Many issues arising from the client-vendor relationship could be viewed as an amalgam of legal, insurance, and ethics issues. The more carefully the terms of a contract specify the conduct of behavior on all sides, the less likely that there will be a dispute. Contracts refer to a meeting of the minds. As long as the parties agree on the terms and the terms are not, on their face, illegal, they are binding on the parties.

In the event of a breach, practical considerations must be weighed against legal rights to determine the appropriate course of action. Have we lost the client already just because there is a dispute? Will we lose the client if there is a lawsuit, and what is their future business worth against the amount of this claim? Do we even want to do business with a client or a vendor that would dispute this issue?

Event professionals are experts in their own discipline. They need to carry that same professionalism into their contractual dealings, no matter who the other party is.

■ SUMMARY

> ➤ Every party in the events industry should do business with a contract. It is professional, it is ethical, and it provides legal protection.

➤ Parties can agree to any terms that are legal and not against public policy, so contracts can include any subject matter of import to the parties.

➤ Contracts should clearly set forth who the parties are, what the expectations of the parties are, and what the financial consideration is.

Chapter

9

Employee Issues

There is no future in any job. The future lies in the
man who holds the job. —George Crane

As they get busier, creative event folk seek to hire others like themselves to carry some of the load, and as more clients have new and
greater needs, new positions are created within the organization to
service them. Before long, new positions are created to service the
organization itself. What was once essentially a one-person show
becomes a company with many employees.

Even more so than with clients, dealings with employees can be
full of legal pitfalls—lots of them. When each employee comes on
board, he or she looks like the answer to a problem, not the source of
numerous others. But as we know from experience, a small percentage
of employees create more problems than one could possibly imagine.
Covering your bases is crucial when dealing with a disgruntled employee or ex-employee. There are statutes, both federal and state, that
can drastically affect the business in the event an employee's claims
are substantiated and the proper paperwork has not been put in place
internally.

It is important to remember that most businesses are run *for profit*
and therefore the employer is at least cognizant of the bottom line. Most
employees are constantly hoping for and often demanding more pay
and benefits. It reaches a point where the employer's interest and those
of at least some employees clash. This can lead to a number of negative
results: an employee being let go, an unhappy employee poisoning the
atmosphere in the entire workplace, an employer giving in to one
employee, which then starts a domino effect, with other employees lin-
ing up for similar perks or raises. The economic interest of the company can fall hostage to workers' demands if the employer is not careful.

Small companies are less prone to the this sort of thing initially.
An atmosphere of teamwork and camaraderie prevails, and everyone

looks out for everyone else. But over time, even the small company is faced with promotion issues and issues of employees wanting more for themselves after contributing to the growth of the company. A small business owner building a great team needs to think ahead to the day when only one or two can be promoted. What does that mean for the others? Have they no future there? Do employees perceive that they cannot advance? This can lead to an exodus of good people, which is a setback. It can be even more harmful if the exodus leads these people to your prime competitors, who are more than happy to get them.

Just as important as the employer-employee issues are those relating to employee dealings with the outside world. It is important to remember that employees are the ones who interface with clients and therefore represent the image of the company. The owner should clearly specify what that image should be and how employees should interact with clients. At the other end of the distribution chain, employees establish and maintain relationships with vendors and suppliers, relationships that are critical to the success of the company. Rules for dealing with vendors should be just as clearly established. Vendors want to hang onto their accounts and therefore need to know the rules by which they are playing.

Handling employee issues is critical to the maintenance of your staff and to the avoidance of lawsuits from disgruntled personnel. Such lawsuits can come from many directions, as the employee can turn to a variety of state and federal agencies for aid in pursuing grievances. The problem can then mushroom beyond belief. One employee claiming that overtime was not calculated correctly can lead to a Department of Labor audit of all employee records, leading in turn to major fines and assessments.

Many times, ignorance of the laws and regulations leads to a problem. But *ignorance of the law is no defense.* Just know that the federal government has vast laws and regulations governing small businesses of all kinds. Rest assured that Department of Labor regulations and at least two or three acts govern your business activities and your relationship with your employees; OSHA, EEOC, the Department of Transportation, and the IRS are involved for sure. State laws and regulations very often cover the same ground as the federal laws.

■ EMPLOYER-EMPLOYEE RELATIONSHIPS

As seen throughout this chapter, there are numerous employer-employee issues, the proper handling of which is important for the survival of any event business.

➤ Employee versus Independent Contractor

Employers are always looking for ways to keep costs down, and because labor is probably the single biggest expense incurred by most companies, they look to limit their full-time payroll as much as possible. This is cost-effective because generally only full-time employees receive benefits such as health insurance. Employers may also take the extra step of treating workers as independent contractors rather than as employees. This saves on payroll tax deductions and workers' compensation premiums, but can add many problems.

For purposes of payroll taxes, the IRS is the final arbiter of who is an employee and who is an independent contractor. Up until 2002, the IRS looked at 20 factors to determine a worker's status. In January 2002, Publication 15-A was issued revising those standards and boiling the 20 factors down to 3: *behavior control, financial control,* and *type of relationship.*

1. *Behavior control.* The more control the employer has over the behavior of the worker, the more likely that the IRS will find an employer-employee relationship. Control can be inferred from the types of instructions given to the worker:

   ➤ When and where to work

   ➤ What tools or equipment to use

   ➤ Which workers to hire or assist with the work

   ➤ Where to purchase supplies and services

   ➤ What work is to be performed by specific individuals

   ➤ What order or sequence to follow

   The IRS also looks at the training the worker has received by the company to perform services in a particular way. Employees usually receive such training—independent contractors do not.

2. *Financial control.* The more the business can control the business aspects of the worker's job, the more likely he or she will be found to be an employee. Areas for review include the extent to which the worker has unreimbursed business expenses, how the business pays the worker, the extent to which the worker can achieve a profit or loss on the work (the independent contractor can), the extent to which the worker makes services available to the marketplace, and the extent of the worker's investment.

3. *Type of relationship.* Facts that show the type of relationship include whether there is a written contract describing the relationship, whether the business provides the worker with any

type of benefits, the permanency of the relationship (if long term or permanent, it points toward an employer-employee relationship), and the extent to which services performed by the worker are a key aspect of the company's normal business. The more important they are, the more likely that the worker will be deemed an employee.

What all of this means to the company is that a misclassified worker can be quite a costly mistake. If the IRS finds there was no reasonable basis for the misclassification, it can hold the company liable for past unpaid employment taxes, including social security, welfare, and other taxes not previously deducted, as well as penalties.

The other aspect of the employee-independent contractor question revolves around workers' compensation insurance. Employees are covered by the employer's workers' compensation insurance; independent contractors are not. The insurance premiums are based on payroll, so employers treating many workers as independent contractors will have lower premiums. But independent contractors must still be covered, and therefore they need to have their own insurance. Employers truly dealing with independent contractors should make certain to get copies of their certificates of insurance for their files. Then, if audited by their insurance company, employers will have correct documentation.

Employers who misclassify workers will most likely be found out during an audit, and they will then be liable for additional premiums.

Those hiring national entertainment, particularly at a high price, should be certain to structure the relationship so that the entertainers are indeed independent contractors. They should have their own workers' compensation coverage, and their contract should clearly reveal that they are independent contractors. Overzealous insurance companies have sometimes tried to treat entertainers as employees for whom a premium is due. This should be avoided at all costs.

The upshot of this chapter is quite simple: If workers should be classified as employees, then classify them as such. That does not mean that they have to be granted full-time status. Company benefits can be structured for full-time employees only, with part-timers entitled only to their hourly wages. But the part-time or temporary employees should have all payroll taxes deducted and should be issued a W-2 form at the end of the year.

True independent contractors should be required to have their own workers' compensation insurance, and the company should have their certificates of insurance on file. They should formally invoice the company for services, and they should receive 1099 forms at the end of the year, documenting the amounts paid to them. Accurate and detailed record keeping make audits a breeze. Proper classification of workers avoids legal problems, aids in morale, and makes a statement about how the company conducts its business.

➤ Employment Contracts

A fine candidate for a position has been interviewed and it is time to make a job offer. The employer would like to ensure that the employee comes on board and stays for a period of time—at least long enough to justify the training and investment the company will invest—and feels that an employment contract is a good way to achieve this. But is it? A potential employee may view an employment contract as a guarantee of salary and benefits and an assurance that the employer values him or her. But is it?

An employment contract can be a double-edged sword. It can work both for and against both the employer and the employee. A mere document is not going to ensure a happy, constructive working relationship. Nor will it in any way guarantee the employee's continued interest in doing a good job or performing in a professional manner. An employer could then be stuck with an unhappy employee who, while not performing up to potential, may not be in breach of his or her agreement. Then the employer has to look for a reason to terminate the contract and the employee.

Generally speaking, employment contracts do not necessarily make sense for the company. There is no good reason for them unless they are required to serve an important company purpose, like convincing a highly desired prospect to take the job. Another, less common instance is one in which the employer may be thinking about selling the business and feels it will have greater value if the key employees are under some kind of binding agreement. Of course, if potential owners do not like these key employees, the reverse will happen.

An employment contract is a written agreement between employer and employee that sets forth the terms of the relationship. It can take the form of a letter signed by both parties or a formal agreement. In order to be at all useful, it should state the expectations of the employer regarding duties, the hours to be worked, and compensation. It should also set forth the term of employment, be it one year, five years, or indefinite. It should also clearly lay out all employee duties and obligations and all employer rights and responsibilities. And very importantly, it should clearly and in detail set forth the conditions under which the contract can be terminated, enabling the employee to quit or the employer to fire the employee without contractual repercussions.

Terms of termination are not necessarily standard. They can be whatever the parties agree to. A company may terminate if an employee is arrested, convicted of a crime, shows moral turpitude, acts in an unprofessional manner (as defined by the employer), accumulates sufficient points under a company disciplinary code, or for almost any reason specified. Sometimes contracts say only "for cause," whatever that may be. An employer can terminate without cause if the employee signs an agreement so stating.

As far as an employee leaving the company, the situation is a bit hazier. Typically, no employer would want to hang onto an employee who does not want to be there. The quantity and quality of work effort will not support the company's best interests. So clauses forcing an employee to stay can be self-defeating. Likewise, the two-week-notice requirement may or may not be of value. Employees who know they are lame ducks may slack off completely or may use the two weeks to copy company files from computers. It might be better to let them go immediately, even if it means paying them for the two weeks.

A hastily drawn employment letter agreement can omit crucial elements that can negatively impact the employer. Intellectual property rights to work done by the employee during the course of employment should be specified in detail. If not mentioned, those rights can, by default, go to the employee, even if this was not the intention. Confidentiality and noncompetition clauses are critical and must be spelled out clearly—courts will not uphold vague, general clauses.

Work duties should be carefully described and a full job description attached. If the employee is expected to drive, it should be so indicated, and it should be stated that a current, valid driver's license is a condition of employment. A copy of the driver's license should be required on hiring and periodically checked thereafter. If any other form of licensing or certification is an ongoing job requirement, the contract should so specify, with a copy attached upon hiring and checked periodically thereafter. The employee should be required to advise the employer of loss of driver's license or other certification. Such loss should be spelled out as a reason for termination or discipline.

➤ Employee-at-Will Doctrine

Currently, in 38 states, an employee without an employment contract is considered an *employee at will*. This basically means that the employee can quit at any time for any reason or for no reason. Likewise, an employer can terminate an employee without a reason. If there is a reason, it can be any reason *except* one in violation of public policy or federal or state law. Even in an employee-at-will state, an employer must comply with the law and may not terminate an employee in violation of it. In the other 12 states, the law states that an employee may be fired for "cause"—cause cannot be in violation of law or public policy.

Public policy exceptions usually involve areas in which the general interest of the public may be at stake. Claims for wrongful discharge of an at-will employee based on a public policy theory have included the following examples:

➤ Filing a workers' compensation claim

➤ Refusal to perform or participate in an illegal activity

➤ Whistle-blowing activity or in other ways exposing employer wrongdoing

➤ Filing a claim under a state human rights law

➤ Jury duty

➤ Military leave

➤ Appearing as a witness at a criminal trial

➤ Filing a labor law violation

➤ Retaliatory discharge for participation in acts that public policy might support

Violation of antidiscrimination laws also qualifies as an unlawful basis for termination. There are numerous federal laws, oftentimes matched by similar state laws. They forbid termination based on discrimination against an employee because of race, color, religion, sex, national origin, age, or disability, on the basis of the filing of a health or safety claim against the company, on the basis of filing a fair labor complaint, and probably several other reasons.

The employee-at-will doctrine, while giving employees freedom to quit whenever they want, does not, in actuality, give the employer quite the same freedom. The employer can certainly fire for no reason, but if there is a reason, it had better not be unlawful or against public policy.

With this in mind, an alternative to an employment agreement is a letter advising employees of their hire date, pay, hours, and the general policies of the company. This will not be construed as an employment contract. A job description can be attached, as can a policy manual, both of which should be signed by the employees indicating that they have received them, read them, and understand them. The letter should state that the employee is an *employee at will,* meaning that either the employer or employee is free to terminate the relationship at any time (subject to the preceding exceptions). An example of a hire letter can be found in the appendix.

➤ Confidentiality/Nondisclosure Agreements

A confidentiality agreement (also known as a *nondisclosure agreement*) is an extremely important tool for business owners to use in the protection of trade secrets and proprietary information. Some of you in the event business may react quickly, thinking that you have no trade secrets, nothing to hide. But everything that makes a business individual in nature is confidential. This includes customer lists, vendor lists, employee lists, and freelance labor lists. It includes databases, software, custom fabrications, processes, inventions, designs, forms literature, and advertising and promotional materials. Each business is in some way unique, and that individuality is worth protecting. An example of a confidentiality agreement can be found in the appendix.

If the employee is signing an employment agreement, the confidentiality (and the noncompete, to be discussed later) clauses can be made a part of that agreement. If not, submit it to the employee as a separate agreement at the time of hiring to be signed as a condition of employment. This creates the necessary consideration for the contract.

Employers should treat their information as confidential if they want employees to do the same. Internal documents can be stamped accordingly, and access should be limited to those who need to see items in order to do their job. Financial statements, employee procedure manuals, policy manuals, production manuals, forms, and photographs should be treated as confidential. Even if all employees are given copies of documents, it should be made clear that they should not be shared with individuals outside of the company. It should also be made clear that when employees leave the company, any such items in their possession are to be returned to the company. The company should get back all customer information and files, all vendor information and files, all computer files, and all address books. Employees should not be allowed to leave with this type of information.

If an employee works at home, there are numerous opportunities to copy company information. This should be avoided wherever possible. Accounting employees should not, as a rule, be allowed to take company books and records home with them, including hard copy or disk, CD or any other electronic format. They should not be allowed to load company software on their computers at home.

Employees who leave the company may retain in their heads much of the information gained while with the company. Under the terms of a confidentiality agreement, they can be required to maintain confidentiality for a reasonable period of time after the termination. Court opinions vary in how long that is, but in many cases one to five years is considered reasonable. An ex-employee's course of conduct is also governed by any noncompete clauses or agreement.

Courts tend to favor narrowly drawn documents. This means that anything too broad in scope or long in duration will be viewed with a jaundiced eye by most judges. Therefore, any confidentiality agreement should cover only that which is truly confidential. Any term for the agreement should be reasonably geared toward keeping ex-employees from taking the secrets to a competitor or making them available to the marketplace as a whole in the short term. That term will ultimately be decided through negotiation and the relative bargaining power of the employer and the employee. If employees come into a company with a tremendous amount of knowledge, they are allowed to leave with all of that knowledge and apply it elsewhere. On the other hand, brand-new employees might have learned everything they know about special events from this one job.

Remember, no matter what your company does in the event industry, you have some confidential information that you would not want your competitors to have. Keep it confidential by making your employees, whether full-time or part-time, sign a confidentiality provision.

► Noncompetition Agreements

Noncompetition agreements go hand in hand with nondisclosure agreements, and the two are typically put together into one document. To reiterate, every employee should be required to sign such a document as a condition of employment. And again, a noncompetition agreement should be narrowly drawn so that a court cannot construe it as a punitive attempt to keep an individual from earning a living. State law varies, but the same general rules apply everywhere. The contract must be limited in time and geographic scope, and the employee must receive consideration for signing it. An example can be found in the sample Confidentiality Agreement in the appendix.

Competition can be viewed in several different ways, all of which can be controlled by an appropriate agreement. While employees are still employed by the company, they can be restricted from carrying on any side business in the same general business areas as that of the employer, from being freelance workers for other companies, and from having any dealings with companies deemed competitive with the employer beyond the scope of their normal business duties. For instance, they cannot advise a competitor of the names of company employees who might switch employment if approached or of vendors who are offering the employer special pricing.

Once an employee leaves, competition can be construed as more than just going to work for a competitor. It can include soliciting customers or employees of the company—or even vendors in some cases. For instance, an employee who is terminated by a technical production company and goes out and starts his or her own technical labor pool, approaching those on the ex-employer's list of employees first, could be in violation. The idea is not to punish an employee no longer with the company, but rather to protect the company, its assets, and its current employees from damage by an ex-employee.

If a special events company works exclusively in a local market, then limiting an ex-employee's ability to go to a competitor within a 50-mile radius of the company would probably not be viewed as excessive. But if the company occasionally took an order from or provided services to someone 200 miles away, it would probably be construed as unreasonable to create a 200-mile noncompete radius.

If an employer is truly just trying to protect the company assets, there may not be any reason to keep an ex-employee from joining a competitor in the local market. As long as typical employees are restricted from using any of the confidential information they were privy to, they can do little harm. They cannot contact ex-clients or even ex-prospects. They cannot try to take employees away. The only harm they can do is to strengthen a competitor by merely working there. If the talents of particular employees are exceptional or unique, then this alone may be a reason to have them sign a noncompetition agreement, as they may have the capacity to start their own company or truly enhance a competitor. It might be wise to have an especially strong version of a noncompete for such unique employees.

What does one do about a breach? Say an owner is told that her recently terminated employee has gone to work for a direct competitor (not prohibited activity) and has contacted all of the company's clients, urging them to follow him to the new company where he can continue to offer what he provided through his old employer. The noncompete agreement should have clauses dealing with breach and setting forth the employer's remedies. Typically, the owner would be able to go to court to get a temporary restraining order or an injunction against the ex-employee's actions, forbidding the ex-employee from dealing with these clients. At a trial, the employer would have the opportunity to show what her monetary damages were.

From a practical point of view, if some of the clients worked with the company only because of the ex-employee and will leave the company for another anyway, it might best serve all interests to try to work out an accommodation. Since the employer is losing him anyway, perhaps she can allow the ex-employee to handle the work for a percentage of the fees; or perhaps they could handle work jointly. Creating a win-win situation is the only one that makes sense for the employer.

Lawsuits, while sometimes necessary, are expensive and often time-consuming. Each party should carefully weigh what it stands to gain and lose in a proceeding and make decisions accordingly.

■ EMPLOYEE POLICY

Having employees means having to comply with many laws at both the federal and the state level. These laws deal with a variety of issues, including nondiscrimination due to gender, color, race, religion, and age (Title VII of the Civil Rights Act of 1964; the Equal Pay Act of 1963, the Age Discrimination in Employment Act of 1967, Title I and V of the Americans with Disabilities Act of 1990, and the Civil Rights Act of 1991); family leave (Family and Medical Leave Act); safety conditions (OSHA); and how employees are compensated (Fair Labor Standards Act). The issues have become so numerous that it pays to have a company policy manual that covers them. Stating the policies in writing, making sure every employee has signed for a copy and has agreed to abide by them, holding company meetings to reinforce them—all of these actions strengthen the company's support of the policies.

➤ What to Consider in Writing Policy

Every company should consult with its attorney and accountant in creating its policies, as the state laws do differ. Also, what is *omitted* from a policy manual not artfully drafted can be damaging to the company. By leaving something out, the company can be accidentally implying something very different from what was intended. Some key areas that need to be considered in drafting policy follow.

Equal Opportunity. First and foremost, companies need to make a statement that they are equal opportunity employers and that they recruit, hire, train, and administer all policies and employees without regard to race, color, citizenship, religion, age, sex, national origin, ancestry, disability, handicap, veteran's status, or any other basis protected by federal or state law. Many sections of the Federal Code come into play, and they are matched by state laws almost everywhere. All of the aforementioned traits are of equal importance, and discrimination based on any of them is actionable. Sexual harassment is the area that is most in the news and the subject of most concern today.

Sexual Harassment Policy. A sexual harassment policy is critical in today's business world. Section 703(a)(1) of Title VII, 42 USC §20003-2(a) states that it is an unlawful employment practice to discriminate based on sex, among other things. In 1980, the EEOC issued guidelines regarding sexual harassment, defining the circumstances under which an employer may be held liable, and offering affirmative steps an employer must take to prevent sexual harassment. The guidelines were affirmed by the U.S. Supreme Court in a 1986 decision.

Again, this is a complex area, and issues of whether sexual conduct is unwelcome or whether a work environment is sexually hostile can be complicated. The stronger the company policy, the fewer gray areas that exist. It should be noted that the policy should be equally applicable to men and women, to heterosexuals and homosexuals.

Here is a sample policy. It is *only* an example.

As part of the Company's nondiscrimination policy, the Company absolutely prohibits sexual harassment in the workplace. This includes work-related settings such as business trips, seminars, and business-related social events.

The term "sexual harassment" refers to any unwelcome sexual attention, sexual advances, requests for sexual favors, and other verbal, visual, or physical conduct of a sexual nature, including

1. *Making unwelcome sexual advances or requests for sexual favors or other verbal or physical conduct of a sexual nature as a condition of an employee's continued employment*

2. *Making submission to or rejection of such conduct the basis for employment decisions affecting the associate*

3. *Creating an intimidating, hostile or offensive working environment by such conduct*

Examples of prohibited conduct include:

- *Threatening adverse employment actions if sexual favors are not granted*

- *Promising preferential treatment in return for sexual favors*

- *Persistent or repeated unwanted and unnecessary physical contact, including cornering, leaning over, blocking movement, and pinching*

- *Excessively offensive remarks, including unwelcome comments about appearance, obscene jokes, sexual teasing, remarks, or questions, or other inappropriate use of sexually explicit or obscene language*

- *The display in the workplace of sexually suggestive objects or pictures*

- *Persistent or repeated unwelcome sexually suggestive looks or gestures, flirting, or pressure for dates*

- *Unwanted sexual advances*

- *Physical assault of a sexual nature*

It is also unlawful to retaliate against anyone who has complained in good faith about sexual harassment or discrimination.

The policy should have a procedure to investigate claims of harassment, with interim remedies available while the claim is being investigated, if warranted. Completion of the investigation should lead to a finding of whether sexual harassment occurred. If it did, there must be some disciplinary measures, based on the company disciplinary code.

Hiring and Firing. It should be remembered that there are a number of key areas where discrimination can occur or can be claimed to have occurred. They include interviewing and hiring. Questions asked during an interview have to be thought through carefully. Many questions are prohibited if answering them could subject an applicant to discrimination. The same can be said for opportunities for promotions. The final area for consideration is in the area of termination. The employer must document the reasons for termination in the employee file, always keeping in mind potential litigation for wrongful termination.

Policy Enforcement. Enforcement of the disciplinary code and other areas of policy enforcement will be closely observed by the employees to make certain that there is no discrimination. Without equal enforcement of all policies, an employer runs a risk of someone feeling aggrieved. It is not a long walk from aggrieved to discriminated against—sometimes talking to an armchair lawyer around the watercooler will be enough. Sometimes this is difficult, as an employer may want to cut a break for the loyal, generally well-behaved employee but not for the constant troublemaker. However, the employer should remember that someone will always be watching, that someone will undoubtedly report the favor to the aggrieved party, possibly stirring up trouble.

Workplace Violence. Another area of great import these days is that of workplace violence. A company should have a policy of *zero tolerance*. Employees should have a reasonable expectation that they will not be subject to violence in the workplace. This means that the employer should have a policy against violence, including possession of weapons. An employer should take reasonable precautions in hiring, such as checking references or even criminal records to determine if there were any previous problems. An injured employee might have cause for action against the employer if the employer knew or should have known of the attacker's violent tendencies.

ADA. The Americans with Disabilities Act is a federal civil rights law designed to prevent discrimination against those individuals who have a physical or mental impairment. It should be noted that this act applies only to companies with 15 or more employees. Employers that are covered by the act must make certain that individuals with disabilities have equal opportunities to apply for jobs and to work in jobs for which they are qualified; that they have an equal opportunity to be promoted once hired; that they have equal access to benefits; and that they are not harassed because of their disability.

Further, under the ADA, employers are required to make reasonable accommodations, making adjustments or modifications to enable employees who have a disability to maintain equal employment opportunities. An employer cannot be forced to make an accommodation if it would pose an undue hardship. The question of undue hardship is individual to each situation and an area best left for discussion with corporate counsel.

Several tricky situations can arise under this act, and the employer has to beware of the slippery slope of the law. Examples would be employees who become HIV positive and deal with the public (e.g., in the catering field) or employees who announce they have a drug or alcohol addiction. There are ways to deal with these situations fairly for both employee and employer, but again, the company attorney should be consulted to assist.

FMLA. The Family and Medical Leave Act applies to private sector employers who employ 50 or more workers in a single location or within 75 miles of a single location for at least 20 workweeks within the current or previous calendar year. To be covered, an employee must have worked in that location and have been employed for at least 12 months and have worked at least 1,250 hours in the 12 months prior to the start of family leave.

A covered employee is entitled to up to a total of 12 weeks of unpaid leave in a 12-month period for the birth of a child and to care for the newborn child; for the placement with the employee of a child for adoption or foster care; to care for an immediate family member with a serious health condition; and when the employee is unable to work because of a serious medical condition.

Upon return from leave, an employee must be restored to his or her original job or to an equivalent job, which means identical in terms of pay, benefits, employment terms, and conditions.

OSHA. The Occupational Safety and Health Act (OSHA) relates to workplace conditions for health and safety. Workplace safety is critical and every employee should be on the lookout for unsafe conditions. Areas of concern range from fall protection to use of power tools to fire and electrical safety to respiratory concerns to toxic chemicals to proper care when spray painting indoors. OSHA covers a wide range, and every area of the company's activities should be reviewed to determine relative safety. If notified of a possible danger-ous condition, OSHA will come in and conduct an audit or inspection, and it may assess a business a fine and demand that the situation be repaired or cleaned up immediately.

FLSA. Last, but by far not least, is the Fair Labor Standards Act, of which most businesses will run afoul. It is extremely important to be aware of the key provisions of this act, as failure to follow it can be costly. It establishes minimum wage and overtime pay and regulates the employment of minors. It does not require vacation, holiday, sev-erance or sick pay—these are benefits an employer grants to em-ployees. It does not require meal or rest periods, holidays off, or vacations—these, too, are benefits. It does not require premiums for weekend or holiday work, pay raises, or fringe benefits.

But what the FLSA does provide is that employees are entitled to time and a half for any hours worked over 40 in a given workweek. This applies even to employees who are salaried and who have a cer-tain amount of overtime figured into their salary.

> **Example:** *A decorator decides to move her key designer to salary from an hourly rate. The designer was earning $20 per hour and averaging 50 hours per week over the course of the previous year. This came to $1,100 per week (40 hours × $20 + 10 hours × $30). The employer gives him a raise to $1,300 per week and tells him that includes as many hours as he is needed. Over the next year, the designer averages 55 hours per week. The FLSA states that the employee is due more money! His average hourly rate is $20.36. Half of that is $10.18 × 15 hours, or an additional $152.70 per week—even though overtime was already figured in to his salary.*

There are some exemptions from the overtime requirements. They include executive, administrative, and professional employees and outside salespeople. Before putting employees arbitrarily into these categories in order to avoid the overtime provisions, there should be some discussion with the Department of Labor local office. There should also be a tailoring of job descriptions to fit the categories and for internal consistency.

Drugs and Alcohol. Issues of drug and alcohol use are fairly common in the event industry. The rock-and-roll mentality pervades, even among many company owners. But safety issues and common sense should prevail. Drug and alcohol use can lead to accidents, causing damage to property or, even worse, to people. Whether in the shop or on an event site, companies should have a strict policy of no drug and alcohol use while employees are on the job—no exceptions. Taking it a bit further, the policy should forbid coming to work under the influence of drugs or alcohol.

> **Example:** *The event production company works all morning on an installation and breaks for lunch, which consists of a buffet that the client put out. There is beer in the drink cooler. Company policy should forbid employees from having a beer if they are going back to work following lunch.*

> **Example:** *A video company is involved in an evening show and has three technicians on-site during the event. There is no heavy lifting or physical work to do, just pushing buttons and rolling tapes. The client has invited the techs to partake in the buffet, which includes alcohol. Policy should forbid this.*

> **Example:** *The tent company crew is heading back to the shop after a long day at work. They stop at a grocery a few blocks from their warehouse, buy a case of beer, and each open one before they return to the shop. Company policy should forbid this, and disciplinary procedures should be followed.*

The issue of drug and alcohol testing is a difficult one. Employees certainly resent the intrusion into their lives, and many feel that what they do on their own time is nobody's business but theirs. If an employer feels the need to have a policy of testing, it should certainly be handled in a nondiscriminatory manner. It would probably be best if agreeing to testing was made a condition of employment. In some areas, the government does intrude, insisting on random testing, as will be seen later in this book.

Right to Privacy. Employees should be made aware that the communications systems provided by the company are and will always remain the property of the company. This includes the telephones and voice-mail system, the computers and all files and e-mail contained therein, and all mail and shipping accounts. There should be no expectation of privacy, and the company has the right to monitor all usage. The company has the right to possession of all employee passwords.

The company also has the right to install video cameras to monitor the business premises for security reasons. Surveillance should not, however, be used where an employee would have a reasonable expectation of privacy, such as in the bathroom.

Company Property. The company may provide an employee with a variety of tools to make job performance more efficient. This can include anything from cell phones and pagers to company credit cards to actual work tools. Issues invariably arise over loss or damage of these items, or in the case of a credit card, spending abuse. The company needs to have a policy that is applied across the board. Pagers are easily lost or broken. Should the employee be responsible for the cost of replacing them? Wrenches are often borrowed from toolboxes and not returned. Should the employee be responsible? A company needs to have a policy on this because it happens on a regular basis, no matter how good an employee may be. If employees know they are responsible, losses may happen a bit less often.

If the company has a policy of employees paying for lost or damaged property, should that apply to vehicles? Or to damage to a client's facility? Business owners pull their hair out over such issues. For them, it is a lose-lose proposition. If they try to force an employee to pay for truck damages, the employee will probably quit; then the employer has to pay for the truck *and* replace the employee. Alternatively, employees may decide they do not want to drive if they are subject to paying for the damage they cause. If owners eat the damage themselves, they have no protection from careless staff. There is no easy solution here.

Dress. Employee dress codes should be relatively easy to create and enforce. Salespeople want to make sales and therefore should want to dress to impress. In today's casual world, a company polo shirt or button-down oxford cloth shirt is neat and comfortable, either for males or females. T-shirts with the company name are fine for warehouse and production employees. Rules about the type of shoes to be worn for safety are acceptable. It makes more sense to have a policy about dress than to occasionally have to speak to an employee whom you feel is dressed inappropriately.

When it comes to dealing with employees, owners may sometimes feel that they are more trouble than they are worth. At other times, their eyes fill with tears of pride at how well the employees perform. But overall, owners must remain objective, treating the superstars and the slackers equally under company policy. Favoritism can be shown in other ways, but should not be shown in unequal policy enforcement, because lurking in the shadows is an unhappy employee and a discrimination lawsuit.

Just as the company loves its clients but subjects them to contracts with detailed terms, so it should treat its employees. Yes, they are team members; yes, there are common goals for the success of the company; and yes, employees should be kept at arm's length when it comes to the company policies and their enforcement.

■ SUMMARY

➤ Companies must understand the difference between an independent contractor and an employee and make certain that all who meet the tests of employee are treated as such for tax, legal, and insurance purposes.

➤ Employment contracts are double-edged swords, and employers should think twice before entering into them.

➤ Employers should understand the term *employee at will*.

➤ Every employee of every company should sign confidentiality and noncompetition agreements for the protection of the company.

➤ Event companies should have clear-cut policies relating to employee behavior and attitudes.

Chapter

10

Insurance

Insurance: An ingenious modern game of chance in which the player is permitted to enjoy the comfortable conviction that he is beating the man who keeps the table. —Ambrose Bierce

Every business would like to be fully insured and to feel comfortable that if anything adverse happens within the company there is appropriate coverage. Unfortunately, the cost of insurance is such that most companies have to compromise, prioritize, and then cross their fingers and hope that situations will not arise that expose areas left uncovered. Many times, companies get their liability and workers' compensation coverage and call it a day, thinking they are covered for the most likely scenarios. Again, until an instance arises for which the company is not covered, that philosophy may seem okay.

Here are some typical situations that may arise fairly commonly in the course of an event company's year:

> ➤ An employee's tools are stolen on a job site and the employee seeks reimbursement.
> ➤ The company's gear is damaged or stolen while in a company truck.
> ➤ The company's gear is stolen off the truck of a hauler.
> ➤ The company's property is damaged beyond repair on a job site.
> ➤ A fire in the company's warehouse damages inventory.
> ➤ An employee embezzles from the company.
> ➤ The company's salesperson slanders another company.
> ➤ The company is sued for copyright infringement for stealing someone's creative ideas.
> ➤ An employee of a subcontractor is hurt on the job, and the subcontractor has no insurance.

➤ An employee of a subcontractor injures a third party, and the subcontractor has no insurance.

➤ A natural disaster damages the company's warehouse or an event site.

➤ A company employee is in an accident while driving a rented vehicle.

➤ An employee's vehicle is broken into while parked at a job site.

Each of the these instances represents different aspects of insurance coverage that may be needed in an event business. It is unlikely that most companies will be covered for everything. Specific jurisdictions and specific types of businesses may be somewhat unique in the types of coverage needed, so this discussion should be viewed as a set of general guidelines that will at least raise issues to be addressed with expert insurance agents.

■ WORKERS' COMPENSATION

Workers' compensation coverage is a very important aspect of a company's overall insurance program, and it is normally required by state law. It is designed to cover employees for injuries they sustain in the course of their employment. It is not based on fault or on the type of injury. Any injury that arises during work and is related thereto is covered. An administrative assistant gashing her leg on an open file cabinet drawer, a warehouse employee hurting his back lifting, a worker falling from a ladder, a stage carpenter getting a splinter—are all compensable injuries. If an employee can show that he or she has high blood pressure due to stress at work, any treatment and medication can be covered. An employee's medical bills are covered, and time missed from work is compensated at a rate set by state statute. There may be some question about whether the workers' compensation insurance or the health insurance is primary coverage, but the employee cannot collect under both. If the health insurance covers treatment before the workers' compensation claim is processed, it may seek reimbursement once the comp claim is recognized.

While workers' compensation was initially designed as a nonadversarial process, insurance companies over the years have contested more and more claims, especially in states where there have been abuses. Sometimes the litigation gets quite contentious, as big dollars are at stake. Exposure to asbestos or hazardous chemicals can be claimed to be the cause of serious medical problems. High-pressure environments have led to stress-related claims alleging both mental and physical injury. These cases can become a battle of expert witnesses. If there is a partial or total permanent disability, the amounts in question can be very large. It should be noted that normally a workers' compensation recovery is the sole remedy that an employee has against an employer. Thus, even if an employer is negligent, the employee often has no additional rights beyond workmen's compensation. Independent contractors should have the right to sue the company for negligent acts or omissions.

Classification of employees is important, as the workers' compensation premium is based on the classification of each individual, and the classification is based on the risk attached to the job. Administrative personnel who never leave the office area are probably the lowest risk, and therefore the premium on them is the lowest. Employees who go out in the field and install equipment, work at height on lifts and ladders, or do electrical work—jobs considered a bit more dangerous—are classified differently and at a higher premium. Employers should look at the classification of their employees very carefully to minimize their premiums. Executives in particular should be careful how they describe their job duties, as mere mention of going out to event sites might cause their classification to change from administrative to a higher-premium classification. Care should be taken in creating job descriptions so that the positions do not appear to be riskier, and hence more expensive, than they really are.

Additionally, it is possible for a single position to have a split rating. If an owner or officer spends 90 percent of his or her time in the office and 10 percent on event sites, the insurance company should be questioned about splitting the rating accordingly to cut down on the premium expense.

As stated in Chapter 9, it is important for event companies to make certain that their subcontractors and their independent contractors have supplied them with certificates of workers' compensation insurance. Otherwise, upon audit, companies will end up paying a workers' compensation premium on their services. Further, if an employee of a subcontractor is hurt on an event site, issues arise if the subcontractor does not have insurance. It is conceivable that the injured party would claim coverage under the event company's policy. It is also possible that the injured party will find a way to sue the event company for negligence if any evidence of that exists.

■ LIABILITY INSURANCE

Liability coverage protects the company from liability for harm it has caused others. This harm is most often a result of things that employees have done that they shouldn't have done—or should have done and didn't—the result of which is injury to persons or damage to property. This can range from a caterer being sued because someone got ill from food served at an event to a lighting company being sued for injuries caused by a light falling on someone's head to a patron slipping on a wet spot on a rental company's showroom floor. It can also cover an employee doing damage to a facility or breaking another contractor's equipment.

In the United States, it is possible to bring a lawsuit for virtually any reason. That does not mean that the party being sued will ultimately be found liable, only that the right to bring the lawsuit exists. Having insurance protects a company against having to spend the money to defend a frivolous lawsuit. There is the suit brought by a dinner guest who leans across the table for the butter, lets his tie fall into a votive candle, and sustains clothing damage and "mental distress," or the guest who, after drinking too much, climbs on to a lighting truss and falls off, blaming the lighting company. Insurance covers the cost of fighting such claims.

Typically, a liability insurance policy will provide a company with a legal defense in the event that the company is sued. Assuming that the insurance company receives notice of the claim in a timely manner, the company will compile information, perhaps negotiate with the claimant or claimant's attorney, and perhaps settle the claim. If that does not work and a lawsuit is filed, the insurance company will provide the insured company with an attorney and full representation at trial. If a verdict or settlement occurs requiring the insured to pay, the insurance company will pay out an amount up to the coverage maximum.

If a company has $100,000 in coverage and a verdict comes in at $50,000, the company will pay it in full. If the verdict is $150,000, the insurance company will pay only $100,000. This means that the company is exposed for the remaining $50,000, and the suing party can come after the company to collect. This can get complicated and ugly. The insurance company is no longer involved, and the company will have to fight this battle using its own counsel, for whom it is paying. Event companies should really have at least $1 to $5 million in liability coverage, as damages and awards get higher every year.

The event company owner needs to be cognizant of what is and isn't covered by the basic liability provisions in the policy. The basic situations described earlier should always be covered. But other, perhaps less common occurrences may not be. Does it cover slander or intellectual property theft claims? Does it cover a claim for pollution or hazardous waste damage?

Companies within the events industry should think about the most likely scenarios for liability problems and then check with their agent to make sure they are all covered. They should also ask the agent to review and explain any other coverage that might be applicable and available to them. A company may discover an area of coverage it had been lacking. The company should also take the time to make clear to the insurance agent all aspects of the business so that the agent has an understanding of all of the risks. Only then can he or she make accurate and complete recommendations. Most people feel that their agent is more salesperson than advisor, so they shy away from extensive meetings and conversations. In so doing, they are not serving their own interests well.

Liability insurance is also necessary on company vehicles. Most states require it by law. If a company owns vehicles, it usually must carry commercial liability insurance on them. If vehicles are leased long term, the leasing company may handle the insurance and just charge it back to the company leasing the vehicles. The company should be clear on that, though. If the leasing company is handling the insurance, the company should still have a copy of the policy and all of the accident report forms, claims information, and anything else needed to prove insurance or to notify the insurance company of a claim. If vehicles are rented on an as-needed basis, the company should either make certain that the rental company is providing coverage or that the event company's commercial liability policy covers rented vehicles.

Finally, businesses have to beware of whether the policy covers workers who drive their own vehicles for business. Employees who make deliveries to customers or drive equipment to job sites, even salespeople who drive to sales calls, definitely fall within this category. If they are in an accident, the company could be sued, so the company should have coverage. Coverage is not automatic, so the company should check with its agent to make certain this is in place.

Many other aspects of liability insurance will probably have to be bought as separate policies. Liquor liability insurance is usually applicable only to facilities or caterers. But planners may want to consider it based on the law in their state. "Dram shop" acts set forth which parties can be held responsible in the event of an alcohol-related accident. If the law could hold them responsible for injuries incurred by a guest or by an innocent party as a result of the alcohol consumption by a guest, planners should look long and hard at that coverage.

Professional liability coverage is most often thought of in relation to doctors and lawyers, who usually refer to it as *malpractice coverage.* While this would not usually be applicable to event companies, check with your agent to determine if any quirks in state law exist that would put your company in need of coverage.

Employment-practices liability insurance covers businesses against claims by their workers that their legal rights as employees have in some way been violated. This would usually be stand-alone coverage and not included in a typical liability policy. This coverage offers protection against employee lawsuits, including sexual harassment, discrimination, failure to hire or promote, wrongful termination, wrongful discipline, breach of employment contract, and infliction of emotional distress.

Directors and officers insurance is another distinct area. Particularly if a company has any outside directors, they may be more willing to serve if they are covered. They then will not have personal liability for any claims based on their actions or lack of action.

In today's litigious world, where juries seem to be sympathetic to injured parties, basic liability coverage may not be enough. Awards keep getting bigger and bigger. Accordingly, companies offer umbrella policies. An *umbrella policy* is supplemental coverage that comes into play only if the liability exceeds the limits of the primary coverage. Umbrella policies are usually sold in high dollar increments, perhaps starting at $1 million. Rather than carrying $5 million in primary coverage, a company should look into carrying a $1 million policy with an umbrella on top of it. It will most probably prove to be much less expensive.

■ PROPERTY COVERAGE

Property coverage can easily be divided into two basic types. The first type is on real estate and fixed property. This insurance covers damage or destruction of a business premises, be it office, warehouse, retail, restaurant, or any other facility. Even if a business does not own the building that it occupies, it is quite likely that the landlord will insist on the business tennant carrying insurance on the occupied premises. Fixtures attached to the building are very often covered by this type of policy. This would include signage, fixed racks, and other attachments. If there are large plate glass windows, the policyholder should determine whether they are covered or whether they would have to be added to the basic coverage.

The real estate itself should also be covered, including sidewalks, driveways, and parking lots. Normal wear and tear is normally not covered.

In terms of destruction of the premises, fire is the most likely cause of that. Therefore, the policyholder should be clear on what is required for the policy to be effective. There may be requirements that sprinkler systems be up to code, that shelving not be too close to the ceiling, or that other steps be taken. Some are municipal occupancy code issues and others are requirements of the insurance company. Proper storage of gasoline and flammable materials is required by both.

The second type of property coverage is on the contents of the facility. This ranges from office equipment, files, forms, letterhead, and furniture to inventory, stock, and equipment. It is very important to think carefully about the amount of coverage required. Should the full value of equipment be insured? Should some older equipment not be insured at all? It would be great to insure everything at full or replacement value, but the cost may be prohibitive. Other obligations may come into play here. Bank loan agreements or equipment leases will require the gear covered by the loans to be insured in full.

In the events industry, gear is on the move all the time. It is critical that the company understand its coverage when it is not in the warehouse. Property is often not covered when it is in transit. Companies need to at least think about covering their equipment when it is in their own trucks, when it is in the trucks of shippers who are transporting it to and from event sites, and when it is at an event site or in the possession of others. Companies that are busy will find that their equipment is more often in trucks and at event sites than in the warehouse. Companies that rent equipment will find their gear in the hands or trucks of others more often than not. Accordingly, they have to be sure that their policy covers these situations. There have been instances in which a company's gear is out on a tour, the tour gets into trouble financially, and all of the gear is seized by a creditor. Even though the company is but an innocent victim in this scenario, their gear is lost to them. Will a policy cover this scenario?

Finally, a company should be clear on whether their property insurance covers the property of others. For instance, a lighting company landing a huge job may rent hundreds of lights to supplement its own gear and spend days prepping this equipment in its warehouse. Is the equipment covered if there is a fire? Employees may leave expensive personal gear in the company warehouse, maybe even park a vehicle or motorcycle there temporarily—is that covered if there is a disaster?

Caterers and florists should query whether spoilage of perishables is covered. Prop shops that build exhibits will want to know whether machinery breakdown is covered. Other disciplines within the industry will have similar concerns that they will have to explore.

A somewhat different type of property insurance involves employee dishonesty. Insurance can be purchased against embezzlement and theft. However, claims under such policies may be difficult to prove. Many of them also require that the policyholder fully prosecute the employee before any payment will be made.

It may be worthwhile to consider coverage for loss or destruction of company records. This would include any data kept on computer, hard copies of accounts receivable, or other monetary or accounting records.

■ BUSINESS INTERRUPTION

Business interruption insurance covers the loss of income resulting from having to shut the business down temporarily due to fire, flood, or other disaster that disrupts the operation of the business. It can also include the additional expense of setting up a temporary facility while the other is being rebuilt or repaired. Damages under this type of coverage are not simple to prove, particularly if records have been destroyed in the catastrophe.

Businesses have to be aware of insurance requirements that exist in a number of other documents and relationships. If the company leases its space, the landlord almost certainly will have insurance requirements. If the company owns its own space but has a mortgage, the mortgage company will have insurance requirements. If the company leases equipment or trucks, no doubt the leasing companies will have requirements. Clients may demand certificates of insurance for certain liability or workers' compensation coverage.

Insurance rates are high because losses are high. That should put every business on alert that suffering high losses without insurance could put it out of business or cripple it drastically. It is important to look at the nature of the business and determine which risks are the most likely or the most potentially damaging to the business and insure against them. If your business is in California, it may be important to determine whether earthquake damage is included in the policy and, if not, whether a separate policy can be written to cover it. If your business is in New Orleans, flood insurance, if obtainable, might be worthwhile considering. In Florida and the Gulf Coast and up the eastern seaboard, hurricane insurance would be valuable, if available.

Whether coverage is available and/or included within policies is important for a business owner to know. Thinking you are covered does no good if in fact there is no coverage. Making sure the company and its insurance agent are acting in unison, using the same facts and the same thought process in deciding the amounts and types of coverage, is important. Owners should pay serious attention to insurance, as boring as it may seem when the agent is explaining it. Having the correct information and the correct coverage may mean the difference between keeping a business or having it die when disaster strikes.

■ SUMMARY

➤ Workers' compensation coverage is normally mandated by state law.

➤ Checking the job classification of every employee will help keep premiums as low as possible.

➤ Liability coverage should protect the company against all foreseeable risks.

➤ An umbrella policy on top of the liability policy is a wise investment.

➤ The company and its agent should review the operations of the business to gain a full understanding of all its activities and how to cover them.

➤ This applies to the activities and to the equipment of the company.

Chapter

11

Labor Unions

*The only thing that will redeem mankind
is cooperation. —Bertrand Russell*

Union issues are particularly prickly for event folk. Many union locals do have a way of taking some of the fun out of putting together a great party or exciting event. This is especially so when their involvement is a last-minute surprise. Many disciplines within the industry cannot fathom how unions can possibly affect them. Who ever heard of a balloon union? Why would carpenters have any interest in flowers? A basic lack of knowledge about how unions operate can cause expensive, time-consuming problems.

When asked what they know about labor unions, the typical event industry respondent would most probably make reference to the building trades. The autoworkers, masons, steelworkers, steam fitters, plumbers, crane operators, and dockworkers all represent large groups of American workers. Other professions, such as hospital workers, grocery workers, and teachers are also unionized. While it should be no surprise that workers servicing the hotels and convention centers are often union members, event people are still surprised when faced with the prospect of having to include them in their event plans.

If a company does enough events in the typical convention cities around the United States, it will inevitably be faced with situations requiring the use of union labor. Sometimes there will be no choice for planners because the venue is dictated to them and the venue is governed by factors outside of the company's control. However, in those instances where a choice does exist for event planners, some due diligence and a basic understanding of the interworkings of the various trade unions in the prospective venue may save the company much money and aggravation.

Unions typically involved in the meetings and events industry include stagehands (IATSE), electricians (IBEW), and the Teamsters, the

Carpenters, the Laborers, and the Decorators Unions. Not all of them have locals in each city, nor do they have the same jurisdictions from city to city. Further, their work rules and wage rates vary. You cannot assume that just because you have worked with the Teamsters in Chicago that the experience will be the same in New York. Nor can you assume that since the Decorators Union constructed props in one city, they would be doing the same in another, or that there would even be a Decorators local in that municipality.

When choosing a venue or being advised of the venue in which an event is to be held, always ask the facility manager whether the building is union. If so, find out which unions are in the building, what their work rules are, and get the names and telephone numbers of the business agents. From them, the union's form contract can be obtained, as well as the work rules and their view of what their local's jurisdiction is. It is also important to get input on the subject of jurisdiction from the building, as its view may be the only objective one to be had. Sometimes jurisdictions overlap, or there are gray areas, and multiple unions will lay claim to the same work. When this happens, either the facility management needs to provide a solution or the planners should choose whichever union works best for them.

In most buildings designated as union, there is either a contract between the various trade unions and the facility or certain protocols to follow that, notwithstanding the fact that there is no contract, make the building a union site. Oftentimes, it is the relationship of the building to the city or the municipality that gives the unions their authority. While this is most often true in the Northeast (Boston, New York, Philadelphia, Baltimore, Washington, DC, Pittsburgh, Cleveland), it also holds true in other large convention cities like St. Louis, Chicago, New Orleans, Los Angeles, and San Francisco.

In each union building, every trade union has carved out an area of work that falls within its jurisdiction. By contract or precedent, these jurisdictional boundaries are enforced. What this can mean for a planner is that the trucks are unloaded by Teamsters, the contents are rolled into the event space by Laborers, and then various parts of the installation are conducted by the Carpenters, Decorators, Stagehands, and Electricians. The unions may have worked out a formula between themselves, such as requiring the hiring of two Laborers for every Teamster, or two Stagehands for every Electrician, and so on. Or unions may split hairs and create weird divisions on a given job (e.g., electricians can light only the part of the event not related to the stage or stage set and the stagehands must light the balance). Since the electricians may be responsible for trade shows and stagehands for stage shows, this split somehow preserves their niches.

Dealing with the same union in different cities will not necessarily yield the same results. Some locals, caught up in interunion politics in their town, will not be as flexible as a local in a city where the competition between unions for the work is less intense. For instance, in some cities the stagehands (IATSE) may have nothing to say about vendors unloading their own trucks and bringing their gear into a facility by themselves. In others, IATSE may be allied with the Teamsters and insist that they will only handle gear unloaded by them. In some cities, a vendor's nonunion employees can work side by side with the union workers; in others, they are not allowed to touch anything. In some cities, minimum calls, minimum crew size, and overtime hours may be negotiable; in others, there is no negotiation. It never hurts to ask for concessions, because any concession can save the client some, and maybe a lot of, money.

In some cities, working with the unions is a pleasure. The workers are skilled, friendly, and happy for the work. They work quickly and efficiently. This is especially so in secondary cities where there may be only one union in a building. In others, the situation is exactly the opposite. There are multiple unions to deal with and they want to show who runs the building. They push for large crew size, perhaps with a nonworking steward or two (who may be nonworking on another crew in the building at the same time, thus getting paid twice for not working!). There are workers who try to avoid working, who take extended breaks well beyond the time limits, who may not be particularly well trained in the work they are doing, and whose biggest motivation is to stretch the workday into overtime. An event company would never hire workers with these habits, yet it has no choice in certain venues.

Before any union contract is signed by a planner or a vendor, it should be reviewed very carefully. First and foremost, the union may be part of a collective bargaining agreement between all of the convention unions and the big convention, trade show, and exhibit companies. Sometimes those companies agree to use the unions everywhere in a city, even in traditionally nonunion facilities. The union agreement may have a clause in it obligating the party signing it to subscribe to that collective bargaining agreement. In effect, the party is lured into agreeing to use union labor everywhere in the city. Once signed, this contract can be extremely difficult to get out of, and the union may be all over the planner wherever his or her events take place. In some cases, it even gives the union local the right to audit the signer's books to make certain that union labor was used everywhere it should have been under the agreement.

Second, the length of the agreement is important. It makes sense from the planner/vendor point of view to have the agreement in force for only a single event. If possible, the dates inclusive of setup and removal should be the time limit of the contract. Dates should be checked carefully before signing. A planner should not be obligated beyond the single event unless knowingly, willingly, and for a good reason. Under no circumstances should the planner sign a year-long agreement.

Third, a party should fully understand the terms of the agreement and what those terms will mean when it comes time to pay the bills. Terms include (1) the basic hourly rate of each type of worker; (2) the minimum number of workers on a call; (3) whether all workers on a call will be working—sometimes stewards or even foremen will be designated as supervisors only, so they will not be working, only watching; (4) the minimum number of hours on a call; (5) the overtime rules; (6) if or when double time may be charged; (7) when breaks and meal breaks are required and the penalties if they do not occur on schedule; (8) the rules for *show call*—the actual union presence required during the event itself; (9) the rule on *shadows*—union workers who, although they don't handle the lighting or audio consoles themselves during an event, sit and watch nonunion techs do it (which prevents union members from being deprived of work by nonunion workers; and (10) the additional hourly charges that must be paid above the actual wage as part of the contract (for annuity, vacation, health, and welfare benefits), often ranging from 25 to 35 percent of the hourly rate. A planner relying on the simple hourly rate when planning budget will inevitably come up short on cash and long on frustration.

Further, other clauses buried in the contract might not be noticed at first glance. One such clause might state that all workers have to be paid within a certain amount of time (e.g., five days or a week) and establish severe penalties for late payment. This becomes a problem if the party responsible for paying the workers planned to do so during that company's next regularly scheduled pay period and that falls outside the time restrictions. Another clause might require arbitration regarding any dispute about payment of wages, with the employer liable to pay the union's attorney if the union succeeds in the claim. Arbitration may actually be a good place to litigate issues, but claims come up for hearing quickly; they involve engaging counsel; unions file hundreds of claims each year, so their attorneys are familiar with the system and the arbitrators; and unions tend to take hard-line positions to set examples.

It should be duly noted that for purposes of a union contract, the party signing it becomes the employer of the union workers for the period of the contract. That means that the company becomes responsible for all payroll taxes. It also means that the employer becomes responsible for listing the union wages as part of payroll and for carrying workers' compensation insurance on that payroll. Thus, whoever signs the contract as the employer has the administrative burden of adding the union workers to employee rosters, of setting them up in payroll, and of making the necessary payroll tax deductions. Additionally, there is the cost burden of the workers' compensation premiums. If a vendor acts as the employer for the planner, the vendor company should figure these costs into its price.

Sometimes planners sign the union contracts without understanding the administrative steps, and once they are made aware, they have no ability to comply. On a large show (a decent-size show can have 50 to 100 different union workers when installation, show calls, and removal involving a number of unions are all factored in), the administrative effort to put all these workers on your payroll can be substantial. Planners do not normally want to touch this, nor do their corporate or nonprofit clients. Therefore, it falls on the production company or on an outside payroll service. (Such payroll services are usually handled by entrepreneurial union members and can be recommended by union business agents or perhaps by the facility or the production company.)

Either way, there is a cost. Union workers get their wages and then some. Typically, benefits (for annuity, health insurance, vacation, etc.) can total from 25 to 35 percent on top of wages. Then there would be a handling charge by the payroll service (for reasonable costs and profit) or by the production company handling this for a client. It can get expensive.

It makes sense to engage someone from the payroll service or someone else to oversee the union workers on the job. That person can be responsible for making certain that work gets done and that union work rules are followed. For example, if union rules require a meal break between four and five hours into a shift, with severe penalties if the break does not happen, it is important to have someone monitor the time carefully. The unions may also be more willing to work under another union person than under the supervision of a nonunion production supervisor.

There are numerous factors that planners and producers weigh in choosing venues for events, conferences, and conventions. Cost is always high on the list. In determining cost, there is more to examine than the facility rental fee and the catering expense. Labor is a large component in the cost of any event. When computing budgets and comparing venues, knowing the costs attached to each venue is critical in making the right decision. The following hypothetical example illustrates this.

Example: *Venue A has a $10,000 rental fee for the space needed by the conference. It is a nonunion venue, and the producer is free* *to use any vendors she chooses. Labor estimates come to $20,000, for a total cost of $30,000.*

Venue B has a rental fee of $5,000 for a similar space. However, it is a union venue with high labor rates and strict work rules. For the same installation, the labor comes to $40,000, for a total of $45,000. Therefore, the gross cost is actually higher in the building with the lower rental fee. The true cost of having an event in a given location can be determined only after considering the cost of labor required to work in that facility.

In a typical nonunion situation, a production company will drive its own vehicles to a facility's dock. Then its own employees will unload the trucks, wheel everything into the space themselves, and perform all of the work necessary for the installation. A single crew will be performing the work at an agreed-upon price and on a fixed budget. The planner/producer has a relatively high degree of certainty about the time and cost involved. Obviously, some surprises can pop up that will affect things, but on the whole, there are few variables.

For the exact same work, it is quite likely that union labor will be higher. First, there will be multiple crews involved, each having a minimum crew size and a minimum hourly call. Based on these two factors alone, there will be many more worker-hours involved in the installation.

Example: *A planner for an event taking place in a nonunion venue hires Event Productions, Inc., to do staging, lighting, audio, the stage backdrop, and room decor consisting of drape and scenic drops. EPI arrives in three trucks with a crew of 12, planning on a 12-hour installation. The crew unloads the trucks, moves everything into the hall to designated locations, splits up, and begins putting everything together. Lighting and audio work together, getting the rigging points in the air, flying the truss, and doing their technical work. The staging crew builds the stage and then switches to the backdrops and draping. The same group of people does all of the work. There is one group of workers, one call, totaling 144 hours.*

Example: *Using the same basic scenario, assume the three Event Productions, Inc., trucks pull up at the dock, where four Teamsters await to unload them. It takes just over one hour to unload the trucks, but the Teamsters are entitled to a minimum of four hours. The client has just paid for 16 hours of work that took 4 worker-hours. Then the Laborers (all eight based on the*

2:1 formula) roll the equipment into the event space. This will take 45 minutes, but they are also paid for four hours, a total of 32 hours paid for 8 hours of work. So far, 48 hours are charged to the client, and work has not yet even begun! The EPI workers are not allowed to work, only to point fingers and supervise.

A crew of three riggers will put the rigging points in for all lighting and audio trusses. Their job is done in two hours, but they get four hours' pay. Stagehands, electricians, and carpenters each have full crews to do the audio, lighting, and stage, each headed by a nonworking steward whose job it is to see that his people work.

Let us say that the installation is done by five o'clock. All that is left is a little bit of lighting focus and programming and some tweaking of the audio system. EPI can handle this with two people. But the union contract calls for leaving people on-site (on overtime, at time and a half) as long as EPI has workers there. Further, for the show itself, the union contract will require shadows, *people sitting next to the audio and lighting technicians throughout the show. This could be on time and a half or even double time.*

On the strike *(the takedown), the same scenario arises. If the strike happens after midnight or on a weekend, it will most certainly require time and a half for all of the union workers.*

As you can see, even if the union workers are skilled and productive, the cost of producing this event in a multiunion venue such as this can far surpass the cost in a nonunion venue. In some union venues, a producer need deal with only one union, and that makes things easier and much less expensive, perhaps even comparable to a nonunion situation.

While it is not necessarily the rule, many union workers are less than enthusiastic about working hard. They can be slow, they can be sloppy, or they can just plain wander off and hide. Vendors rarely have a say in which union workers they have on their crew, so it is hard for them to plan or predict how long the work will take and how well it will be done. Union workers are chosen for assignments by seniority. Those with the most seniority tend to get the best assignments. "Best" can be the largest shows with the best chance of substantial overtime, or it can be a sweetheart deal in a theater. If there's a lot going on in a city on the days when union labor is needed for a client's event, there is a good chance that the event will land labor from pretty far down on the union's list. This will mean less experienced and less skilled help, meaning slower setup and more supervision. If, by chance, the client's event is the only event requiring union labor, the top crew will be on call and things may go remarkably smoothly.

In nonunion scenarios, vendors will very often give a client a firm price for a production, including labor. The vendor will stick by the contracted price, even if its actual labor cost comes in higher than estimated. However, in a union situation, union stewards or business agents, as a rule, will not put a cap on the number of hours they anticipate, nor will they agree to a contract price. If the crew happens to be slow or unskilled, the cost can get quite high. Furthermore, whoever makes the union *call* (arranging for the number of workers needed) has no control over which workers are assigned. Oftentimes, corporate shows are viewed as prime work because they are perceived as having big budgets, which means lots of overtime.

Another scenario that can arise is when work falls in a gray or overlapping area, where two unions feel they are each entitled to the same work. This type of dispute can lead to a shutdown of work on the site until it is resolved, obviously an expensive proposition. Sharon Moore, president of Moore Events, Inc., outside of Philadelphia, always insists on a "pre-con meeting" with a facility representative and representatives of all unions involved. Jurisdiction can be discussed, as can order of work, estimates of time, and any other unusual situations. According to Moore,

> *While I know that nothing said in the meeting is binding on the unions, I do want to establish a sense of accountability on their part. I also want to show that they cannot take advantage of me because I am a woman. By laying the ground rules out before work actually begins, I definitely get a much more efficient installation. It also helps to hire a well-respected union member as production manager for the job. Workers respond better to one of their own than to an outsider.*

One other item that Moore recommends is to determine whether the union claiming jurisdiction over a certain type of work is actually skilled in that work. Moore recounts a situation where the union claiming jurisdiction over the installation of intelligent lighting instruments had no workers on the crew who knew the first thing about intelligent lights and the way they were to be hung and cabled.

Planners who are shopping venues need to be aware of the cost of working in a union facility before choosing it. They need to include all the preceding factors into their working budget. Do not take a production company's quote for working in a nonunion building and stick it into a budget for a union building. The labor costs will be very inaccurate. Sam Cavell, who heads up production for the Vega Group, a New Orleans destination management and event company that works all over the United States and around the world, has had quite a

bit of experience in union venues. Her approach is somewhat different. Here's what she has to say on the subject:

> *I would never make a venue decision based on whether a building
> is union or nonunion. Unions are almost a given in many cities,
> so the idea is to go in prepared and organized and knowing what
> to expect. Frame of mind is important, and going in with the right
> approach will make a world of difference. Go in expecting a con-
> frontation, and you will probably get one. Go in without doing
> your homework, and you may get clobbered. But if you go in with
> a straightforward attitude, acting pleasantly, showing you know
> what is what, it should go well. I have never had a bad experience
> with the unions as a whole.*

Clearly, the more experience planners have in union venues, the
more aware they are of how matters should proceed and how situations should be handled. A planner having confidence in his or her
position and showing knowledge is in a much better position than a
novice. Also, planners with experience in working with unions know
how to budget for their expense. Novices can get themselves in big
trouble if their budget is based on nonunion estimates—or even on
calculating union costs without taking into account all of the techni-
calities of the agreement.

Remember that all of the labor is geared toward getting equipment
loaded into a facility and installed for use. The equipment itself can be
a big part of a budget also. When working in a union venue, most
often an outside production company will be bringing in the gear. It
will be allowed to supervise the union workers in the installation, but
only rarely will it be allowed to be hands on. Production company
employees have a vested interest in taking care of the gear, handling it
carefully, and installing it properly. Union members may not have
that focus. The production company must spend time carefully supervising the union to ensure that the gear is looked after.

If nonunion production company employees are allowed to operate the equipment (usually audio and lighting consoles or video
equipment), union shadows may still be required to sit beside them as
though they were actually the operators. This is in lieu of letting the
union workers actually operate the consoles, which they may or may
not know how to do. With many of the complicated shows of today,
there is no thought of using union lighting and audio crews to actually
operate the consoles. Many production companies bring in hotshot
lighting designers to plot the show, program the lights, and operate
the board.

In a few instances, union production companies own gear. They may be able to offer a better overall deal on their labor than in working directly through the union itself. Because they own the equipment, they can factor an equipment discount into a package that can be palatable for a planner. If working in a union venue, consideration should be given to any union production companies for at least a proposal, assuming that they have a reputation for quality gear and work.

In some simpler scenarios, a facility may have only a single union working there, fulfilling multiple functions. In such instances a planner may find that the union knows the facility well and works cooperatively with outside companies, which can be very cost-effective. In others, the key unions are well-trained, skilled workers who can get work done in a cost-effective manner. In still others, the number of unions and their rigid work rules can make for an expensive experience.

On a big show, unions can be a good and necessary source of somewhat skilled labor. In some cities the unions are the best source of skilled labor. But they can also add layers of expense. It is incumbent upon the planner or producer to be well informed about the venues in which he or she is considering booking a conference, convention, or event.

Finally, if a labor dispute arises, it is quite likely that the union involved will threaten a job action or picketing. A job action can mean that the union will refuse to work and refuse to let other unions or nonunion workers work until issues are resolved. Obviously, this has the impact of putting things well behind schedule on an event site and will most certainly cause moments of panic and heart palpitation among planners. While negotiation is called for, unions oftentimes feel they have a strong advantage in this situation, so they are unwilling to give up too many of their demands.

The threat to picket is another weapon in union arsenals. No event planner wants union pickets outside their event space as guests arrive. It definitely does not create the desired impression. What to do? The planner should be in touch with counsel as quickly as possible to determine the legal options. Often, this is dependent on state labor law, which sets forth the circumstances under which job actions and picketing may be warranted. While pursuing a peaceful negotiation, the planner's team should be determining what steps need to be taken to get a temporary injunction against the union.

The National Labor Relations Act, established back in 1935, is still the strongest relevant federal statute. It gives employees the right to organize, to form unions, and to join in collective bargaining. It established the National Labor Relations Board, which has the power to preclude employers from engaging in unfair labor practices. However, the state statutes are probably the most relevant, particularly in the typical emergency situation an event person might be facing.

The planner should also be consulting with the facility to determine what has happened there historically and what options have been employed in the past. Facility representatives may be experienced in living through these difficult situations and may know the best way to approach them.

In summary, when working in a new venue, determine whether union labor is required. If so, gather information and determine the best course of action. Base budgets on realistic numbers, taking into account all costs. Negotiate as much as possible, and oversee union workers carefully. With good management and a bit of luck, the event can be a success.

■ SUMMARY

➤ In many large venues in large convention cities, unions are a fact of life.

➤ In most such venues, unions will add a fair amount of expense to the cost of the event.

➤ Planners should understand the union cost before booking a venue.

➤ If planners are locked into a union venue, they should carefully review union contracts and jurisdictions.

➤ Unless a company works with the same unions week in and week out, it should be careful about signing a union agreement for longer than a single event.

➤ Somebody has to be the employer of record for the union workers, responsible for paying them and for deducting taxes from their checks.

➤ Unions may threaten job actions and picketing if they are unhappy with situations on an event site, and clients want to avoid them.

Landlord-Tenant Concerns

Why so large a cost, having so short a lease, does thou upon your fading mansion spend?—William Shakespeare

Most special events businesses do not own their own buildings. Accordingly, they find themselves in the position of being tenants subject to a lease with a hopefully benevolent landlord. However friendly and accommodating a landlord may appear, business owners should look carefully at any proposed lease and be prepared to negotiate. Small one- or two-person event planning offices do not need much space. Sometimes this is a disadvantage, as small spaces are hard to come by. Because there are so few on the market, these small spaces may be relatively expensive on a square-foot basis. On the other hand, if a landlord wants to fill up the space, it may be had at a bargain price. Timing (which includes the factors of supply and demand) is everything. Companies that need a small amount of space may also find opportunity in subletting from other companies who may have some extra space within their offices.

Those that need a larger amount of office space will certainly have far more choices in a variety of price ranges. Office space comes in all types of edifices, from modern high-rises to converted factories. Event people convey all types of images. Some are truly buttoned-down business people and fit right in with the lawyers and investment bankers in their buildings. Others are very hip and edgy, preferring to inhabit space that makes that statement, such as a loft space or an old commercial space upgraded for funky offices.

Some companies prefer to be in buildings that provide flex space. *Flex space* is basically a combination of office and warehouse space, with the percentages being based on tenant build-out. There are loading docks and unfinished space for storage, while the space used for offices is finished nicely. Space like this is often found in industrial and business centers.

Then there are pure warehouse buildings, which tend to be the least expensive spaces. They are unfinished spaces designed to house large inventories of props, technical gear, tents, and carpeting. The office spaces contained therein are generally more functional than beautiful.

All of the different types of space have a role in the event industry. Each company must determine what type of space best suits its needs. For many, rent is the second biggest expense they have after payroll. For that reason, care should be taken in choosing the right home for the business.

■ TENANT DUE DILIGENCE

Real estate is a cyclical business, dependent to a great degree on the health of the economy. When the economy is booming, businesses are expanding and space may be at a premium. When things are a bit tougher, companies are contracting or going out of business and there may be more space on the marketplace.

Both landlords and tenants have to think about the state of the economy when they sit down to discuss the terms of a lease. Tenants have to decide whether they should lock in for a long term at a given rental rate, hedging against a tighter market and increasing rental rates, or sign a shorter lease, hoping prices will drop in the next few years. Landlords have the same issues to consider, obviously from the opposite point of view.

If space is tight in the marketplace, then landlords certainly have the upper hand in negotiations. They don't have to give up much because they know there is demand for space. If the market is flaccid and space abounds, landlords may be anxious or even desperate to move the space. Therefore, they may give some concessions on the rental rate, on build-out cost, or even throw in some rent-free months.

Based on these factors, the event company tenant should get a sense of the marketplace before signing any lease. Local newspapers report on vacancy rates, as do local business magazines and journals. Real estate agents will also have a very good handle on the local market. The event company should have an agent working on its behalf looking for the type of space needed by the company. To make the process as simple as possible, the company should have a sense of how much space it needs, of what type, and some general ideas about location and price range.

As is often said, real estate is all about "location, location, location." This may or may not hold true for an event company. The individual business must assess the advantages of locating in a particular neighborhood or city. Planners who rely heavily on local corporate business will want to locate close to the potential client base. Florists who seek to provide flowers for the homes of the wealthy will probably want to locate nearby or in a spot where the shop will be convenient and noticed by the potential clients. If a city is a very competitive market, then a company may need to decide what factor gives it a leg up on competitors—being conveniently located or being located in a low-cost area and keeping prices low.

Special events companies go from one extreme to another in choosing event space. Some go for large spaces with nice offices, spacious warehouses, and buildings they are proud to showcase for clients. They really look at their space as a marketing and sales tool. Others pack themselves into tight little spaces lacking real offices and with just barely enough room for gear. They look at their space as a cost and not a benefit. Most companies probably fall somewhere in between. They should have a handle on what purposes their facility will be put to before actually choosing a space. Some companies have multiple offices, most of which are the in-home offices of a salespeople or representatives in remote markets.

Prospective renters should be doing price comparisons of various spaces within each area so they will know the going rate. They should compare the features of the buildings in which they have an interest with regard to their business needs. They should check traffic patterns from each office to the city and the major highways at rush hour and at other times of the day. They should know if any of the areas have flooding during heavy rains or are susceptible to road problems, electrical outages, and so on.

Once a company finds a space it feels could work, it should get a list of other tenants and should check with them to see what kind of a landlord this one would be. Is the fitting out of the space handled in a timely and professional manner? Are complaints dealt with promptly? Is maintenance done on time? Is the parking lot shoveled during the winter? Does the landlord care about the appearance of the building?

■ LEASE NEGOTIATIONS

If the answers to the preceding questions are positive, then the tenant and the landlord can begin lease negotiations. Most landlords use form leases. In many instances, these forms can be purchased in a legal-stationery store, and they are structured to favor the landlord in every way. Other times, the forms are created by the landlord's counsel for use on all of his or her properties. They, too, are designed to favor the landlord.

Even the form leases have some blanks that need to be filled in. These will include the size of the leased premises, the lease term, and the rental rate. In some states the rate is described as the cost of each square foot over the course of the year. For example, 20,000 square feet at $6 per square foot is $120,000 per year, or $10,000 per month. In other states, the rate is expressed as the cost per square foot per month, so the same facility at the same price would be rented at $.50 per square foot. Tenants need to understand how the rate is being expressed to fully understand what they are paying.

Clients should also understand how the size of the space is derived. Is common space with other tenants included? Is there a shared loading area? Is there a blended rate, meaning one rate for office space, a lower rate for warehouse space, with the two blended into a single rate for the overall space?

Oftentimes, the cost of fitting out a space is included in the lease rate. Inquiry should be made into the cost of the space with and without it being fitted out. Perhaps the difference may justify the tenant doing the construction work itself. Tenants should get full information on what different aspects of construction cost, because with knowledge, they can decide what to include or omit. They may discover that some of their requests that the landlord so willingly granted are costing them a lot of money.

If the construction of loading docks or a drive-in bay is a necessity for a tenant, and the landlord agrees, the tenant should make certain that the landlord is paying for it. The same goes for items like parking lot lighting, outside lighting, or a security fence to make the premises safe. These items should by provided by the landlord and treated as a necessity and a condition of the tenant accepting the lease.

The *term of the lease* also needs to be discussed and negotiated. If one party wants a long lease and the other a shorter one, compromise may be in order. An option for a second term may be requested by the tenant. Another device used by landlords to protect themselves if the market price escalates is to put in a renewal price at a higher rate or to escalate the rent slightly each year during a term. Sometimes a tenant looking to grow into a space can request a lower rate in the early years of a lease and a higher rate later in the term. All of this can be negotiated.

As painful as it may be, somebody needs to review the lease clause by clause. It is important that the business know what responsibilities the lease creates and what actions it forbids. A landlord may be willing to negotiate certain clauses if reasonable argument is made, and these discussions can save some pain later. Issues such as responsibility for the heating, air-conditioning, and plumbing are of importance. If the tenant accepts full responsibility, it could be in for some major expense down the road. If the landlord won't budge on that responsibility, the tenant should at least insist that the landlord do a full inspection of the systems and have them certified to be in good shape by an acceptable contractor. This should hold true for any major system that the tenant is responsible for maintaining—plumbing, heating, air-conditioning, or alarm systems.

Rollup garage doors also require regular maintenance, and tenants should seek to make them the responsibility of the landlord. The landlord normally assumes responsibility for the building structure, and the tenant needs to make the argument that the doors are part of the structure. Typically, landlords will not accept responsibility for windows, and plate glass is a tenant responsibility. Skylights on roofs can become issues.

The tenant should also have the landlord certify that the premises are free of environmental and hazardous waste problems, and if any are found it will be the landlord's responsibility and expense to fix them. The roof should clearly be the problem of the landlord. The landlord should also be responsible for making sure the building is free of insect infestation prior to the tenant assuming the space.

If a company has special needs (a lighting company needing additional electrical power, a caterer or florist needing a walk-in box), it should be so stated and agreed to in the lease. A pyrotechnics company may need additional precautions in its warehouse, which should be set forth in the lease. A landlord should always be made fully aware of the uses to which the premises will be put and should agree to them in the lease. If the landlord is to be responsible for effecting construction to accommodate for these needs, the lease must so state.

Landlords may want to keep the space free from certain activities and may forbid such things as storing certain materials and chemicals, maintaining a painting operation inside, or operating certain machinery. Event companies should be aware of all prohibited activities.

Items like parking spaces need to be specified. In a multitenant building, parking may be at a premium and tenants want to be assured that their employees will not be hassled about parking, which can become a big issue. Tenants should verify the number of spaces they are entitled to, and perhaps even have them marked with their name.

■ ADDITIONAL RENT

The rental rate per square foot is not necessarily the only rental cost. Landlords have certain ownership expenses that they normally pass on to their tenants. The landlord's most obvious expenses are real estate taxes, insurance, utilities and maintenance. Typically, tenants will find themselves paying these ongoing expenses, called a *triple net charge,* billed either quarterly or yearly. They should have a sense of what that will amount to and figure the cost into their budget.

Other landlords may have something called a *common area maintenance* (CAM) charge. This would be the cost of mowing lawns, plowing snow, and any other general maintenance. This is usually apportioned among tenants based on their percentage of the overall rental space. Tenants should, at the very least, try to place a cap on this so they know what their maximum exposure might be.

As a further assurance, the lease may require tenants to maintain specific levels of insurance on their leased portion of the premises, naming the landlord as an additional insured. The landlord may insist on receiving a current certificate of insurance for each year of the lease.

■ LANDLORD DUE DILIGENCE

The prospective tenant should not be surprised if the landlord requests financial information before agreeing to a lease. Landlords want to protect themselves and make certain that before they spend money moving in a new tenant, the tenant is financially capable of handling the lease payments. Accordingly, it should be no surprise if landlords ask for one or two years' worth of financial statements. Companies do not like to share their private information and may fight that request, but if the landlord is adamant, there is little choice.

Landlords may also request additional financial assurance from a tenant. This can include a security deposit of anywhere from one to three months' rent. It can also include payment of the first month and last month of the lease in advance. All told, this can amount to five months' rent, which may well tax companies without strong cash flow.

Landlords also like to put acceleration clauses in the leases. Such clauses allow the landlord to accelerate payment of the rent for the entire balance of the lease if the tenant defaults, meaning that if a tenant misses a month or two of rent payments, it might find itself immediately owing years of future rent. Tenants have to be cognizant of this situation and of how strictly the landlord enforces the provision.

Other provisions may kick in when tenants default. Tenants may be locked out of the building and thus denied access to their inventory and records. Their inventory may be seized. Prospective tenants should have a very clear understanding of what they may be in for if things go bad for them.

■ OTHER ISSUES

A big issue that needs to be considered is the right to sublease. If tenants find their business growing rapidly, they may have to think about moving into a bigger facility prior to the completion of the lease term. Most landlords are quite amenable to this if the tenant is willing to move into another space within the building or another of their buildings. If the business has to look outside the landlord's holdings for space, however, the landlord may not be so quick to tear up the lease.

In a down real estate market, the landlord may have a hard time finding another tenant for the space, especially a financially sound one. In such circumstances, letting a good tenant leave early could leave the space vacant for a long while. Therefore, the landlord may be stubborn about freeing the tenant from the lease. Anticipating this, the tenant should have made certain before signing the lease that the right to sublease was included. This allows the tenant to re-lease the space to another party. Normally, the landlord would maintain the right to approve any subtenant.

Even if the tenant is paying $5 per square foot and has to sublease for $4 per square foot, it is much less expensive for the tenant to pay the landlord the difference of $1 per square foot than to be on the hook for the entire amount. Tenants are still liable for the full amount of the rent, and if the subtenant defaults, the tenant is responsible for the full amount.

On the other hand, if the tenant finds that business is contracting and less space is needed, a subtenant may be brought in to take over the unused space. Sometimes a tenant will find that it can actually charge more to subrented space than it is being charged under the basic lease.

Another area of concern is the lease's definition of the term *fixtures*. Normally, leases state that any fixtures installed by the tenant become part of the realty and remain the property of the landlord. This can include shelving affixed to the walls, installed ovens, cold-storage boxes, and so on. Any such planned alterations should be discussed in advance with the landlord before the signing of the lease.

■ CONCLUSION

Leases are much like other contracts. Terms should be negotiated before signing, as no bargaining power exists after signing. While the landlord maintains the better bargaining position, the tenant has the ultimate ability to walk away. Short of this, the tenant should go through every clause and fight for its interests, knowing where it can give in and where it will not.

Most landlords are reasonable, although not necessarily on every point. If a company finds a facility it likes in a desirable location at a fair price, every effort should be made to come to agreement. But the event company must make certain that it can conduct its business the way it needs to in order to be successful. If the landlord will not negotiate on the points necessary to make that happen, then despite a favorable price and location, the space is not the right one.

■ SUMMARY

> ➤ An event company should analyze the type and the amount of space it needs to function at the present time and for the number of years of the lease, taking into account projected growth of the company.

> ➤ The potential tenant should perform due diligence on the location, the landlord, the specific building, the neighbors, the real estate market, and the economy.

> ➤ The landlord will perform due diligence on the finances of the prospective tenant.

> ➤ Tenants should calculate the true cost of the lease, including the triple net portions and all common-area charges and other items.

> ➤ Security deposits may be required.

> ➤ Leases, being contracts, are negotiable. Since the forms tend to favor the landlords, tenant or tenant's counsel should read the lease carefully and attempt to adjust unfavorable provisions.

> ➤ Tenants should make certain that they have the right to sublease.

> ➤ Tenants should clearly understand the rights of the landlord should they default.

Chapter

13

Trucking

Don't mistake motion for action. —Ernest Hemingway

It is always a source of pride when the event company buys its first vehicle, even if it is a secondhand van. The truck represents a hard asset that is used for actually doing business. It is a bold statement that says, "I am really in business."

When a company starts out small, there are few issues in truck ownership. As long as the company carries insurance and makes certain that its drivers have valid drivers licenses, there is little to worry about. But as the company grows, trucks get bigger and travel farther, state lines are crossed, and more reporting requirements come into play. As in other areas of doing business, a company's trucking issues grow as its business grows. The types of trucks change, the types of driver's licenses of those driving them change, and government interest in the company's truck-related activities changes.

■ INTERNATIONAL FUEL TAX AGREEMENT

The International Fuel Tax Agreement (IFTA), a road tax collection system, is an agreement between the 48 contiguous states and all Canadian provinces except for Northwest Territories and Yukon. The purpose is to simplify the reporting of fuel used by motor carriers operating in more than one jurisdiction. A company registers its vehicles in its home state or province and receives decals from that jurisdiction. The decals qualify the holder to operate in all member states or provinces without the need for additional permits. The home jurisdiction collects all road taxes due by that company, even if some are due in other states or provinces. It will then distribute the taxes owed to the other jurisdictions. If a company has several fleets registered in multiple jurisdictions, the jurisdictions may allow the company to choose one base jurisdiction and file a consolidated return.

IFTA applies to any vehicle having two axles and a gross vehicle weight exceeding 26,000 pounds or three or more axles regardless of weight.

Each company with an IFTA license must maintain a complete record of all fuel purchased, received, and used in the conduct of its business. The fuel records should contain, at the least, the date of each fuel receipt, the name and address of the person from whom fuel was purchased, the type of fuel, the amount of fuel, and identification of the vehicle into which the fuel was placed.

Quarterly tax returns must be filed containing all the preceding information. Included in the return is detailed information pertaining to distance, fuel purchase, and fuel usage records for each vehicle. These reports should include records of fuel purchase in each jurisdiction, the usage of fuel in each jurisdiction, and the distance traveled in each jurisdiction in which the vehicles were operated. The law requires payment of a tax equivalent to the rate per gallon times the amount of fuel used on the highway. Credit is given for tax paid on fuel purchased. Thus, if proper records are kept showing tax paid on each gallon, there should be no additional tax payments due.

Leased vehicles are subject to fuel tax and tax filings the same as owned vehicles. Leased vehicles take several forms—long-term lease from a truck leasing company; short-term lease from a truck leasing company, or the leasing of a vehicle and its driver. Some companies do not own their vehicles outright—they lease them for one to five years. Additional rentals may take place for a day, week, or month—this is a short-term rental. A company may also hire a tractor trailer with its driver for one or more trips. There are rules that apply to each of these situations. The transportation department in each jurisdiction can provide a manual setting forth all rules.

There are exemptions in certain jurisdictions from the licensing requirement. Each state and province may have different exemptions, so it is important to be familiar with the jurisdictions in which the company operates.

There are IFTA record-keeping requirements for all qualified vehicles, and the records must support the information on the quarterly tax returns. The documentation of all mileage traveled is required by date of trip, trip origin and destination, routes of travel and state-line odometer readings, total trip miles, mileage by jurisdiction, vehicle identification number, and vehicle fleet number.

In addition to mileage verification records, the company must also maintain records on all fuel purchased. To obtain credit for the retail tax paid per gallon, a receipt is required. Acceptable forms of receipts include receipt, invoice, credit card receipt, or transaction listing.

■ CDL LICENSING REQUIREMENTS

By passage of the Commercial Motor Vehicle Safety Act of 1986, the federal government created the requirements for a commercial driver's license. The purpose was to ensure that drivers of large vehicles are qualified to operate them and that those who are unsafe and unqualified are removed from the highways. The act established the minimum standards for both written and driving tests for persons operating commercial vehicles. It was left to the states to issue the licenses, administer the tests, and create laws within their jurisdiction consistent with the standards contained in the federal statutes. The Federal Highway Administration has defined the standards for testing and licensing.

Under the law, a Commercial Driver's License (CDL) is required to operate any vehicle with a manufacturer's gross vehicle weight (GVW) of more than 26,000 pounds or a vehicle towing a unit with a manufacturer's GVW of more than 10,000 pounds when the GCWR exceeds 26,000 pounds. If a driver either fails the air brake component of the general knowledge test or performs the skills test in a vehicle not equipped with air brakes, the driver is issued an air brake restriction. A driver operating a vehicle with a double trailer must get an endorsement on his or her CDL.

A CDL license can be issued only by the state where the driver maintains legal residence, and an individual with a CDL license can have no other driver's license in any state. There are a few exemptions to being required to have a CDL, such as for those on active military duty with military licenses and firefighters with licenses for emergency vehicles.

There are eligibility requirements for CDLs in every state. Typically, drivers must be at least 21 years of age and possess a valid medical certificate. They must also qualify for the license based on their driving record. Anyone disqualified from commercial driving privileges anywhere, anyone with a currently suspended, revoked, or canceled license, or anyone with a conviction for driving while impaired in the past 24 months is ineligible for a CDL.

States develop their tests based on the minimum standards set forth in the federal law. The general-knowledge portion must contain at least 30 questions, and applicants must answer at least 80 percent correctly. The skills test must be taken in a vehicle representative of the type of vehicle that the applicant expects to operate. Applicants must successfully perform all of the required skills.

If the employee with a CDL has a moving violation, the consequences are severe. A simple moving violation can lead to a suspension of the license. Two or more within three years can lead to a long suspension. Driving under the influence or leaving the scene of an accident can lead to a suspension of three years or more.

Some companies discover the need for a CDL when they load a big show onto a truck for the first time. When it's weighed, they discover they are over the non-CDL limit and must rent a CDL truck. Then they are told they need a CDL driver. Oops, don't have one. Bigger loads require bigger trucks. Bigger trucks probably mean CDLs. The license is required for driving the truck within one state only or in intrastate commerce.

Companies that find themselves needing to rent or lease CDL trucks should make certain that they have CDL drivers. Some companies make it a requirement for all who drive for them. Others find a lack of enthusiasm on the part of employees for obtaining a CDL and do not really feel they have the leverage to force their employees to comply. The requirements for a CDL are tougher, and the consequences for violation greater, than for a regular driver's license. Companies may have to consider an incentive for the drivers to obtain their CDLs. On the other hand, in some companies, the fact that a CDL is a job requirement is enough of an incentive.

Many states have different classes of CDLs, with tractor trailers, for instance, being in a different class from the 26,000 GVW truck. It may be hard to justify keeping a tractor trailer driver on staff, but they are certainly available on a per-trip basis.

■ TRUCK LOGS

Every interstate driver is required by the Federal Motor Carrier Safety Regulations to maintain a *Record of Duty Status,* affectionately known as a truck log. The purpose of this requirement is to limit the hours of service to promote safer driving, because tired drivers are not safe drivers. The first limitation is on driving time. There can be a maximum of *10 hours of driving time,* after which the driver must take 8 hours of rest. The only exception is if drivers encounter bad weather or traffic conditions that they could not have anticipated, there can be a two-hour extension.

The next rule is *15 hours on-duty time*. This states that drivers cannot drive after they have been on duty for 15 hours until they have had eight consecutive hours of rest. There are no exceptions to this rule.

The third rule is *60 or 70 hours of service maximum*. If the company operates vehicles six days per week, a driver may accumulate a maximum of 60 hours of on-duty time in any seven consecutive days. If the company operates vehicles seven days per week, the driver can accumulate up to 70 hours of on-duty time in any eight consecutive days.

Drivers have to keep logs showing their on-duty and their off-duty hours. The information required includes the date, total miles driven on that date, truck number, name of company, driver's signature, 24-hour-period starting time, total hours, main office address, remarks, name of codriver, if any, and shipping document numbers. Drivers are required to keep their logs up-to-date as of the last change-of-duty status, which mean the records are supposed to be current at all times. Drivers must submit a copy of the logs to the company. Drivers must keep their own copy for seven days, and the company must keep its copy for six months.

It should be carefully noted that the company can be responsible for the violations of its drivers if it had or should have had the means to detect violations. Intent is not a necessary element of that liability. Companies are deemed to have permitted violations by their employees if they do not have the management systems in place to prevent such violations. Further, the company can be found to be liable if drivers falsify their records and the company has accepted the false documents.

Rumors persist that some drivers actually falsify records by keeping two sets of logs, so authorities do not see rule violations. Company managers may wink at their drivers and treat this as an insider's privilege, even a right of passage.

■ WEIGH STATIONS

Each state has its own criteria for enforcement of the laws regulating the trucking industry. While they may differ from state to state, they are all designed with highway safety in mind. The weigh stations are set up to verify that tractor trailers and other trucks do not exceed the maximum gross vehicle weight or axle limitations.

Drivers who are pulled aside at a weigh station will, at the very least, be expected to produce their truck log, CDL, and medical card. Drivers will be pulled aside at the scales for random inspections (perhaps one out of every 100 to 150 trucks) or because an inspector has noticed something wrong with the equipment. There are different levels of inspection, ranging from a North American Standard Inspection, which is a full inspection of the driver's paperwork and the truck, to Driver-Only Inspections, where just the driver's paperwork is reviewed.

Needless to say, state departments of transportation, which normally control the weigh stations, may find irregularities in the paperwork, or they may find that a truck is overweight or poorly loaded. At the very least, this will require the driver to shift his or her load. If the truck is overweight, it will not be allowed back on the road until the weight is brought back within the law. This will involve waiting for another truck to come to the station and take on part of the load. Drivers whose paperwork is wrong or who have driven their full 10 hours will be held at the site, "out of service," until they meet the rest requirements.

■ DRUG AND ALCOHOL TESTING

The Department of Transportation requires drug and alcohol testing for all those whose position requires a commercial driver's license, even if they are not driving. The types of testing include preemployment (for drug use only), random, reasonable suspicion, postaccident, return to duty, and follow-up.

The regulations read that those being offered positions requiring a CDL shall have a preemployment test. During the course of employment, drug and alcohol testing may be required of an employee under the following circumstances: (1) when that employee in the course of performing a safety-sensitive function is involved in an on-the-job driving accident that results in the death of a person or results in a citation for a moving traffic violation and any vehicle requires towing from the scene; (2) when the employee is observed using drugs or alcohol while on duty; (3) when a supervisor formally trained to recognize physical appearance and behavior of persons under the influence of alcohol or illegal drugs observes an employee exhibiting such behavior and appearance during, immediately preceding, or following the workday period in which the employee is performing a safety-sensitive function; (4) when the employee is selected pursuant to a random process; (5) when an employee returns to a safety-sensitive position after having been diagnosed by a substance abuse professional as needing assistance in resolving drug or alcohol problems.

Safety-sensitive functions include the entire period from the time a driver begins to work or is required to be in readiness to work until that driver is relieved from work and from all responsibility from performing work: (1) all time at the physical plant waiting to be dispatched; (2) all time a driver spends inspecting or servicing any commercial vehicle; (3) all driving time; (4) all time other than driving time in a commercial vehicle except for time in a sleeping berth; (5) all time loading or unloading a commercial vehicle, supervising or assisting in loading or unloading, or remaining in readiness to operate the commercial vehicle; (6) all time repairing, obtaining assistance, or remaining in attendance on a disabled commercial vehicle.

The federal regulations prohibit any alcohol or drug use that could affect performance of a safety-sensitive function, including (1) reporting for duty or remaining on duty to perform safety-sensitive functions with a blood alcohol content of 0.04 or greater; (2) use while performing safety-sensitive functions; (3) use during the four hours prior to performing a safety-sensitive function; (4) use during the eight-hour period following an accident or until a driver undergoes a postaccident test, whichever happens first; (5) refusal to take a required test.

Drugs to be tested for include marijuana, cocaine, opiates, amphetamines, and phencyclidine (PCP). A driver may not report for duty to perform a safety-sensitive function if (1) the driver tests positive for controlled substance use; (2) the driver refuses to take a required test; (3) the driver uses one of the controlled substances—unless prescribed by a doctor who has advised the use will not adversely affect the driver's ability to operate a commercial motor vehicle.

This is a very important area for employers. Federal regulations require employers to meet all applicable requirements of the law and make them responsible for all actions of their representatives in carrying out the regulations. Alcohol and drug testing does not sit well with the event industry because there are too many owners and managers for whom alcohol and drug consumption is normal, and in addition they do not wish to pry into their employees' personal lives. Unfortunately, the rights of privacy and personal freedom conflict with the government's overriding interest in preserving highway safety and cutting back on accidents. Hippy values need to be set aside in the face of the DOT's awesome power to enforce its regulations and to fine heavily those who do not follow them.

Several private companies throughout the United States will implement a testing program according to the federal regulations for event companies. They have affiliated testing centers throughout the country. They will provide all necessary paperwork, and they will make sure that all of the employer's legal obligations are met.

Speaking bluntly, many employees believe they can outwit the average drug test and continue their drug use by doing so. Chemicals are advertised in magazines and on the Internet that can supposedly remove traces of all of the suspect drugs from the urine. Whether they work is irrelevant. Owners should be sympathetic with the purposes of the laws and should discourage this type of attitude. If an innocent party were to die as a result of an employee driving while impaired, reality would be driven home in a horrible, devastating manner. This is an area where being a rebel has no value and no place.

■ MISCELLANEOUS ISSUES

Several other transportation-related issues merit mention. It pays to be thoroughly familiar with your responsibilities under the law or to consult with someone who is.

➤ Hazmat

The Code of Federal Regulations does speak to the transportation of hazardous materials on America's highways. Those who deal with such materials should be cognizant of the relevant sections. Compressed gases, even carbon dioxide in tanks, are regulated. Tunnels are restricted, as are some bridges.

There are relatively new sections of the code dealing with the transportation of fireworks. Extra care should be taken here.

➤ Trailer Permits

Some businesses in the event industry own or rent portable generators for event use. Some travel on their own trailers, which need to be hitched to the back of trucks. State laws dictate the size of the vehicles required to tow such trailers.

➤ Financial Considerations

Event companies should beware of situations where they are sending a lot of gear out on a tour in a truck or trucks owned by a client or another vendor. If for any reason the owner of the truck is in financial trouble and the truck is seized by a creditor, the company may have a hard time getting its gear back. Event companies should check with their attorneys to determine what steps are required to perfect and maintain their interests in their own equipment.

Used trucks generally hold up better than used cars. Trucks are made to last longer. Nonetheless, when purchasing used vehicles, check maintenance records and have a mechanic go over the vehicle. If vans have trailer hitches, find out what they have been towing and compare the weight to the type of suspension and the towing package on the vehicle.

■ CONCLUSION

The Department of Transportation has a very complete web site where much free information can be obtained. Most states have DOT web sites and telephone numbers to call for assistance. Much information is available. For new business owners, asking to be made aware of anything they might need to know as commercial vehicle owners will open the door to discussions and information that otherwise they might not have.

There are too many ways to run afoul of the Department of Transportation to just sit back and act ignorant. Commercial vehicle owners need to be proactive—ask truck leasing companies, insurance agents, and the state departments of transportation for information. Otherwise, large fines and, even worse, serious liability may be incurred.

■ SUMMARY

➤ IFTA is a fact of life throughout the continental United States, and its provisions must be addressed by all companies operating vehicles with a gross vehicle weight in excess of 26,000 pounds.

➤ CDL trucks are those with a gross vehicle weight in excess of 26,000 pounds.

➤ CDL trucks must be driven by drivers with Commercial Driver's Licenses.

➤ CDLs have stringent requirements, both to pass the test and to maintain the license.

➤ By federal statute, there are limits on the number of hours a CDL operator can drive in a given day.

➤ Accurate truck logs must be maintained and kept available in the truck for inspection.

➤ There are highway restrictions for vehicles carrying compressed gas and other materials considered to be hazardous. These restrictions include tunnels and bridges.

Intellectual Property

Ideas are the beginning points of all fortunes. —Napoleon Hill

Much of what is done in the special event industry is based on creative thought, which is expressed in a variety of ways. Sometimes the creativity is reduced to writing or other recordable forms such as proposals, scripts, music, photographs, and video. People in the industry range from very concerned to downright paranoid about the theft of their ideas. They want to protect what they view as their biggest asset, their creativity, from theft by others who will turn it into commercial gain. Event professionals would like nothing more than to find an easy way to sue and obtain damages from everyone who steals their ideas or takes their proposals and produces them themselves.

Intellectual property is definable in a variety of ways, one of the simplest being any product of the human intellect that is subject to copyright, patent, trademark, or trade secret protection; licensable know-how; research findings; compilations of information in particular formats, whether text, spreadsheets, databases, graphics, digital images, audio, video, or multimedia, in either written or electronic form.

By creating a broad definition to protect the creations of special events professionals, a converse obligation is created for those same professionals to honor the rights of others. This obligation comes into play in software licensing and in the use of music, photography, and video created and copyrighted by others.

Both sides of the issue are discussed in this chapter.

■ EVENT COMPANY CONCERNS

Every event company has competitors. Just as every company believes that it is most deserving of a client's business for one reason or another, its competitors feel the same way for the same or different reasons. Accordingly, companies want to preserve their edge between themselves and their clients. Even then, they can be nervous if they do not know a client well or do not trust the client 100 percent. If Company A feels that it can come in at the lowest price because it already owns much of what is needed to fulfill its proposal, it wants to keep that price a secret so no competitor matches or undercuts it. If Company B has a wonderfully creative approach to a problem that gives it the edge, it wants to keep that approach solely its own.

What if the client likes Company C best of all, based on previous history, on reputation, or on promised kickbacks? What if the client shows Company C the proposals of A and B, requesting that Company C incorporate the best of both into its proposal? What protection do the others have?

What if the client is a hotel or a casino and who gets the proposals and realizes it can actually produce Company A's proposal in-house without using Company A? What can A do?

Suppose that Decor Inc. lands an extensive production job at the science museum that will truly showcase its talents and, with the client's permission, arranges to have the event photographed. To cut down on the expense, the company enlists the caterer, lighting company, and facility to share the cost. The event is spectacular and the photographs truly capture it. All parties involved receive copies to include in their portfolios. What happens when the facility uses the pictures to try to woo a corporation into holding their event there and at the same time recommends a decorator or lighting company other than the ones pictured? What happens if one of the companies goes to Kinko's to make color copies rather than getting them from the photographer? What if the photography company uses the pictures to market itself? Who owns what rights?

There are numerous examples of event companies seeking to protect their creativity. Can this be accomplished? If so, how?

■ COPYRIGHT

Copyright is a type of legal protection afforded by federal statute (title 17 of the U.S. Code) to the authors of "original works of authorship." This phrase includes the following types of works:

> ➤ *Literary works.* Included in this category are novels, short stories, magazine articles, newspaper articles, prose, poetry, manuals,

catalogs, brochures, ad text, compilations, training manuals, software documentation and manuals, and computer software.

➤ *Dramatic works.* Plays, operas, and skits, including accompanying music.

➤ *Musical works.* Songs (including any words), advertising jingles (including any words), and instrumentals.

➤ *Pantomimes and choreographic works.* Ballets, modern dance, jazz dance, and mime works.

➤ *Pictorial, graphic, and sculptural works.* Posters, photographs, maps, paintings, drawings, lithographs, graphic art, works of fine art, statues, display ads, cartoon strips, cartoon characters, and stuffed animals.

➤ *Motion picture and other audiovisual works.* Movies, documentaries, travelogues, training films and videos, marketing films and videos, television shows, television ads, and interactive multimedia works.

➤ *Sound recordings.* Recordings of music, sound, words, or a combination.

➤ *Architectural works.* Building designs, either in the form of plans and drawings or the constructed building itself.

The reason for offering copyright protection is to give creators the fruits of their creative efforts: recognition and fair financial reward. Copyright holders are given the incentive to create and distribute their creative efforts without fear of unauthorized use. They secure their reward, and the public secures the reward of enhanced lives through the enjoyment of the copyrighted works.

Copyright protection begins the moment the work is created in fixed form (i.e. a form in which the work can be read or visually perceived either directly or with the aid of a device or machine). The copyright is the property of the creator of the work or of any deriving their rights through the creator (a license, assignee, or heir). It affixes automatically—no steps need be taken. If the work is created over time, the portion of the work recorded or fixed on a given date constitutes the created work as of that date. The copyright need not be registered in order to be valid. However, the copyright needs to be registered before an infringement suit may be filed. There are two other benefits. First, if registration is made within three months after the publication of the work or prior to any infringement, statutory damages and attorney fees will be available to the copyright holder in court actions. Second, registration allows the owner of the copyright to record the registration with the U.S. Customs Service for protection against importation of infringing copies.

Copyright holders have the exclusive rights to use or authorize others to use the work on agreed-upon terms and conditions. The holder of the copyright has the right to either authorize or prohibit (1) the reproduction of the work in various forms, such as printed publication or sound recording; (2) its public performance, in the case of a play, musical work, motion picture, dance program; (3) its recording in the form of compact discs, DVDs, cassettes, or other tapes or videotapes; (4) its translation into other languages or its adaptation, such as from novel to screenplay; (5) modification to create a new or derivative work; (6) public display of the work directly, by means of a film, slide, or television image in a public place, or by transmission to the public.

To obtain the benefit of copyright protection, the first requirement is that the work be *original*. This requirement is fairly simple, as the definition of originality is quite broad. As long as the work owes its existence to the author and was not copied from any preexisting work, it is deemed original. No creativity or uniqueness is required. When a work is created through the compilation of preexisting material, the copyright will extend only to the original portion. Facts are not considered original. A compilation of facts, however, may be original in the way it is chosen, coordinated, arranged, and presented.

The second requirement for a work to be copyrighted is that the work be *fixed*. Section 101 of the Copyright Act says a work is fixed when it is made "sufficiently permanent or stable to permit it to be perceived, reproduced or otherwise communicated for a period of more than transitory duration."

There are limitations on the rights of a copyright holder, giving others the right to have limited use of copyrighted works. The copyright protects against the unauthorized taking of a work's "expression," but does not protect the ideas, concepts, principles, processes, or procedures in the work. It does not protect facts, no matter how laboriously collected.

The largest exception is that of the *fair use* of a copyrighted work. While not defined by the Copyright Act, Section 107 of the Copyright Act states that fair use is to be determined by balancing the purpose and character of the use; by the nature of the copyrighted work; by the amount and substantiality of the portion used in relation to the totality of the work; and by the effect of the use on the potential market for, or value of, the copyrighted work.

The doctrine of fair use first came into being via judicial decision, and it was subsequently codified in the Copyright Act. The courts were trying to balance the interests of copyright holders against the interests of society in socially important areas such as education, research, reporting, and criticism. When the law was changed to adopt the doctrine, fair use was not defined clearly, so case law has provided conflicting interpretations. For purposes of the special events profession, there is no clear doctrine of fair use, and a copyright attorney should be consulted before relying on fair use as a basis for copying a portion of another's work.

Violation of any of the exclusive rights of a copyright holder is called *infringement.* The holder of a copyright may sue an infringer and can recover actual monetary damages as well as, in some cases, statutory damages. The courts may also issue injunctions to restrain or prevent copyright infringement and can further order the impoundment and destruction of infringing works.

How does this apply to the industry? The photographer whose photos appear in someone else's brochure without his permission has a cause of action. The songwriter or scriptwriter whose work is taken and used without her permission has a cause of action. The big question—what about proposals? Proposals vary so much in content and style that no blanket answer is possible. Remember that copyrights do not protect ideas alone. If event professionals feel that their work is original and has been infringed upon, they should consult a copyright attorney to review for the possibility of bringing suit. Few cases exist, so there is not really a body of case law on the subject. Case law with any real authority comes from appellate courts. This means that cases have been brought in a trial court, and then appeals have been taken from them to the higher court. Lawsuits have been brought, but few are tried and fewer still are appealed. It is unlikely for an event company to expend the time, energy, and money to take a case this far.

Under the current law, copyright life for works created by an individual is equal to the life of the author plus 70 years. Under some circumstances, copyrights may extend to either 95 years from the date of first publication or 120 years from the date of creation.

Two copyright issues remain. The first pertains to international protection. U.S. authors automatically have copyright protection in all countries that are a party to the Berne Convention for the Protection of Literary and Artistic Works or the Universal Copyright Convention. Most countries belong to at least one of the two.

The second issue is the effect of the Internet on copyright. Two treaties finalized in 1996 at the World Intellectual Property Organization (WIPO), the WIPO Copyright Treaty (WCT) and the WIPO Performances and Phonograms Treaty (WPPT), were passed to supplement existing copyright rights related to the dissemination of protected material over digital networks such as the Internet. Basically, the two treaties decisively clarify that copyright holder rights do apply in the digital environment. Through the World Trade Organization, an additional agreement was created, the Agreement on Trade-Related Aspects of Intellectual Property Rights (TRIPS). It is the most comprehensive multilateral agreement on intellectual property, establishing standards of protection for copyrights, trademarks and service marks, industrial design, and patents; providing standards for enforcement of intellectual property; and prescribing a binding dispute-resolution procedure.

When all is said and done, a copyright may not offer the protection that an event person would like to have. Is there anything else that can be done? If the proposal is the big issue, perhaps there is. A lesson can be learned from the software companies, which require users to click on "I Accept" in the licensing agreement before they can install the software. An event person can do the same. A cover letter can create a license, giving the client the right to read the proposal and hire the vendor to produce the ideas contained therein. It forbids the client from taking the ideas, sharing them with others, and/or producing the ideas without the creator or without paying the creator a licensing fee. This may be easier to enforce than a copyright action. The vendor has to consider the impact of such a cover letter on a proposal: Would the client be insulted? Angry? Understanding? An example can be found in the appendix.

The use of photographs calls for a written agreement. Photographers have every right to expect that they will remain the owner of their images. However, if the client has other plans, it should be dealt with up front. The client should specify any wish to own the images, the negatives, and any rights thereto. The photographer should charge accordingly. If the client then decides to share with other vendors, the terms should be laid out clearly, also in written contractual agreements. A copy of such an agreement can be found in the appendix.

■ TRADEMARKS

A *trademark* is a distinctive sign, word, name, device, symbol, or combination of any of these identifying certain goods or services to indicate the source of the goods and distinguish them from the goods of others. A service mark is the same as a trademark, except that it identifies the source of a service rather than a product.

A trademark provides protection to its owner by ensuring the exclusive right to use it to identify the goods. It rewards the holder with recognition and financial reward, and it hinders others (unfair competitors) from using deceptively similar marks to market different or inferior goods.

A trademark is registered by filing an application with a national or regional trademark office. The application must contain a clear reproduction of the sign and must contain a list of the goods or services to which it will apply. The sign must be distinctive so that consumers can distinguish it as identifying a particular product. It must neither mislead nor deceive. Rights applied for cannot be the same as or similar to rights already granted to another trademark owner.

In the United States, trademarks can be protected under both the federal statute, the Lanham Act, 15 U.S.C. §§ 1051–1127, and state statute and court decisions.

A trademark is good in the country in which it is registered. The WIPO administers a system of international registration of marks. This system is governed by two treaties. The first is the Madrid Agreement Concerning the International Registration of Marks, and the second is the Madrid Protocol. By initially registering a mark in a member country, a person can obtain registration of a mark internationally in those countries (approximately 60) that are parties to one or both of the agreements.

A mark does not necessarily have to be registered. Rights can be established based on the legitimate use of the mark. But trademark registration gives the holder the right to bring an action in federal court based on the mark and the ability to file the U.S. registration with the U.S. Customs Service to prevent importation of infringing foreign goods.

Once a party claims rights in a mark, it can use the ™ (trademark) or ˢᴹ (service mark) designation to give notice to the public of the claim. The federal registration symbol ® can be used only after the Patent Office has registered a mark—not while an application is pending.

Event companies may invest much money in designing a logo, a tagline, or a particular look to their literature. Especially in the case of a national or international company or a firm that wants to do business on a national basis, identifiability is critical to success. The Creative Design Group will need a catchy logo and presentation to distinguish itself from others in the industry, because the name will be similar to that of many other companies.

Event companies may design similar marks for clients for events, meetings or conferences, or advertising campaigns. The client's campaign or conference may be extremely important to it, and therefore the clear identification of the campaign and its distinctiveness from others must be assured.

■ PATENTS

Patent law has a long history in the United States, going back to Article I, Section 8 of the Constitution. The Patent Law can be found in Title 35 of the U.S. Code, and it is administered by the U.S. Patent and Trademark Office.

A *patent* is the grant of a property right in an invention. The invention must be of practical use; it must show an element of novelty; it must show an inventive step; it must not be obvious in light of prior patterns and known technology; it must be useful; and it must be accepted as patentable under the law. The invention must show some new characteristic that is unknown in the body of existing knowledge in its technical field. This body is referred to as *prior art*.

The patent owner has the right to decide which parties may have use of his or her invention during the period of its patent protection. The patent holder may license the use of the invention or may sell the patent rights. In order to receive the patent, the owner must disclose in detail how to make the invention work and how it is used.

The patenting process is somewhat more complicated than the copyright and trademark process. Patent attorneys are quite often needed, and the applications are typically very detailed. It may take some time for a patent to be issued. Typical of patented technology in the event industry would be intelligent lighting instruments and controllers, audio speaker technology, audio consoles and processing, and video projectors.

■ INDUSTRIAL DESIGNS

An industrial design is the ornamental or aesthetic aspect of an item. The design can consist of three-dimensional features, such as the shape or the surface of the item, or two-dimensional features, such as patterns, lines, or color.

To be protected under the law, industrial designs must appeal to the eye, meaning that they are primarily of an aesthetic nature. They add to the value and marketability of the item in commerce.

As a general rule, an industrial design must be registered in order to be protected under the law. To be registerable, the design must be *new* (meaning that no identical or very similar design can be found to have previously existed) and it must be *original*. If protection is granted, the registration generally applies for five years, with possible periods of renewal. It is also conceivable that under some national laws an industrial design can be protected as a work of art under copyright law.

Protection under industrial design law is usually limited to the country in which protection is initially granted. There is an international treaty, the Hague Agreement Concerning the International Deposit of Industrial Designs, administered by the WIPO. Under it, an applicant can make a single international filing, thus protecting the design in the countries that are party to the treaty.

■ TRADE SECRETS

A *trade secret* is any information that derives its value from being known only by the company owning it. Trade secrets can be formulas, processes, methods, techniques, pricing information, customer lists, and so on. Patents and trademarks are by definition inconsistent with trade secrets, as the former must be revealed in detail, and the latter is designed to increase recognition. However, material that can be copyrighted can also be held to be a trade secret. Computer software is an example.

Trade secrets are primarily protected by state law. Most of the states have adopted the Uniform Trade Secrets Act, which was drafted by the National Conference of Commissioners on Uniform State Laws, as amended 1985. The act allows for injunctive relief for actual or threatened misappropriation. Misappropriation is defined as follows:

> *(i) acquisition of a trade secret of another by a person who knows or has reason to know that the trade secret was acquired by improper means; or (ii) disclosure or use of a trade secret of another without express or implied consent by a person who (A) used improper means to acquire knowledge of the trade secret; or (B) at the time of disclosure or use knew or had reason to know that his knowledge of the trade secret was (I) derived from or through a person who has utilized improper means to acquire it; (II) acquired under circumstances giving rise to a duty to maintain its secrecy or limit its use; or (III) derived from or through a person who owed a duty to the person seeking relief to maintain its secrecy or limit its use; or (C) before a material change of his position, knew or had reason to know that it was a trade secret and that knowledge of it had been acquired by accident or mistake.*

Under the act, damages can be obtained for misappropriation, including damages for any actual loss as well as the amount of any unjust enrichment gained by such misappropriation. If damages cannot be computed in any other manner, they can be assessed as a reasonable royalty on the misappropriator's unauthorized disclosure. There are instances under the act whereby exemplary damages can be collected in an amount not greater than twice the award of actual damages. Further, the opportunity for either party to collect attorney fees exists under the act.

■ WORK FOR HIRE

In the event industry, business owners are looking to hire individuals who can produce outstanding work that will enable the company to acquire new, exciting, and lucrative clients. Of course, in order to do that, the employees need to show originality and creativity, as does their work. In fact, the work done by employees may have great commercial value. The big question is, to whom?

The general rule is that the person who creates a work is the author of the work and therefore the holder of the copyright to that work. A *work for hire* arises when a person creates a copyrightable work but does not own it. Under the Copyright Act, the copyright can go, not to the creator, but to the person or company that hired the creator. The act states the following:

> A *"work made for hire"* is—
>
> (1) a work prepared by an employee within the scope of his or her employment; or
>
> (2) a work specially ordered or commissioned for use as a contribution to a collective work, as a part of a motion picture or other audiovisual work, as a translation, as a supplementary work, as a compilation, as an instructional text, as a test, as answer material for a test, or as an atlas, if the parties expressly agree in a written instrument signed by them that the work shall be considered a work made for hire. For the purpose of the foregoing sentence, a "supplementary work" is a work prepared for publication as a secondary adjunct to a work by another author for the purpose of introducing, concluding, illustrating, explaining, revising, commenting upon, or assisting in the use of the other work, such as forewords, afterwords, pictorial illustrations, maps, charts, tables, editorial notes, musical arrangements, answer material for tests, bibliographies, appendixes, and indexes, and an "instructional text" is a literary, pictorial, or graphic work prepared for publication and with the purpose of use in systematic instructional activities.

Determining whether a particular work falls into the category of a work for hire is based on the relationship of the parties. If the creator is an employee, the work would generally be considered a work for hire. If a work is created by an independent contractor, then the work is specially ordered or commissioned. It is deemed a work for hire only if it falls within one of the nine categories listed in part 2 of the definition in the act and there is a written agreement between the parties specifying that the work is a work for hire.

If a work is deemed a work for hire, then the employer owns the copyright. The term of a copyright for a work for hire is 95 years from publication or 120 years from the date of creation, whichever comes first.

Event companies that use independent contractors to design their web sites should be very careful to have a work-for-hire agreement. Otherwise, they may find they do not own their own web sites. The same can be said for brochures and other traditional marketing pieces. A sample work-for-hire letter can be found in the appendix.

■ TURNABOUT IS FAIR PLAY

The same event professionals who are concerned about protection of their intellectual property also need to be concerned about the protection of others' rights. On a daily or regular basis, event professionals come into contact with intellectual property owned by others.

The foremost example is in computer software. Many companies buy one copy of a piece of software that contains a single-user license and install it in multiple computers. This is copyright infringement. The typical rationalization involves the self-pitying "small company versus giant software Goliath" argument. But, it is nonetheless viewed as infringement.

The use of music, be it a short snippet or an entire recorded work, is common, either as a sound effect, walk-in music, background music for an event, support for video modules, or as an evening's entertainment. ASCAP and BMI were discussed in Chapter 8, and the obligations to those organizations should not be forgotten.

Likewise, video clips are often pirated to create dramatic effects or entertaining moments. Technically, much of this is copyright violation and should be avoided.

Use of photographs without permission or without crediting the photographer can also be interpreted as infringement, and event professionals should be fastidious in doing the right thing.

There are enough double standards in the world without creating new ones in the event profession. Care should be taken to preserve the rights of others. The laws exist to protect all whose work comes under them, and event people should no more be the victimizer than the victim.

■ SUMMARY

- ➤ Intellectual property encompasses a broad spectrum of products of the human mind.
- ➤ Copyright does not protect ideas, but it may protect the illustration, explanation, performance, and production of ideas.
- ➤ A work is considered to be copyrighted as soon as it is in a fixed medium, but the copyright needs to be registered before the owner can pursue an infringement action.
- ➤ A trademark provides the owner with the exclusive right to use a logo or identifying mark.
- ➤ A trademark must be registered.
- ➤ A patent grants a property right in an invention.
- ➤ Whereas copyrights, trademarks, and patents are protected by federal law, trade secrets are protected under state law.
- ➤ A work for hire is work created by an employee or an independent contractor that is owned by the company employing or engaging the creator.
- ➤ Event people wanting their intellectual property respected shouldrespect the intellectual property of others.

Chapter

15

Accounting

There's no business like show business, but there are several businesses like accounting. —David Letterman

Accounting is a most mysterious part of business for event professionals. While they understand revenue and expenses and the need for the former to be greater than the latter, most event company owners would rather leave the numbers to others so that they can work on their creative pursuits. Accordingly, others in the organization must have a grasp of accounting and the procedures that must be established to create a sound internal financial system. This chapter makes no attempt to explain any basic accounting principles, but rather focuses on a few areas where big problems can develop if unwatched.

As discussed in prior chapters, the correct accounting software package is critical to the successful operation of a business. Along with that comes the need for the right individuals to enter the data into the system in a timely, accurate, and thorough manner. Without both of these assets, the *technology* and the *people,* business owners cannot possibly receive the information they need to operate their businesses in an informed manner.

Poring through scads of accounting information is not a task near and dear to the hearts of most event people, so company owners need to ascertain what information they need and in what form to give them the snapshot they want of their business. It is then up to the internal accounting department or the outside accountant to create and enact the procedures to make this happen.

Simple reports can be created for owners, backed up by the typical monthly statements—cash flows, income statements, and balance sheets. Owners may not like accounting data, but they need to care about the state of their business. They need to force themselves to understand what is going on internally. They need to learn to rely on their own observations as well as on the statements and observations of others in their company. Owners must remember that nobody cares about the company as much as they do.

Key areas of concern are billing and accounts receivable, ordering and account payables, budgeting, and taxes.

■ ACCOUNTS RECEIVABLE AND BILLING

From one point of view, clients or customers are the lifeblood of the company. They provide the revenues that pay the salaries and the bills and put profit in the pockets of the owner. They fuel the growth and also provide the company's employees with the work that gives them their job satisfaction. On the other hand, clients can be demanding, can cause all sorts of disruption, can cause job cost to go through the roof, can be slow to pay or not pay, and can lead to the bankruptcy of the company. The trick is to keep them on the positive side and as far away from the negative side as possible.

Assuming the sales and marketing staff employs the proper principles and thought process to locate the best clients for the business, the company is off to a good start. But certain procedures need to be implemented from the beginning and followed no matter how badly a company desires a client's business.

Clients should be asked to fill out the company credit application, which should be kept current in each client's file. The credit application should contain all of the information needed to determine the type of terms and credit limit that should be proffered to each client.

The company should have accounting policies and procedures in place that apply to all new clients and all established clients. These procedures should include doing business only on receipt of properly signed contracts, receiving deposits in a timely manner, and receiving final payment when promised. New clients should be required to pay a deposit on signing the agreement, with the full balance of the contract price due before the event starts. Too many event companies have billed for the balance due and have never seen it.

Too many event companies fear the loss of clients to the extent that they apply no policies or procedures to them, or they ignore their own policies when clients complain a bit. This is sheer insecurity on the part of event companies. Event professionals, as professionals, should stick to their procedures no matter who the client is. Big corporate clients have procedures of their own that they must adhere to, so they should understand the need of event companys to adhere to theirs. If the corporate client signs the contract stating that final payment will be made prior to the event, it should be held to that contract.

The excuse of not having the check should hold no sway. The contract calls for it. The event does not begin without it.

For those whose terms give them 15 or 30 days to pay the final balance of their bill, the start date should be made absolutely clear. Many clients will wait for the invoice to start counting, even knowing what their balance is. Relying on the contract itself to prompt payment obviously will not work in such cases. Accordingly, the client should be given either the final invoice or instructions to pay the balance on the contract, with terms running from the date of the event.

Clients should be billed in clear, concise terms, referencing the event, the date, and any client identification number. The salesperson from the event company should have found out early on the exact name and address of the party to whom any invoice should be addressed. Clients buy time by stating that they never received the invoice, so it is important to make certain correct information is obtained. A follow-up call to that person after mailing, or a faxed invoice sent on the date of mailing will serve as extra insurance that the client received the invoice promptly.

It also helps for the salesperson or production manager to contact the client after the event to make sure there were no negative issues. If there are, discussing them and making any adjustments to the invoice, if necessary, will facilitate being paid in a timely fashion. It will also eliminate, or at least diminish, any ill feelings that the client may have developed.

One way to ensure that the client will come back is to offer a discount on the client's next event rather than on the one just completed. It gives the event company another opportunity to redeem itself and get back in the client's good graces.

What if the client doesn't pay within terms? There should be procedures in place to handle this. Telephone calls should be made to find out why. If the client has a history with the company and a short-term situation, it may be handled one way. If the client has no history or a difficult history, it may be handled in another way. There must be decisions made about whether to continue to do business with a client while payment is overdue. Credit risks have to be weighed, and the company has to know when to cut off a client.

If a client cannot pay but is willing to go on a payment plan, a company should weigh the risks. Interest should be added to the payments even if it was not called for in the initial agreement. The payment plan is a new agreement.

Some slow-paying clients will end up having their accounts sent to a collection agency. While such agencies charge a fairly hefty percentage on funds they collect, it may be worth it for an event company that has little success with telephone calls and letters.

If ultimately it becomes clear that the client is unwilling or unable to pay, decisions have to be made about how to proceed. Should a lawsuit be filed? If there is a decision that a lawsuit should be brought, the company will be relying heavily on its original contract with the client. The contract should call for interest, attorney's fees, and court costs. It should also provide for the lawsuit to take place in the venue most convenient for the company and/or under the law most favorable to the company.

It is important to manage receivables with care, as they are the company's operating cash. A company that is too forgiving may find itself operating on fumes, having to stretch out vendors, or worse. Additionally, banks rely on receivables as collateral for financing, but only current receivables. As receivables hit 45 or 60 days, the bank will not count them, and the company may find itself in trouble with its bank in having insufficient receivables relative to the size of the outstanding loans. Banks look at cash on hand plus receivables to determine whether there is sufficient cash flow to pay the debt service on their loans. If they feel that there is not, they can call the loans, putting the company into default and triggering all sorts of problems for the company.

Weekly receivables reports should be prepared for management, sales, and accounting, and every client on the list should be contacted and payment dates confirmed. While the larger amounts are the obvious targets, small ones should not be allowed to slip through the cracks, as many small ones can add up quickly. Receivables should be kept as current as possible. If after 60 days some have not been paid, they should be sent out for collection; if there is no luck in collecting after a fixed period, those receivables should be sent out for the filing of suit. Do not ever forget that these receivables mean the difference between having cash or having one big problem. Kindness and generosity as a policy is theoretically admirable, but practically very dangerous. Exceptions may be made for the best clients, but as a rule, toughness is the order of the day.

■ ACCOUNTS PAYABLE

Timely payment of obligations is important to the smooth running of a business. Companies work hard to establish credit with vendors, with credit card companies, and with other important relationships such as the utility companies, landlords, leasing companies, and truck rental companies. Maintaining a good credit record is a function of paying bills in a timely fashion. This, in turn, is a function of having the cash to do so. The cash comes from sales followed by the collection of the receivables from those sales. If sales are insufficient, bills will not be paid. If collection of receivables is insufficient, bills will not be paid.

Event companies need to have a purchasing policy to avoid buying what they cannot afford. Purchase approval has to rest with qualified managers. Purchases should be made by purchase order, which can in turn be matched to packing slips, bills, and monthly statements. Only when all the paperwork matches up should payments be made to vendors.

Invoices should be scheduled for payment in an orderly and planned fashion. Discounts can be sought for early payment if cash flow allows. In fact, the best time for event companies to negotiate better terms is when cash flow allows for early payment, preparing for the day when cash flow will be tighter. When cash is tight, the weekly payables schedule should be carefully reviewed and logical decisions made on payment. The usual issue is whether to pay a few vendors in full or to pay a portion to all. In general, the latter approach will probably provide the most mileage for the company with the most suppliers.

Event company owners should always keep an eye on any obligations for which they may have personal liability. They do not want to see the company fall behind on those payments. These include loan payments, possibly equipment lease payments, credit card bills, 401(k) contributions, and withholding taxes. A clear head must be employed to analyze a situation. A short-term glitch is one thing. But if the company is having an increasingly difficult time meeting its obligations and is falling further behind, with receivables shrinking and payables growing, it is important for someone to recognize it and take actions to keep these obligations current, even if it means stiffing vendors or shutting down.

■ JOB COSTING

Job costing was discussed in Chapter 6 in some detail, so it will not be covered in depth here. However, it is important to note that the accuracy of the costing for each event is critical to being able to gauge cash flow. The job costing should show which portion of the price derived from the client will go to pay direct costs, which portion will cover overhead, and which portion will be free cash (not having any cost allocated to it).

Thus, the cumulative job costings will, or at least should, reflect the cash flow of the company. Therefore, the formulas used, the percentages applied, and all factors included should be reviewed on a regular basis for accuracy. Likewise, the costings should be compared to postevent actual costs to make certain that the estimators are doing their job well. Job costings are a useful tool only if they bear a relationship to reality.

■ FINANCIAL STATEMENTS

With a reasonable accounting software package, internal company accounting personnel should be able to produce all of the daily, weekly, monthly, and quarterly reports that management could possibly require. Which reports will be the most important will vary from event company to event company.

Clearly, cash flow statements, receivable reports, and payable reports are critical. Sales reports showing event bookings may give a sense of the future, and some planning may occur based on them. Profit and loss statements and balance sheets are standard accounting tools and contain valuable information for those who read and interpret them.

Yearly budgets, broken down to individual monthly budgets, should be a great aid to those charged with analyzing them, with regard to both revenue and expenses. Sales reports, by salesperson, may give valuable information on how each individual is doing and, in conjunction with the budgets, will give a deeper perspective.

Inventory reports will help determine how well the company is doing in protecting its assets. Items in repair reports can give a sense of the condition of the working inventory. Depreciation reports or hours-in-use reports can help managers decide when certain items should be sold or replaced.

Individual companies will have their own reports or statements peculiar to their business or to the owner's management style or information needs. Whatever works in keeping management informed and involved is a positive.

Some reports are required by outside agencies. Lenders require yearly financial statements prepared by outside accountants—usually either reviewed or audited. Landlords may have similar requirements. If the owner is contemplating selling the company in the near future, accurate and complete financials should be available for at least three historical years. If the company has thoughts about going public at some point, a total and complete record must be accessible for review by the marketplace and potential investors.

■ TAX ISSUES

Event companies, like other businesses, have a variety of tax obligations. Managers have to be aware of them and make certain that all appropriate returns are filed and taxes paid. Some of the issues can be a bit tricky, particularly for companies that do business in more than one state. First and foremost are payroll taxes, both federal and state and, in some cases, municipal.

➤ Payroll Taxes

Employers are required to make payroll deductions from the paychecks of their employees and to deposit the withheld amounts with the appropriate tax agencies. On top of that, the employer is responsible for paying certain additional amounts based on what the employees are paid. The two categories together comprise the company's payroll tax obligation. This obligation includes federal, state, and local income taxes, social security and Medicare taxes, federal and state unemployment taxes, and possibly disability insurance taxes.

Withholding is the means by which taxing authorities compel employers to collect taxes (via payroll deductions) owed by their employees. The employer has the obligation to withhold tax and also to deposit the withheld amounts with the appropriate authorities in a timely manner. Employers should be acutely aware of the fact that they become personally liable for the taxes if they are not properly withheld or deposited.

Federal income tax withholding is determined from simple tax tables. Certain withholding exemptions are available under the law, and each employee should fill out a W-4 form and provide it to the employer to claim the exemptions. Federal deposits must be made on a monthly or semiweekly basis.

State and local income taxes are to be withheld as well, based on a fixed percentage of income, on a fixed percentage of the federal withholding, or on wages. Many states that have a state income tax (41 do) have their own exemption certificates similar to the W-4. Local taxes are not as common as state income taxes. But in those states where local taxes are permitted, the employer is required to withhold for them.

Social security and Medicare taxes are mandated under the Federal Insurance Contributions Act (FICA). Under the law, the employer is required to withhold and also to pay an employer's share. Each of the FICA taxes is imposed as a flat rate. Employees pay 6.2 percent for social security tax and 1.45 percent for Medicare tax, and the employer matches that. These taxes are unaffected by exemptions. There is a ceiling on the social security tax, which is adjusted annually for inflation. However, there is no ceiling on Medicare tax. These taxes, like federal withholding, are to be deposited on a monthly or semiweekly basis.

For federal payroll taxes, the employer has an obligation to file periodic returns. Form 941, Employer's Quarterly Federal Tax Return, is required to report federal income taxes withheld and FICA taxes withheld and paid.

The Federal Unemployment Tax Act (FUTA) places a payroll tax obligation on employers based on wages paid to employees. This money is not withheld—it is owed by employers. The FUTA tax is a flat 6.2 percent on employee wages up to $7,000 in a given calendar year. Once an employee has earned $7,000 there is no further FUTA liability for that year. Employers do get credit for state unemployment taxes paid in a timely manner—the credit is 5.4 percent of federally taxable wages, effectively dropping FUTA to 0.8 percent. FUTA taxes are typically required to be deposited on a quarterly basis.

For FUTA taxes, Form 940 must be filed annually. This return is due on January 31 of the following year, although a 10-day extension may be available.

State unemployment taxes vary from state to state. In virtually every state, the tax is the responsibility of the employer, not a withholding amount from employee payroll. Each company should have its accountant determine whether the company has a state unemployment tax liability. Most states charge a simple percentage, making the tax easy to compute. However, the percentage each company is charged may be based on what states call an *experience-rating system*. Basically, these systems assign a lower unemployment tax rate to companies whose workers have suffered the least involuntary unemployment and higher rates to those whose workers are subjected to the highest levels of involuntary unemployment.

Only six jurisdictions in the United States require an employer to withhold or pay disability insurance taxes. These jurisdictions have state-mandated temporary disability insurance programs.

After all of the taxes have been withheld and paid and all returns and reports filed, an employer still has an obligation to maintain the records substantiating that payroll taxes have been paid. For federal tax purposes, records must be retained for four years after either the due date of the return or the date the taxes were paid, whichever is later. For state purposes, the record-keeping requirement varies from state to state.

The records that should be kept include (1) the name, address, and social security number of each employee; (2) the total amount and date of each payment of compensation; (3) the period of service covered by each payment; (4) the portion of each payment constituting taxable wages; (5) copies of each W-4; (6) date and amount of tax deposits made; (7) copies of returns filed; (8) copies of any undeliverable W-2 forms.

➤ Sales and Use Taxes

Sales and uses taxes are a somewhat more complicated area. While most states do have a sales tax, they do not all administer it the same way. Nor do they all define *taxable sale* the same way. Therefore, there is often confusion. Many event companies are not clear on whether their services are taxable in whole or in part. Many have been advised that if they present their invoices one way, their services are not taxable, but if they present them another way, they are. Rental of equipment may be taxable, but labor may be nontaxable.

Exemption certificates can be filled out, allowing for certain transactions to be tax-free. Nonprofit organizations may not be required to pay sales tax. Companies that are resellers may not have to pay tax on their purchases but may have to charge tax on their sales.

> **Example:** *IBM hires Anna the Planner to produce an event. She, in turn, hires the Surefire Production Company to actually put it all together. They hire Dwight's Lights to handle the technical side. Does Dwight charge Surefire tax on its services? Does Surefire charge Anna? Does Anna charge IBM?*
>
> *In many jurisdictions the tax law states that goods or services in a chain, such as in the example above, should be taxed only once. So Dwight, as long as he has a resale certificate from Surefire, should not charge it tax. Nor should Surefire charge Anna tax on any services coming under its contract, as long as it has her resale certificate. The entire proposal of Anna's, including the services of subcontractors, should have tax added to it for IBM to pay. Anna is then responsible for collecting and submitting the amount of the tax to the state.*

Being aware of exemptions that apply in each state of operation is important for every event company. Making sure to have the required filled-out exemption certificates on file is also important in case of audit.

Another complicated area of sales tax involves companies doing business in more than one state. Companies in certain areas of the country will most certainly be involved in more than one state. The tristate areas of New York, New Jersey, and Connecticut; New Jersey, Pennsylvania, and Delaware; New Jersey, Delaware, and Maryland; and Maryland, Virginia, and the District of Columbia are all local, yet multiple-state business areas. It is highly likely that event businesses located in these areas will be filing sales tax returns and paying tax in all three, or even four jurisdictions. This means that income tax returns will need to be filed there as well. Finally, it may mean that owners will have to file personal tax returns in those states, particularly if their company has filed a Subchapter S election or is a sole proprietorship or partnership.

Many event companies do events all over the country. It would not be atypical for a regional or national company to be involved in one or two events per year in each of 10 or 20 states. Must they file sales tax returns in each state? Federal law allows states to impose taxes only when certain conditions are met. One of the conditions is that a "substantial nexus" must exist between the taxable entity or event and the state. *Substantial nexus* is defined as a "definite link or minimal connection." Typical of the connections that provide that nexus are having employees within a state; having independent commissioned agents or representatives in the state; making regular deliveries in a state using the company's own vehicles; dropping shipments into a state; having a physical presence in a state. If a company attends trade shows in a state and does business at the shows, it may qualify as a nexus if the company is in the state for more than 14 days.

Based on the preceding, the company that does one event per year in a number of different jurisdictions is probably not subject to sales tax concerns in those jurisdictions. However, if there is any doubt, an accountant should be consulted.

Sales tax is an area in which an accountant's guidance is required to help with several different questions. It is important to settle the issues quickly and clearly to avoid confusion and possible liability down the road. If possible, obtaining an opinion letter from the accounting firm on the nature of the company's sales tax obligations would be a good idea.

➤ Miscellaneous Taxes

There are certainly other potential tax liabilities that an event company might have in its home jurisdiction, or even in others where it does business. Mentioned in Chapter 13 was the IFTA tax. Corporate income tax at both the federal and state level may be due, depending on the form of the company. There may be franchise taxes or business privilege taxes. It is important to determine in which jurisdictions a company may be taxable and then research the taxes that may be due within those jurisdictions.

■ POTENTIAL AUDITS

Another good reason to maintain detailed, accurate accounting records is that you'll need them when the inevitable audit is scheduled. The big fear is always that the IRS is going to come in and audit the books, but the fact of the matter is that several other audits are many more times more likely. Event companies should expect to be audited on a yearly basis for at least one or two separate reasons. Being audited, no matter by whom, is no fun. The specter of owing additional sums of money looms large. Payroll and sales records should be kept in good order in the course of business, but also in preparation for the inevitable audit. The event company should have a designated person in charge of meeting with any auditor. That person should have a good handle on the financial areas that will be under review, as well as access to and an understanding of previous audits and their results.

The other major preparation for an insurance audit is to make certain that all independent contractors have filed certificates of insurance with the company. These will be very relevant in making certain that money paid to them will not be treated as payroll. No company wants to pay a premium on individuals who are not their employees.

If the insurance company offers a premium discount for the company taking certain proactive steps in its operations (e.g., the creation of a safety committee), evidence of having completed those steps should be available so it can be taken into account in figuring the final premium.

➤ Insurance Premium Audits

Insurance carriers audit their workers' compensation and liability policies on a regular basis. Premiums are typically based on the sales of the business or its payroll. Accordingly, the premiums for the coming year are based on estimates of what the payroll or company sales will be. At the completion of the policy period, the company arranges to come out to the business and audit the books to get the actual sales or payroll amounts.

Company owners need to have a game plan when it comes to estimating the relevant figures. If cash flow is traditionally weak at the start of a premium year, a company may knowingly estimate low numbers so that the premiums will be lower. As cash flow improves, the company can go back to the carrier or agent and raise its estimates, thus adjusting premium levels. Some agents throw in lowball numbers to make their estimates look low in comparison to others, only to have the company owe a huge amount after audit. Other companies estimate high and bear the cost throughout the year to avoid a large audit premium later.

In an audit of the *workers' compensation policy*, the designated event company employee handling the audit should be well versed in all aspects of the company's operation. He or she should be quite familiar with each position within the company. A key part of premium determination is employee classification, with each classification bearing different premium rates. Keeping the employees in the correct classification is an important task.

> **Example:** *The president of Event Planners, Inc., does primarily sales, entertaining clients and writing proposals from her office. She does, on occasion, go out to event sites. Some auditors may classify her at a higher rate because, by going to event sites, she is at greater risk. Others may see her job as primarily administrative and rate her lower.*

Floral decorators may be treated one way because their risk of getting hurt or injured on the job is slight; yet decorators working with props and sets may be treated very differently because they lift heavy objects and work with power tools. Salespeople or account executives should be classified as low risks, as should all administrative personnel. Companies should look into whether their carrier allows them to split an individual's position into two classifications. If so, the records must be able to document the percentage of time the worker spends at each type of work.

Furthermore, there may be another opportunity for discount if there is substantial overtime on the books. Most states allow these numbers to be reduced to straight time for purposes of audit, so if those hours can be easily broken out, there is an opportunity for a nice discount.

Liability insurance audits are often based on the gross sales of the company. Depending on the particular state, it may be possible to deduct the cost of subcontractors from the gross sales. Producers or planners who subcontract almost everything should determine whether the law requires them to pay premiums on just their fees or on all charges passing through their books.

Event companies should fight hard for the proper classification of their employees and the correct amount of payroll to be considered. Using the correct figures can save the company a substantial amount of money.

➤ Tax Audits

The area of wage tax was addressed earlier in the chapter. It is quite possible that a municipality that levies a local tax will audit companies, particularly those from outside the municipality that often work within it.

> **Example:** *An event company in the Philadelphia suburbs works on events in Philadelphia almost every week. Philadelphia has a wage tax that applies to those who live in the city and those who work in the city, whether they live there or not. The event company has the responsibility of deducting the municipal wage tax from the pay of any employee who has spent time working in Philadelphia.*

Another area of audit is sales tax. The state agency will want to make certain that the event company collected and paid tax on every transaction for which it was required. Again, paperwork needs to be in order. All tax-exemption certificates should be filed where they can be found for auditor review.

Of course, it almost goes without saying that the state and federal governments can audit for income tax purposes.

➤ Miscellaneous Audits

Some other audits that are less likely to occur, but still quite possible, can be a source of discomfort for event companies. Any event company having a union contract may find itself subject to audit by the union to determine whether the company has used the union on all events within the union's jurisdiction. There are probably damage provisions in the union contract that subject the company to fines for not using the union where it should have.

The Department of Transportation has the right to come into a company and audit whether the company is in compliance with all requirements of the drug and alcohol testing program required by law. Fines for noncompliance can be very high, and companies truly need to shoot for full compliance.

■ CONCLUSION

It is amazing how many accounting, finance, and tax issues exist in small companies. Even the simplest operation must deal with a large number of issues, many of them primary to the health and continued well-being of the company.

While the accounting department is not directly involved in the primary activity of the business, it is essential to its ongoing operation. Even the smallest company must deal with the accounting functions discussed in this chapter. Importance should be attached to choosing the right accounting team for the organization, one that will carry out all of the functions with enthusiasm and attention to detail.

■ SUMMARY

➤ Keeping track of accurate information is critical to the event company manager.

➤ Managers should determine what information they need to do their jobs and have the accounting department create a report for them with that information.

➤ The right accounting software package is a very important tool.

➤ Qualifying clients before doing business with them is the best start to a sound accounts receivable policy.

➤ Creating and enforcing credit policy is important to keeping receivables at an appropriate level.

➤ Accurate billing information includes the correct person in the correct organization at the correct address with the correct account number and job reference. This information should be confirmed prior to the event, and the due date of payment should be made clear on the bill.

➤ Collecting receivables is like feeding the business. Are you willing to go hungry for clients that aren't paying?

➤ Being able to pay bills on time can be a function of collecting receivables on time.

➤ Companies need a purchasing policy so they do not purchase what they cannot afford.

➤ An internal job costing system is important to enable companies to price their event services correctly and to make sure that their overhead is covered.

➤ Someone in each event company must generate, and others must read, the financial statements that will give management an accurate picture of the company's current condition.

➤ Taxes are ubiquitous. No company can avoid them. To avoid penalties and interest, companies should be aware of which taxes and returns are owed when, schedule them, and pay them.

➤ Payroll taxes, unemployment taxes, sales and use taxes, and fuel taxes must all be tracked and dealt with.

➤ Any of the taxing authorities, as well as insurance carriers, may audit an event company. Keep good records.

➤ Event companies must keep good records!

Chapter 16

Legal Liability

The minute you read something you can't understand, you can almost be sure it was drawn up by a lawyer. —Will Rogers

It is a well-known fact that any person can sue any other person or company for any reason at any time. The American judicial system is open to anyone to bring suit, even if the suit is later deemed to be frivolous. The most common actions brought against businesses are civil in nature, meaning that resolution of the issues will involve damages and/or possibly injunctive relief as opposed to criminal penalties. Typically, these corporate actions involve either a breach of contract or an act of negligence resulting in injury to person or property. Lawsuits are a distraction to a company whether the company is the plaintiff (the party suing) or the defendant (the party being sued). Nobody within an event company has managing, directing, and handling lawsuits as part of their job description. Whoever is assigned those tasks is being pulled away from regular responsibilities and is probably not happy about it. Being a party in a big lawsuit causes a lack of focus on the business at hand. Avoid being in court whenever possible.

■ CIVIL ACTIONS

In civil cases, the damages sought by the party bringing suit are, for the most part, monetary in nature. Sometimes there is a request for an injunction involved. Most often, suits will be brought by a client, vendor, competitor, or financial institution. That means that a fractured relationship is involved, which likely means emotions are running high, and common sense may not always prevail.

Many states have judicial systems in which cases under a certain dollar value are heard by arbitration panels. Chances are, these will move through the court system more quickly than a larger case. Cases alleging damages in larger amounts are heard by a judge or judge and jury. Court backlogs could keep these cases from coming to trial for months or maybe years.

Breach of contract cases involving special events companies arise in two ways: (1) A client did not get what was bargained for in the contract and thus sustained damages. (2) A vendor did not receive payment in part or full and thus sues for damages. These types of lawsuits would not normally be covered by a company's liability insurance policy, so the company would be responsible for engaging its own attorney and paying its own attorney fees, court costs, and any potential settlement amount or verdict.

Most instances where one party claims damages as a result of a breach of contract result in a settlement well before the case goes to court. In those instances, the alleged breach is obvious and it is only a question of the amount of damages. There is likely to be a compromise on the amount and the case is settled. In instances where the parties cannot even agree on the facts, meaning that the alleged breach is not a given, then threatened litigation, the involvement of attorneys, and actual litigation will follow. Unless a substantial amount of money is at stake, the case will be painful for both sides, involving time, expense, and, at best, a minimal amount of satisfaction in the result.

In some instances where the breach of contract claim is for nonpayment, the case will sail through the courts because the party sued does not have the desire or the money to defend. The defendant knows it owes the money, but it just does not have the means to pay, nor does it have the means to contest the claim. Normally, in such an instance, a default judgment will be entered in favor of the suing company. With judgment in hand, the winning company then has to decide how to proceed. It can try to collect on the judgment through state court procedures or it can try to work out a payment plan. It all depends on the financial condition of the debtor.

The second type of civil action that event companies are likely to become familiar with over the course of their existence is a *negligence action*. Event companies carry liability insurance to protect themselves in the event they are faced with negligence claims. These claims can range from accidents involving company vehicles and/or company employees to trip-and-fall cases on company property to injury to an innocent person due to carelessness during installation or removal of event products and services to an individual being hurt during an event. A rental company can be negligent in the way it maintains its equipment, and if someone is injured as a result of that negligence, a lawsuit can result. It doesn't matter whether the equipment is a ballroom chair or a piece of lighting truss. If a court determines that there was negligence and that the negligence was the primary cause of someone's injuries, a verdict will result in favor of the party bringing the suit (the plaintiff).

If an accident occurs, the company should have a procedure in place for reporting it. The reports should include thorough recounting of what happened by all the participants and witnesses from the company. The company should maintain a file on all accidents and should report them to its insurance agent immediately. If the company then receives notice that the injured party is making a claim, it can renotify the insurance agent, who will then contact the insurance carrier. Timely notice is a condition of coverage in many policies. Therefore, companies should waste no time in notifying their agent and should record the date, time, and person to whom the accident was reported.

The insurance company will do an investigation, gather all the facts, and then decide whether to try to settle or to defend. When the carrier is unwilling or unable to offer money in settlement of the claim, it is possible that the claim will escalate to a lawsuit. The carrier will then engage counsel on behalf of the event company, and the case will be settled or tried at the expense of the insurance company. The one instance of concern for the event company is a verdict in excess of the amount of insurance coverage. In a serious case with a high-award verdict, the injured party's attorneys may go after the company for the balance of the verdict that exceeds the policy amount. They most likely would have a right to do so. Accordingly, the company could be in jeopardy. This is a good reason to carry a high-limit liability policy and an umbrella policy.

■ BUSINESS TORTS

Other, less common lawsuits may be brought. They arise from causes of action called *torts*. A tort is a civil (as opposed to criminal) wrong between two parties that the courts have recognized as a basis for filing a lawsuit and collecting damages. Tort law is formed by the courts, not by statute. Therefore, the law will vary from state to state as the different courts write their opinions. Torts recognized by the courts in some states are not recognized in others. In order for a tort to be recognized, the court must find a duty existing between the two parties; the defendant must have breached that duty; the plaintiff must have sustained damages; and the breach of duty must have been the direct cause of the damages.

Business torts are usually intentional acts by one company that negatively impact the business rights of another. They can be placed into several different categories.

➤ Disparagement

If an employee of an event company makes statements, either orally or in writing, that are untrue and that damage an individual or business, the company could be subject to a lawsuit for slander or libel. The elements of one type of trade libel would be publishing false information about another's product, services, or business that result in third parties refraining from doing business with the defamed company and that cause the defamed company to suffer economic loss or damages. The elements of a second type are present when one falsely publishes information that denies or casts doubt on another's legal ownership of property, thus causing the owner to suffer a financial loss with respect to the property.

Another issue that will be filling the courts in the years ahead will be that of defamation in cyberspace. Publishing false and defamatory information in cyberspace can make one liable for damages. However, it appears that a party *distributing* the false and defamatory information will not be liable. It remains to be seen whether entities such as online information services that allow individuals to post such information can be held liable.

Each company will have to carefully peruse its insurance policy to determine whether it provides coverage in such cases. Employees should be trained not to use negative selling techniques that put down their competitors to make themselves look better. While such cases are unusual in the event industry, the behavior leading to such suits is not. Unfortunately, many individuals in the event industry do not practice either good business or good ethics. Any company without insurance coverage that is found liable in a lawsuit will quickly understand pain.

➤ Wrongful Interference

There are two types of wrongful interference torts. The first is *wrongful interference with contractual relationships.* This tort occurs as follows: A valid, enforceable contract exists; a third party is aware of the contract; the third party induces a party to breach the contract; and the purpose of the inducement is the advancement of the financial interests of the third party.

> **Example:** *Company A has the exclusive lighting contract at the local art museum. Company B convinces the museum to breach the contract, stating that it will offer cheaper prices and will contribute a percentage of each event dollar to the museum.*

Likewise, if an event company employee should *tortiously interfere with an existing business relationship* involving a competitor, a suit could be brought. In this instance, the courts try to draw a line between legitimate competitive behavior and what they consider to be predatory. The requisite elements of this behavior that must be proved are that an established business relationship existed; a third party brought the relationship to an end by acts that were predatory and intentional; and the plaintiff suffered financial damage as a result of the third party's actions.

➤ Appropriation

Torts of appropriation occur when an individual or company, without permission, uses the name, likeness, or any other identifying characteristic of another to derive business benefit. The law does not require that an *exact* likeness be used, as long as it leaves little doubt regarding whom it is intended to portray.

This situation is very rare in the event world. It could occur when one company comes out with a new technology or product that is immediately successful. A second company quickly follows with a very similar product under a similar name, hoping to create and capitalize on the market's confusion about the originator.

The Lanham Act, a federal statute (15 USC 1125), protects against misappropriation and the likelihood of causing consumer confusion. Remedies under the statute include injunctive relief, an accounting, damages, attorneys' fees, and costs.

➤ Racketeer Influenced and Corrupt Organizations (RICO) Act

RICO was originally intended as a purely criminal statute. However, civil damage provisions come into play if a person or business damaged by the business practices of another can show that the damages were caused because the other party engaged in a pattern of fraudulent activity over a substantial period of time.

■ PERSONAL LIABILITY OF OWNER

Business owners try to set up their affairs in such a way that their personal liability is nonexistent or severely limited. However, if they are not careful, they can fall into situations where they are terribly exposed through their own actions or inattention.

➤ Personal Guarantees

The potentially most serious personal liability can arise from personal guarantees that the owner makes in the course of doing business. These are routinely demanded in loan, equipment leasing, and financing documents. If the company has credit card accounts, the owner may have to personally guarantee the master account, or all amounts on all of the individual company cards. These guarantees are often requested as part of credit applications for normal business terms with trade vendors, and owners may sign them without even realizing what they are. Owners are always optimistic and believe the guarantees will never be relied upon. When things go bad, owners can find out how quickly they will be relied upon. They may be further surprised to find out how many guarantees they have signed over time.

Joint guarantees of husbands and wives can be devastating if the company gets into financial trouble. Under these situations, even the family house can be in serious jeopardy, as can joint bank accounts.

➤ Trust Fund Taxes

As discussed in Chapter 15, businesses are required to pay a variety of taxes to the federal and state governments, including those deemed to be *trust fund taxes,* so named because businesses collect and deposit those taxes in trust for the governments. The money collected never belongs to the company, but rather to the taxing authorities. These taxes include payroll and sales tax.

When companies get into cash flow difficulties and financial trouble, they may be tempted to rely on the cash collected for these taxes to come to their aid and thus fail to pay it to the taxing authorities. To increase the likelihood that these funds will be paid, the taxing authorities have imposed personal liability on the "responsible persons" within a company (Section 6672 of the IRS Code). These are individuals connected with the business who have the authority, power, and/or control to ensure proper payment of taxes. There can be more than one responsible party in a given company. The IRS and many of the states require a showing of intent or willfulness. The main evidence of such intent is the payment of other creditors rather than remittance of the funds to the taxing authority.

A person found to be the responsible party and thus liable is obliged to pay the unpaid taxes along with accrued penalties and interest. Some states may even impose criminal penalties. And even more bad news—the obligations to pay trust fund taxes are not dischargeable in bankruptcy.

➤ Gross Negligence

Gross negligence is generally defined as reckless disregard of the safety and lives of others that is so great as to be a conscious violation of the rights of others. It almost rises to the level of an intentional act. Whereas negligence is normally covered under liability insurance policies, gross negligence is most often not covered. A party found to have acted with gross negligence can also be found liable for punitive damages on top of actual damages found to have been suffered. Such a person can also be found to have acted outside of the scope of the corporate protection and therefore be personally liable.

■ CRIMINAL ACTS

It should go without saying that any company owner or manager can be found personally liable for criminal acts. Violation of the various statutes discussed throughout this book does not, in most cases, put the violator in jeopardy of criminal liability. However, any number of criminal acts can occur within the business context that can lead to personal liability.

These acts include receiving stolen goods, larceny, embezzlement, mail and wire fraud, bribery, money laundering, bankruptcy fraud, theft of trade secrets, and computer crime.

Business owners, admirably, will do almost anything to help their business. Lines have to be drawn short of criminal behavior, however. Care must be taken to avoid any criminal activity. Cooking the books and other accounting-related activities should be avoided with the aid of the outside accountant, and the company attorney should keep everyone on the straight and narrow.

■ CONCLUSION

Business owners should set up their companies to avoid personal liability. They should, with as much diligence as possible, make certain that they do not enter into any business activities that might subject them to liability. Businesses should be set up to serve the needs of their owners, and the owners should not mistakenly allow the business to drag them into an abyss from which they cannot escape.

■ SUMMARY

➤ Civil suits involving event companies usually fall into one of three categories. They are breach of contract, negligence, and intentional business torts.

➤ Breach-of-contract actions are most often based on nonperformance of contractual duties, including failure to pay.

➤ There is usually no insurance coverage for a company sued for breach of contract.

➤ Negligence actions are based on a breach of care owed to the injured party. A company's liability insurance policy should provide for the company's complete defense, counsel, and payment of any settlement or verdict.

➤ The event company may have liability for any amount of the verdict above the maximum limits of the insurance policy.

➤ Business torts involve disparagement (the various forms of slander and libel), wrongful interference, and appropriation.

➤ Business owners must be aware of situations exposing them to personal liability—and avoid them at almost all cost. These situations include nonpayment of trust fund taxes, the signing of personal guarantees, gross negligence, and criminal acts.

Chapter 17

Ethics

The reverse side also has a reverse side. —*Japanese proverb*

Ethics is not an area that most businesses spend a lot of time contemplating. This is not to suggest that companies are necessarily unethical. Rather, companies focus on business—bringing in the sale, producing the work, and getting paid. That is substance. Ethics is ether.

However, the ethics of the company as a whole may have a major impact on the success of the company in many ways. An ethical framework within a company will help determine how to deal with clients, vendors, employees, and the public. Further, an ethical framework within an industry will create a business milieu imbued with trust, confidence, and professionalism.

The special events industry is relatively young as a profession. It is only since the 1980s that the concept of an industry based on special events took form. Since those early days, there has been a push to have the industry viewed as a profession, on a par with the legal, accounting, medical, engineering, architectural, real estate, and public relations professions. What does that mean? What is a profession? There are any number of ways to define *profession* and *professional,* but certain traits or characteristics seem to epitomize these terms.

A *profession* seeks to separate itself from other groups in the business world. First, its members have specialized knowledge and skills. Second, they hold themselves to higher ethical standards than other groups in society. Third, they self-govern, regulating entrance into the profession, monitoring the performance of its members, and expelling or disciplining those who abrogate their responsibilities. Fourth, they provide important benefits to society. Fifth, their fees are based on the value of their services. Sixth, they comply with regulations intended to protect the health, safety, and welfare of the general public. Seventh, they have an agency or fiduciary relationship with their clients.

Ethics is concisely defined as moral principles or rules of conduct. *Professional ethics* thus relate to rules of honorable conduct to be adopted and practiced by a given profession. They are important because they provide a means of self-regulation, provide a measure of status for the members of the profession, and provide the general public with an assurance of high standards of service, quality, and propriety. In order for professional ethics to have legitimacy, there must be professional accountability—that is, cases of misconduct should be dealt with and discipline imposed. Without this accountability, they merely become a guide to behavior.

The International Special Events Society created "Principles of Professional Conduct and Ethics" for the profession. This code, with its attendant disciplinary procedures, has helped move the event industry forward. It is short and simple. Its directives are fairly broad and general, but relatively easy to interpret. It reads as follows:

➤ Promote and encourage the highest level of ethics within the profession of the special events industry while maintaining the highest standards of professional conduct.

➤ Strive for excellence in all aspects of our profession by performing consistently at or above acceptable industry standards.

➤ Use only legal and ethical means in all industry negotiations and activities.

➤ Protect the public against fraud and unfair practices, and promote all practices which bring respect and credit to the profession.

➤ Provide truthful and accurate information with respect to the performance of duties. Use a written contract clearly stating all charges, services, products, performance expectations and other essential information.

➤ Maintain industry-accepted standards of safety and sanitation.

➤ Maintain adequate and appropriate insurance coverage for all business activities.

➤ Commit to increase professional growth and knowledge, to attend educational programs and to personally contribute expertise to meetings and journals.

➤ Strive to cooperate with colleagues, suppliers, employees, employers and all persons supervised in order to provide the highest quality service at every level.

➤ Subscribe to the ISES Principles of Professional Conduct and Ethics, and abide by the ISES bylaws and policies.

Questions of ethics are not always black-and-white. Often they involve difficult questions without easy answers. These questions can be made complex by an event person trying to distinguish one situation from many others in order to justify the desired result. Sometimes the answers can be obtained by employing an easy multipart test that does away with obfuscation and fancy footwork and brings the issue back to the basics.

Can you, as an event professional, look yourself in the mirror and tell yourself convincingly that the position you wish to take or action you have okayed is acceptable? If not, you should stop right there and rethink your position. If so, then the next step is to determine whether you could look your parents in the eye and explain yourself to them. Parents are used in this example because they know you better than anyone—your quirks and the little physical traits that show up when you're not being honest. If your chosen action or position does not pass the parent test, you need to stop in your tracks and reconsider the ethics of the situation. If you can pass the parent test, you have done well, but you still need to examine the situation under one more microscope. You need to picture yourself on national television, explaining yourself to an investigative reporter or a courtroom full of people, or even to a congressional committee, with the whole world watching. Can the position taken stand up against this? If it can, then it is most likely an acceptable ethical stance. If it cannot, then more thought is required.

Another way of examining a course of action involves asking a few different questions. Could this be explained to the company's board of directors? What would the company's lawyer and accountant say? What would you say if your biggest competitor were doing what you are about to do? Is this a professional action—would it cast honor or dishonor on you and the event industry?

Professionals need to project to their clients that, in hiring them, the clients' interests will be protected. Clients need to know that they are getting the services they have bargained for, that they are paying a fair price for those services, that those they hire are capable of performing in the expected manner, and that those they hire to represent them will act in an honorable manner that won't embarrass them or cause them to lose face or standing in the community.

Where does professionalism begin? It begins with each company gaining an understanding of what it stands for, what its mission is. That mission should be clearly enunciated by ownership and management, drilled into employees, repeated to employees, made clear to employees by actions as well as words. Professional ethics start at the top. Ownership sets the tone and should be the shining example.

The company's mission statement should clearly set forth the values of the company. It and other messages from management should give the employees of an event company the ammunition they need to help them make the right decisions, decisions consistent with what the company believes in. Management must be careful to act in accord with its words. Consistency is critical. If employers want the respect of their employees and the concomitant quality of performance, they should work hard every day to earn that respect.

Employees should not have to guess what is right and what is wrong in a given situation. When two or more company values conflict, the ethically correct course of action should be obvious to a company employee. A company should not hang employees out to dry by making them wrong no matter which option they choose to follow. If an employee opts for the wrong course of action based on the "least unethical" value, it is not normally a character failure on the part of the employee, but rather a failure on the part of management to be clear about what is right, what is ethical, and what is acceptable to the company.

Example: *The economy is slow and business is hard to come by. Cash flow is tight and The Catering Company is hurting. In the morning sales meeting, the company owner urges his salespeople to go out and bring in some business by hook or by crook—by any means possible. Joe, the salesman, takes the words to heart and hits the streets. He calls on some old clients who have drifted away to other caterers. Two of them say that they like Joe's work, but XYZ Catering is cheaper and is kicking back 10 percent to them personally. If Joe matches the deal, he can have the business back.*

Joe knows the company needs the business desperately, but also knows that the owner has, without any contradiction, without any exception, strictly forbidden the type of kickbacks requested of Joe here. Even though the company is hungry for sales, Joe knows (doesn't guess, but knows without doubt) that the owner's ethical positions rank higher in the company value system than landing new business. Accordingly, Joe knows he will have to think of other ways to win back the client. He should not pay the kickbacks, because the owner has drawn a line in the sand when it comes to kickbacks.

In a different company, where the owner has never discussed the issue of kickbacks, Joe could easily decide that bringing in business under any conditions is the ultimate goal, and he might very well agree to the terms.

Ethics should not be elastic. It should not matter who the client is, what the event is, what the time of year is, what the state of the economy is, what the dollar value of the event is. The codes of ethics of other professions do not specify a sliding scale based on a variety of factors. Neither should special event ethics, not if special events people want to be taken seriously as professionals. Certain courses of action that exist in certain geographic markets have made certain ethical violations commonplace. Event professionals rationalize their behavior by saying, "Everyone is doing it." Would such a rationalization work for theft? Embezzlement? Of course not, so there is no reason why it should be acceptable for ethical violations. It shouldn't take a law to stop improper behavior.

■ PAYING AND RECEIVING COMMISSIONS

The area of commissions has been one of the most controversial ethical quagmires for a number of years. Seminars have been given at industry conventions, and debates have been held in many forums. Numerous possible scenarios are wrapped up in this issue, and that adds to the confusion. Within this large issue lie numerous answers, not just one. Commissions per se are neither ethical nor unethical.

> **Example:** *An event planner lands a nice piece of business and decides to offer work on the exciting event to a group of vendors. She tells them that they have the work—it will not be put out to bid—but each vendor must pay a commission of 20 percent of their contract price to her. She tells the vendors that she got the job because she charged the end user a small fee. She says that she expects to make the rest of her money by taking the commissions. She does not specify how they should price their services, does not ask for good pricing, does not state whether the 20 percent should be added to the contract price or come off the top of the regular pricing. She specifies only that she will forward their contracts to the end user, who will pay them. She would then expect to receive their checks following their payment in full for the event services.*
>
> *What are the issues? This scenario is rife with issues. First, is anyone getting hurt? Second, is deception involved, and is it a key factor in who gets the work? If the end user is paying more because of the arrangement, it is wrong. Someone is getting hurt. If the end user is coerced into hiring the planner because of the "low fee" or told to use the suppliers, not because they offer the best value to the client, but because the planner is getting a commission, it is*

wrong. If planners' charges appear to be low because they charge a low fee but get paid well by supplier kickbacks, the client is deceived, and that is wrong.

What would make this ethical? The planner could offer the client two options for payment on his contract: (1) a straight fee based on either estimated time to be spent on the event or an hourly rate, (2) a 20 percent markup on all event services. The client would have a clear picture of how the planner was being paid, and there would be full disclosure and informed consent. The planner would be acting professionally by handling fee arrangements in a professional manner. Event professionals must believe that services they provide are of value to the client and charge for them accordingly, in an above board manner. Only in this way will clients come to appreciate the value of event professionals.

Planners should either bid the subcontractor work or decide whom to engage based on who would do the best job for the client, not who would pay a commission. Planners, who are representing end users, should negotiate the fairest price they can from each vendor and present contracts at those prices to the end users.

Commissions are not unethical per se. How they are handled will determine that. They should always be paid by company check. The receiving party should be given a 1099 at the end of the year for all amounts paid. The paying party should work out with ownership or management of the receiving company how the check should be made out, preferably to the company, not to an individual. If an employee of the receiving company requests that the commission be paid directly to him or her, the paying party should check with management before doing so.

When looking at the ethics of commissions, the actions of both the payer and the payee have to be examined. The payer may offer a commission as an inducement so he will be awarded the event. Is the commission coming out of the vendor's regular price, thus coming out of her profit? Or is it being added onto the regular price? The former is a reasonable action. The latter is unethical, because the client will be hurt, paying 120 percent for a 100 percent product or service. The client does not derive the benefit in this scenario, the planner does. The planner is being unethical because he is not looking after the best interests of his client, only his own interests (unless he has notified the client of his intention and the client agrees to it). A planner can put a vendor in a very untenable position if he has beaten up the vendor to get a rock-bottom price and then proceeds to demand a commission as well. The vendor then may have to face a choice of (1) refusing the work because she doesn't want to lose money on the

194 ◄ THE SPECIAL EVENTS ADVISOR

event production; (2) adding a commission to her price solely for the benefit of the planner, thus acting unethically; or (3) advising the planner of his pricing structure, educating him on what it costs to do business, and trying to give him a measure of understanding of the conundrum in which she has been placed.

Referral fees are slightly different from commissions. The referring party is not necessarily a decision maker in hiring the event company. It may just put the event company's name before the decision maker in some manner. In fact, some planners have been known to let the client choose from among three or four competitive vendors and then demand a referral fee from whichever one the client chooses. In this instance, the party asked to pay the commission should know whether it is the exclusive referred party, whether the referring party actually controls the business, and whether the end user is being hurt in any way. Vendors can protect themselves in some sense by having an agreement with the planner that they will pay commission only for an exclusive referral.

Some event professionals feel it is a breach of ethics for one company to try to hire the employees of another. While this may certainly create some bad feeling, this type of behavior is consistent with what seems to be an overall acceptance of free agency in the business world. Doctors move entire practices from one hospital to another; lawyers move from firm to firm; and business executives go where the money is. This is more a statement about society as a whole than an ethical conundrum.

What about the vendor that bids on the same event with more than one planner? This is a touchier area, but one that merits discussion. The vendor is in a nice position if multiple parties seek bids for the same event. It means that the vendor is well thought of and highly desired. If a vendor does bid with more than one company to play it safe, it should advise each planner that others have asked for proposals and give assurances that no information about the planner's overall vision will be shared. If the identity of the planners bidding on the project is not public knowledge to the other bidders, the vendor should be circumspect about releasing the identity of the others.

Suppose a vendor's specialty is video. The request for proposal sent to the planners specifies the exact video requirements of the event, so creativity or uniqueness of design is not much of a factor. Is the vendor who proposes to multiple planners obligated in any way to provide them with the same price? The vendor should know that by giving one a lower price than the others, it may be giving that planner a competitive advantage in the bid. This is a tough issue. But look at hotel chains and airlines, for instance. The same hotel room or seat on a plane may be sold at very different prices to different users, based on a variety of factors, including business relationships. Large trade associations earn discounts for their members because of buying power. An event vendor may have a different relationship with one planner than another. Should a planner with which it does $500,000 in business per year be given the same price as one with which it does $10,000? It would seem that the bigger and more reliable client is more valuable to the vendor and therefore deserving of a better price. This is part of building business relationships. Certain clients merit discounts, while others pay retail.

There are too many potential ethical issues to discuss them all. They can involve the unauthorized use of ideas contained in a proposal (a client using the proposal as a bid specification for others; a client asking one vendor to produce another's proposal); negative selling; a vendor of a planner soliciting an end user on the planner's event site; a vendor bidding on an event with two planners and sharing with each of them the other's ideas. Vendors may try to pass others' ideas off as their own, showing pictures or making claim to work that others have produced. A vendor working for a planner might pass out business cards on the planner's event site without the planner's permission. End users may try to go around planners and make contact with and hire vendors directly, cutting out the intermediary.

There are ways to deal with a lot of these situations. Remember, under contract law two parties can contract and reach agreement on anything that is not illegal or against public policy, so planners and vendors can put in their contracts whatever clauses they want to protect themselves against anticipated unethical behavior. Taking such action reflects your stand on ethical issues and gives your company a legal backup.

In our society, several layers of rules govern behavior. First and foremost are the laws of the land, clearly establishing what actions or inactions can subject individuals to criminal sanction. Criminal activity is certainly unethical, and the legal penalties are consequently more severe. Second are court decisions that impose civil penalties in the form of damages and injunctive relief. The law recognizes that certain behavior, such as a tortiuous act, is wrong and requires recompense. At least in the case of business torts, it can be said that unethical behavior is involved as well. Finally, there is unethical behavior that does not rise to the level of a crime or a business tort. The only remedy for this behavior is through professional self-regulation. Organizations such as ISES have procedures in place for hearing ethics complaints and determining whether the complaining party has a valid grievance. If so, the offending party will be reprimanded in some way. Historically, professional ethics issues have subsequently been addressed by judicial systems or legislatures, and certain behaviors are determined to be violations of civil or criminal law.

Lawyers must continue their education throughout their years of practice, and each state sets standards for continuing education. The same is true for doctors. Event professionals need to continue their education on an ongoing basis as well. Of course, every company should make sure that its employees receive ongoing education, both formal and otherwise, in its particular discipline. There should be internal training sessions, and employees should be sent to training courses given by experts around the country. Beyond that, companies should see that their key employees gain a broader understanding of the industry as a whole. They should understand the other disciplines and what it takes to work well with them. They should learn what it takes to be a team player.

Being good at creating and presenting food is a wonderful talent. But without knowing how to integrate food service into an evening's program, how to coordinate with entertainers and their sets, how to communicate with a facility or a tent company about the amount of space needed for an event, and how to communicate with an electrical services provider about the electricity needed for the coffee urns and the stoves, the caterer has not learned enough. It takes a team working together, not individually or at cross purposes, to handle an event successfully. It takes an understanding of how the pieces all fit together, and it takes an understanding that everyone involved in an event can be touched by its success or its failure. The client's interest should be the goal of everyone involved, and all should work toward it. No single vendor should be satisfied that it fulfilled its role well if it stood by and let the event falter.

Events are wonderful celebratory occurrences made more wonderful when the planner and the vendors are on the same wavelength, understanding their individual and joint missions and pursuing them with vigor and enthusiasm. For the client, the event might be a once-in-a-lifetime happening of the utmost meaning or importance. To members of the event team it may be but one of hundreds of events in a row, but if they treat it as important, they can take pride in their efforts, in the results, and in the client's happiness.

■ SUMMARY

> ➤ Ethics begin in the office with top management. Owners should set the tone and should make sure every employee knows and understands the company's priorities, its values, and its ethics.

➤ Event people should always act as if everything they do can be viewed by others and not act in any way that they wouldn't want their clients, vendors, or employees to know about.

➤ Ethics are not situational. Standards should not be abandoned to land a particular client or event. Unfortunately, it is easier to adjust ethics downward than upward.

➤ Always consider the client's interest and remember that there exists a relationship of trust.

➤ Professionalism demands and requires ethics.

➤ Act professionally and the clients will value event professionals.

➤ Every company should find ways to enforce its ethical standards through its contracts. Numerous provisions can be put in to regulate the behavior of the parties to a contract.

➤ Breaches of ethics can be brought to the attention of the professional associations, such as ISES, or the multitude of other organizations and discipline can be imposed by such a society.

18

Exit Strategies

*Affairs are easier of entrance than of exit; and it is but common
prudence to see our way out before we venture in. —Aesop*

One of the issues that event company owners need to address at a
fairly early stage in their company's existence is how they are going to
get out of the business. This is not in recognition of having made a
mistake and wanting to recover from it. Rather, it is an understanding
that the business is serving a function in the life of the owner and that
once that function is achieved, the owner can, and perhaps should,
move on with his or her life. At some point, if you're an owner, you
will be ready to convert the fruits of your labors into cash and ride off
into the sunset. How can you plan for this day? What can you do leading up to it to maximize the value of your business?

As an owner, you can decide to sell your business by the time you
reach a certain age. You may decide that once the company achieves a
certain value, you will sell. You may decide not to put in any additional capital or take out any additional loans and sell if it appears
that such steps may be necessary in the near future. You may have it
in mind to create the largest company in the industry and not to retire
until you have done so. Whatever the motivating factor may be, a road
map for getting to that point is required. Keep in mind, however, that
plans and conditions do change. As an owner, you may see the beginning of a trend that you do not think bodes well for your business and
feel the need to speed up the timetable.

Exit strategy will and should have an effect on how the business is
managed and grown. The first question that owners must ask themselves is how they hope to exit. If they know that they want to grow
large enough to attract a takeover from a large company, then they will
want to increase the value of the company as much as possible, perhaps by building or purchasing hard assets or creating a distribution

system that will be of value to a purchaser. They should be thinking about what would make the company valuable to the anticipated type of purchaser. If owners feel that the business will most likely be purchased by a competitor, they might instead focus on building a strong marketing presence and client base, which will be of more value than facilities or equipment similar to the potential purchaser's. If owners want to preserve the company for the next generation of their family or for some key employees, then planning for that will have to begin well before retirement.

Exit planning, like any other type of planning, has to be flexible and will be subject to many changes beyond the control of individual owners. Changes in the economy, new trends in the market, technology changes, and actions by others within the same or parallel product or geographic market may affect an owner's well-laid-out plans. Even within your own company, you may discover that your heir would rather play guitar in a coffeehouse than take over the reins of the company or that the well-chosen and trained successor is not quite as honest or as talented as you thought. Plans must then change and the owner must adapt.

Exit strategy fits right into the overall planning that a company owner must do. Owners should have a vision of what they want from the company, what their personal goals are, and what the company will have to do in order for them to achieve these goals. Thus, the second question for an owner is, "What do you hope to attain?" As stated by Peter Engel, author of *What's Your Exit Strategy: Seven Ways to Maximize the Value of the Business You've Built,* "It's not a question of getting out. It's thinking about maximizing the value at whatever time you intend to get out." Engel goes on to say, "Develop an exit strategy that ties into the business feasibility and your personal goals. If it can't do that, get yourself a different business, because you'll be miserable."

Remembering that many event companies bear the name of their owner or have been marketed solely around the owner's unique skills and persona, it is not hard to believe that the transfer of such businesses may present some interesting issues. In general, it may be more difficult to sell a business that has been built around a personality. An all-star decorator may have a booming business, but when that person wishes to leave, what is left? He or she may have a talented staff and wonderful props and vases and urns, but what value will be put on those assets? Certainly, the business is not worth enough to satisfy someone who has put heart and soul into a company that has now become synonymous with that person. The same could be said of a catering business that has built its reputation and clientele around the flamboyant chef, who now wishes to move to Tuscany. A company that is viewed as a one-person show will not create good value for the owner, if that person is the one wanting out.

Because of the diversity of the companies within the event industry, it is difficult to talk about it as a homogeneous entity and to offer general rules that would apply across the board. Many companies are mom-and-pop operations, single units managed by the owners. Some do a regional business from either a single operation or multiple units. There are relatively few industry giants. In the late 1990s, there appeared to be a trend toward consolidation in the event industry. A few companies began merging and acquiring competitors. One or two even went public, and a few more prepared to. With the consolidations taking place in a variety of other industries in the 1990s, it seemed that big companies might come to dominate segments of the event industry. With that happening, other companies began reevaluating their own planning. They began to think about either growing rapidly in order to compete or making themselves attractive as an acquisition candidate.

Well, the industry behemoths, for the most, faltered, and once again many company owners took a deep breath and began to rethink. Companies are living, breathing organisms, and plans must be altered, adjusted, and tweaked.

There are a number of ways that event companies can be classified. One way is by event discipline—floral decorators, set design companies, draping companies, lighting companies, audio companies, video companies, caterers, planners, producers, destination management companies, transportation companies, and so on. Another way of classifying them is to distinguish between those that are heavily invested in equipment and those that are more invested in ideas. Some deal in recognizable hard goods, like tents, tables, chairs, and linens, while others provide creative design ideas, logistical plans, lighting plots, and room layouts. Some are trade-based, relying on electricians, carpenters, and riggers to do their work. Others are service companies, providing transportation, entertainment, actors, speakers, script writing, and a variety of other services.

Event companies generally offer a blend of creativity of design, quality of service, and quality and quantity of event equipment of some sort. All three are important to varying degrees in every company. In a rental company, the quantity and quality of equipment would come first, followed by quality of service, with quality of design ranking third. In a decorating company, creativity of design and quality of service are more important than equipment. This type of analysis becomes relevant when a company owner sits down to think about an exit strategy. The question becomes, "What is the purchaser actually buying and how can the value be maximized?"

Example: *Floral decorator Natasha is the hottest designer in New York. She does $10 million in business per year, virtually all of it coming to her company because of her industry reputation. She wants to retire and move to Holland to grow tulips. Her inventory of floral props is worth $250,000. She has a talented but unknown staff. What is her business worth?*

If she does not want to stay on at all, the entire draw of the business is gone. The value is nowhere near what it would be had she stayed on. Natasha probably needs to set her ego aside and spend a year or two promoting her young associate designers, introducing them around town, speaking publicly of their talent, transferring her best clients to them, laying the groundwork for a transition. Once this is done, her company will not be a one-person show, but a multitalented group that can bring in business and service it without Natasha being there, thus enhancing its sale value.

Some companies derive their value mainly from their inventory. A rental company with 2,000 place settings of the best china and glassware and 2,000 each of four different chairs may have a huge competitive advantage based strictly on its inventory. If the inventory is kept in prime shape, the company is salable on the basis of inventory alone. Add in a top-notch sales team, an up-to-date inventory control and rental software package, and an operations manager who makes sure rental deliveries and pickups happen when and where they are supposed to, and the business should have maximum value, even with the owner who set everything in place walking away immediately after the sale. In this instance, the company itself is the star, not the owner. All of the value remains in the business even after the owner leaves.

Some companies fall in between. Full-service lighting companies in the top rank provide creative design, quality technicians for installation and operation, and quality, up-to-date equipment. Their business is creativity and equipment, service, and quality. Smart owners will position themselves out of the necessary mix in valuing their company. If they are top-notch salespeople, they should make sure they maintain a crack sales team around them to hand clients off to. If they are the chief designer sought out by clients, they should begin acclimating clients to other designers within the company over time. It is best for the business in the long run.

There are a variety of ways that owners can voluntarily divest themselves of the business and exit gracefully:

1. *Sale to a family member.* The owner can plan on leaving the business in the hands of one or more family members. This is

ideal for some, seeing their legacy carried on by a son or daughter, niece or nephew. If this is part of the thought process, there should be a process for the heir to grow in the business—that is, a long training and motivational period. Some business owners require that their heirs learn business in someone else's company first, perhaps a large company with a formal training or sales training program. However it is done, it requires planning and preparation. How to fund such a transfer is a big issue that needs to be addressed early. Will the heir have the cash to effect a purchase? Will it have to be a payout over time? What happens if the payments stop coming? If the company is already leveraged, there is little opportunity for the heirs to borrow money to buy out the owner. Perhaps one of the goals of the owner in the years approaching the hoped-for departure is to pay off as much debt as possible so that the successors will have room to borrow against the firm's assets to raise the money to make the purchase.

2. *Sale to one or more key employers.* The thought process for this plan probably develops a bit later in the history of the company, as the owner sees which employees are strong enough and qualified enough to run the business. Sometimes an owner will bring in someone from outside of the company with the specific intent to have that person take over. Owners have the same financial worries in this instance that they do in the case of family. Do the buyers have the cash for a cash deal? If not, how will a financing or a payout work, and what protections will be in place for the owner if the successors don't succeed? There are companies with employee stock ownership plans (ESOPs), although this is not common in the event industry. This type of plan creates a means for the employees to buy the business. Over time, the owner sells stock to a trust with the employees as the beneficiaries. The trust is funded by employer contributions based on a percentage of payroll. There must be strong future management in place for this to be realistic. ESOPs must be *qualified,* which is a technical subject to be discussed with legal and accounting counsel.

The same thought process should be followed to lower the company's debt in the years leading up to the takeover so that the business purchase can be financed. Hopefully, the future owners will be involved in the management of the business in the years leading up to the owner's exit, and they can familiarize themselves with the financial end of the company and guide it toward that point when they can take over and be able to pay the departing owner.

3. *Sale to a competitor.* This is a tricky area, as any qualified buyer is going to want to review every facet of the business, including, of course, all financial information and client lists. Showing all of this information to a competitor that may just want to learn more about your company can be very disconcerting. Even obtaining signed confidentiality documents does not offer a reasonable comfort level. An example of such a confidentiality agreement can be found in the appendix. As a general rule, the lack of trust does not bode well for this type of transaction to take place.

   However, a competitor in a different geographic market wishing to expand into new markets may provide a higher comfort level. So might a company offering a complementary service that wishes to broaden its offerings. Just as businesses have to qualify customers before granting them credit and doing business with them, so, too, must prospective purchasers be qualified.

4. *Sale to a client.* In the event industry, disciplines sometimes cross into the areas of other disciplines. Many decorators do their own lighting, and many caterers have gone into rentals or decor, ostensibly to spruce up their food presentation. Some caterers develop exclusivity in a venue, take over the management of the venue, and then bring in and own all of the event services therein. Some destination management companies come to own props and theme decor. Thus, a vendor of a specific service may find prospective purchasers among its clients. The big concern is whether the vendor's clients, who are probably competitors of the prospective purchaser, will remain with the company if purchased by the client. This could be a risky purchase for the client. Due diligence would have to be employed by the seller, as the prospective purchaser may not get an honest response approaching competitors who happen to be clients of the vendor's business. What would prevent telling a competitor that you will continue to use Company A if you purchase it and then switching vendors after the purchase is made?

5. *Sale to a supplier.* This is the reverse of selling to a client. There can be great integration of product lines and services. It can just become an issue of client attrition. If a company that rents plants and trees to many of the floral decorators in a given area decides to buy one of the premier floral decorating companies, will the others in the market continue to use it for their rentals? The answer may vary from situation to situation. If the company has a near monopoly on rental plants and trees, the competitors may have no choice. If the rental company is willing to sacrifice

the tree business, just keeping the greens for its use alone, it will not care how competitors react. But if the prospective purchaser is hoping for a synergy and to hang onto its clients, it may be in for a rude awakening when those clients have other options available to them.

6. *Sale to a megacompany.* This could be a dream come true, having a major industry player purchase the company. How good a scenario this actually works out to be may be a function of timing. When the conglomerate is beginning its acquisition binge, it may be willing to pay more for certain companies to gain a foothold in a marketplace or to establish itself in a certain market segment. Or it may not really know the value of companies and may overpay in its eagerness to grow. Later in the life cycle of the company, after having purchased the first few leading companies it desires, the conglomerate may be a lot more picky about the companies it purchases and may not be willing to pay as much. Further, if the top dog wants to buy a company of a certain type or in a certain geographic location, it may actually pressure the seller to sell for less by fanning fears that it may purchase a competitor instead, thus hurting the small seller's competitive position and lowering the value of that company.

7. *Sale to an individual buyer.* Individual buyers are often high-net-worth individuals, meaning that they have the liquid assets to effect a purchase—or at least sufficient assets to get financing to make the purchase. Some are previous business owners looking to get back into running a company. Others are ex-employees of large corporations who have been downsized or who have been struck by the entrepreneurial spirit and are now looking to make a statement of their own. They can be good prospects, assuming they are financially qualified. It is unlikely that selling to such an individual will be part of a long-term planning process, as finding such an individual can be more luck than anything else, and relying on luck is not really sound planning. The business owner would have to ask, "If this buyer can afford my business, why would he want it?"

8. *Sale to a venture capital group or an angel investor.* At any given time, there are investors scouring the market for companies to purchase as an investment. These investors are looking for income, growth, or a combination of both. Rest assured, they will have an exit strategy of their own and will be looking for specific criteria in a company that will help them achieve it. As part of your owner's strategy with regard to such potential

purchasers, you need to give them a picture of how they can exit with the desired profits.

9. *Going public.* This is not as clean an option as a sale. An initial public offering (IPO) may help owners derive some cash for their sweat equity, but it may not enable them to retire immediately. Even if they are successful in going public, owners may need to stay with the company for several years. They may also find that their shares are restricted and that they cannot cash out for a number of years. Finally, they most likely will find that small companies do not generate much market support from analysts and therefore their stock will not trade heavily. Its price may drift lower and lower over time, making the value of the owner's equity less and less. Owners who are ready to retire may find that their shares are not worth nearly as much as they had hoped. On the other hand, the company could catch the public's fancy and the stock could take off, making sellers far richer than they could have hoped.

Any of the preceding options may prove to be the way to go. A lot of the success in selling a company or realizing value from it can be attributed to luck. Timing, changes in the economy, or a chance meeting with the right person can all factor into the equation. But luck is not a sound foundation for an exit strategy. The planning portion should be much more influential, which is why the exit plan has to be flexible and adaptable to market changes. Owners have to have a sense of what they need to do to attract the purchasers they desire and then build their business around those factors. This flies in the face of the concept that the owners need only to work hard, build a solid company, and someone will be there to buy it at the right time. Owners cannot be that random.

The other type of exit is involuntary in nature. Owners can be forced out of business involuntarily due to bad health, disability, or death; natural disaster, such as earthquake, fire, or flood; or financial/economic disaster, such as bankruptcy, foreclosure, loss in a major lawsuit, embezzlement, bankruptcy of a large client, or a failed investment or acquisition. Can owners protect against any of these by careful planning?

A key-executive policy can provide a business with cash on the death of its owner—cash to pay heirs for the value of the owner's shares in the business. If such a policy does not exist, then the question of payment of the heirs of the deceased owner is a bit more difficult. The administrator or executor of the estate will have to sort out the situation. Should the business be sold? Who should run it in the interim? What additional controls and oversights will be required to protect the asset? If there is a shareholder agreement in place, it should specify terms for the purchase of the decedents' shares. But a meeting of the shareholders and the board of directors will need to be held to vote on a replacement for the owner and on filling key roles. Deceased owners may have had a detailed plan worked out for their succession, but unless it was written down and in the hands of the board, that plan may never be implemented.

Surviving a natural disaster is a different story altogether. It is important to have adequate insurance to cover the facility, its contents, and business interruption. Can company records be reconstructed? Without adequate insurance it may be impossible for the business to recover from a disaster. If inventory was financed, the provider of the financing is going to want to be paid even though the goods may no longer exist. Truck leases, insurance premiums, and a multitude of other business expenses continue on a monthly basis despite the fact that the business has been damaged to the point that it cannot operate.

The financial disasters may be harder to prepare for and to fight off once they occur. Decisions that seem wise at the time, that seem consistent with the business plan and the exit strategy, can backfire and lead to disastrous consequences. Once these decisions have been made, all management can do is monitor their results carefully. Along the way, all known risks can be constantly assessed by management and minimized to the degree possible. The extent of a disastrous financial situation may not be obvious at first. Business owners are notoriously optimistic, and they may truly believe that things are not as bad as they appear or that they will work themselves out. When it finally sinks in that the situation may not be retrievable, owners should minimize the pain of that exit by making sure that all areas where they might be held personally liable are addressed within the business first.

Given that businesses are supposed to serve their owners and give them what they want in life, it is incumbent on owners to know and plan for those things. If they do, exiting from a business can proceed smoothly, leaving them where they want to be in life and leaving the business in good shape for the next owners.

■ SUMMARY

> ➤ Planning an exit strategy should begin with the start-up or purchase of the business.

➤ The exit strategy may be a major component of the operational and growth plans of the business.

➤ Owners have a number of choices in how they maneuver toward their exit.

➤ Involuntary exits can be planned for to a degree by having a written succession plan approved by the board of directors, by having key-executive insurance, and by having insurance covering all damages in the event of a disaster.

Chapter

19

The Last Word

*They are surely to be esteemed the bravest spirits who, having the
clearest sense of both the pains and pleasures of life,
do not on that account shrink from danger.*
—Thucydides, History of the Peloponnesian War

A lot of individual areas have been covered in this book, separated by
headings, paragraphs, or chapters. They could just as easily have been
jumbled together in one big mass, and that mass would be recognizable as a day in the life of a special event company manager or owner.

Virtually all of management's time is spent dealing with employees, clients, vendors, and inventory or equipment. Of course, government can't be excluded from the mix, and that includes federal, state,
and local authorities. All of these areas have been touched on to high-
light situations in which managers may have to anticipate or deal
with problems arising in the course of their normal business day. Such
issues represent the bulk of a manager's time.

This volume does not devote much time to the positive aspects of the
business: the joys of the creative process, the elation of having a proposal on a big event accepted, the thrill of getting in the door to meet
with an exciting prospect, and the high of seeing new equipment or
inventory arrive in the warehouse. Nor was much verbiage devoted to
the ultimate satisfaction of a job well done, an event praised by the
client and the attendees. With all the day-to-day challenges, the payoff
is that joy, whether fleeting or long lasting. But managers rarely need
assistance in dealing with the good moments, just the challenging ones.

The event business is not for everybody. It is not for someone looking for a nine-to-five position. It is not for someone desiring to keep
weekends free for leisure-time pursuits; in fact, it may not be for those
desiring leisure time at all. But within the profession, there is room
for a broad spectrum of personalities and skill sets. Sales and marketing types, technicians, designers, thinkers, creators, craftspeople, and

managers all have leading roles. Accounting people, administrators, and tacticians fill key positions.

Solving the problems that event companies face is fulfilling in and of itself, but it also makes for a more joyful atmosphere within the company. A positive environment breeds better results. Stress levels are reduced, cash flow is improved, and employee productivity increases.

The information contained in this book should help you start solving those problems, hopefully before they have become too serious. The rest is up to you.

Chapter

20

Important Documents Checklist

Good order is the foundation of all good things. —Edmund Burke

Every company has a number of documents that it should treat as important. Copies should be kept in an accessible location for easy reference and access. Documents that require the signature of one or more parties should be *signed* copies. The signatures themselves may be relevant one day. Blank copies may prove to be worthless in the event of litigation.

These documents should be kept in folders stamped CONFIDENTIAL. Any copies of the documents kept in files throughout the company records should themselves be stamped as confidential. Remember, for the company to claim the documents to be confidential in any litigation, they have to be treated as confidential by the company.

Most of these documents continue to be relevant even after the owner has sold the company or retired.

The following lists may seem like a lot of information, but it is information critical to the company and therefore worthy of being kept in a safe place.

Formation or Purchase Documents
1. Articles of incorporation or LLC operating agreement
2. Bylaws
3. Shareholder meeting minutes
4. Board of directors meeting minutes
5. Federal ID number
6. Documents showing Subchapter S election being granted
7. Any amendments to item 1—name change, registered address change

8. Any partnership agreements
9. Shareholder agreements
10. Purchase agreements if the owner bought an existing business
11. Company stock certificates

Employee File Documents: Documents to Be Kept in Each File
1. Signed confidentiality agreement
2. Signed noncompete agreement
3. Signed employment contract or hire letter
4. Signed policy manual acceptance form
5. Signed reviews and reprimands and other disciplinary action
6. Records of pay changes
7. Job description, including language showing any exemption under the Fair Labor Standards Act
8. Copy of current driver's licenses if driving is a job requirement
9. Records of drug and alcohol testing
10. Any unemployment filings by ex-employee and responses by the company

Payroll Records
1. All payroll records from employees for past four years
2. All 1099s for past four years
3. All payroll checks for past four years
4. All expense reimbursement forms for past four years

Bank Documents: Term Loans and Lines of Credit
1. Loan documents
2. Guarantees
3. Notes
4. Security agreements
5. Copies of UCC-1 filings
6. Pledges
7. Payoff statements

Tax Returns
1. All annual federal and state returns
2. All quarterly returns for withholding tax, unemployment tax, and so on
3. All municipal tax returns
4. IFTA filings
5. Correspondence with taxing authorities
6. Audit results

Financial Statements
1. Package of income statements, balance sheets, and supporting reports for each year of the company's operation

Pension Plan or 401(k) Documents
1. Plan documents
2. IRS approval of documents
3. Correspondence from plan management company and IRS

Computer System Information
1. System passwords and individual user passwords
2. List of access level of each employee
3. Software licenses
4. Code for proprietary software
5. Backup tapes or CDs of accounting data
6. Web site hosting and ISP contracts

Business Licenses and Permits
1. Sales tax license in each jurisdiction
2. Business licenses
3. Building permits

Agreements with Professionals
1. Letters of engagement with CPA
2. Opinion letters from CPAs
3. Retainer letters with attorneys
4. Contracts with Realtors
5. Contracts with consultants
6. Contracts with business brokers and investment bankers

Trademarks, Patents, and Copyrights
1. All applications sent by the company
2. All correspondence between the company and government agencies
3. All documents awarding the company the desired protection

Leases
1. All real estate leases and renewals
2. All equipment leases and guarantees
3. All truck, generator, trailer leases

Insurance Policies
1. Liability
2. Comprehensive

3. Property
4. Vehicle
5. Workers' compensation
6. Group disability
7. Medical and dental insurance
8. Key-executive life insurance

Union Contracts
1. Any year-long or multiyear contracts
2. Any per-event contracts

Litigation Files
1. Where the company is the defendant

   Notice of claim letters

   Letter notifying the insurance agent or company of the claim

   Correspondence from counsel

   Legal pleadings
2. Where the company is the plaintiff

   If a breach-of-contract suit, a copy of the contract and any other supporting documentation

   If a business tort, copies of any writings that prove the case

Dealer Contracts
1. Original dealer contract
2. Any supporting documents showing sales requirements, geographical territories, and other important information
3. Renewals or nonrenewals to contact and correspondence relating thereto
4. Copies of all correspondence serving as written notice required by any contract or lease

Sales and Marketing
1. Detailed client list
2. Detailed prospect list
3. Marketing plan
4. Sales plan
5. Company commission structure
6. Detailed information on marketing vendors

   Literature (graphic artists, copywriters, printers)

   Letterhead and logo

   Web site

Promotional advertising suppliers

Photographers and videographers

Company apparel creators

Miscellaneous
1. Proprietary forms
2. Company manuals

   Policy and procedure

   Sales

   Technical

   Training
3. Company credit card account agreements

   List of employees holding cards

   List of cards taken back from terminated employees and a record of the cards being canceled.
4. Copies of titles and registrations of all company vehicles
5. Extra set of keys to each company vehicle
6. List of employees with office and warehouse keys and their alarm codes
7. List of all company laptops, pagers, and cell phones and which employees have which devices
8. List of all employees entrusted with photo albums or company CD photo disks
9. Mission statements
10. Business plans

The preceding lists are fairly comprehensive. Putting copies of these documents all together and within easy reach of management will involve a bit of effort, but the effort is well worthwhile. From time to time, virtually all of these items will become at least temporarily relevant to management. Compiling this data before you need to will make things go more smoothly within the company and will also signal that management has its act together.

There's an old adage in the event industry: "Hope for the best but prepare for the worst." It is better to be ready for that unexpected demand for information than to be scrambling through files and boxes and dumpsters looking for the information you desperately need.

It is quite conceivable that various taxing jurisdictions require you to maintain records for a specific number of years. Check with your professional advisors or with the various arms of government. Should you sell your company, a decision must be made about which party keeps which records. If the sale is a stock sale, the purchaser will be inheriting all of the company's liabilities and should keep the company records. As the seller, you should determine what ongoing issues you might have after the sale and keep copies of any relevant records. And certainly you should maintain records related to any issue over which you might have personal liability. You may want to have a provision in the agreement of sale that allows you access to any records from your period of ownership should the need arise. This would include both hard copies and computer data.

Purchasers who accept certain liabilities in the stock purchase agreement should make certain that the records related to those issues are available. If there are issues that the seller was supposed to settle before transfer, then any settlement documents, court orders, release of liens, and similar documents should be made available to the purchaser.

Appendix

Sample Documents

CONFIDENTIALITY AND NONDISCLOSURE AGREEMENT

THIS AGREEMENT made as of _____ (date), by and between **ABC PRODUCTIONS, INC. (ABC)** and **123, INC. (123)**.

WITNESSETH:

WHEREAS, ABC and 123 are discussing the possibility of an acquisition of ABC by 123 in the form of a merger, acquisition, or other business combination; and in connection therewith 123 has requested financial and other information from ABC which may include confidential business information, trade secrets, and proprietary data of ABC; and

WHEREAS, ABC is willing to disclose such confidential information if 123 agrees to maintain the confidentiality of such information as provided in this Agreement;

NOW, THEREFORE, in consideration of the promises herein contained and intending to be legally bound the parties agree as follows:

1. <u>PURPOSE.</u> ABC may disclose Confidential Information (as herein defined) to 123 for the purpose of permitting 123 to evaluate the possibility of a merger, acquisition, or other business combination between ABC and 123.

2. <u>DEFINITION.</u> "Confidential Information" means any customer information, pricing information, financial information, and employee files disclosed by ABC, which is designated in writing at the time of disclosure to be confidential or proprietary. Confidential Information does not include information which: (i) is in possession of 123 at the time of disclosure, (ii) before or after the time of disclosure becomes part of the public knowledge or literature, or (iii) is approved for release by ABC.

3. <u>USE LIMITATIONS.</u> 123 agrees not to use the Confidential Information of ABC for its own use except as set forth in Section 1.

4. <u>NONDISCLOSURE.</u> 123 agrees not to disclose the Confidential Information to any third parties except those persons who are shareholders, officers, and/or directors of ABC, or employee, accountants, attorneys, and consultants of 123 who have a need to know the Confidential Information for the purpose described in Section 1.

5. <u>COMPULSORY DISCLOSURES.</u> Nothing in this Agreement shall prevent the disclosure of Confidential Information if required by judicial or other governmental compulsion; *provided, however,* that 123 shall advise ABC promptly of the receipt of any subpoena or other document requiring such disclosure.

6. <u>RETURN OF MATERIALS.</u> Any materials or documents which are furnished by ABC, and all copies thereof, will be returned by 123 promptly following

the termination of this Agreement; *provided, however,* that 123 may retain one copy of such information for its archives, which, 123 agrees, shall remain subject to this Agreement and shall not be further copied.

7. <u>TERM.</u> This Agreement shall become effective as of the date written above and shall apply to Confidential Information received by 123 prior to any termination of this Agreement. This Agreement may be terminated by ABC in writing to 123. The provisions of this Agreement shall apply to all Confidential Information disclosed under this Agreement prior to termination and shall survive for a period of two years after the date of this Agreement.

8. <u>CONFIDENTIALITY OF NEGOTIATIONS.</u> ABC and 123 each agree to keep the fact of their negotiations confidential and not to disclose that fact to any person other than their respective shareholders, officers, and/or directors, and/or to those of their respective employees, accountants, attorneys, and consultants who participate in or as-sist with such negotiation, unless and until a binding agreement for merger, acquisition, or other form of business combination is executed by ABC and 123, or by the shareholders thereof. The provisions of this Section 8 shall survive termination of this Agreement.

9. <u>GENERAL.</u> This Agreement sets forth the entire understanding and agreement of the parties with respect to the subject matter hereof and supersedes all other oral or written representations and understandings. The formation and interpretation and performance of this Agreement shall be governed by the laws of the Commonwealth of Pennsylvania, excluding its conflict-of-law rules. This Agreement may be amended or modified only in a writing signed by the parties. This Agreement shall not be construed as a joint venture or other business relationship. This Agreement shall be binding upon the successors and assigns of the parties hereto.

ABC, INC.   123, INC.

By: _____   By: _____
          President   President

Attest: _____   Attest: _____
         Secretary   Secretary

SHAREHOLDERS AGREEMENT

THIS IS AN AGREEMENT (Agreement) effective as of _____ (date) between **WILLIAM WILLIAMS (WW)** and **JOHN JOHNSON (JJ),** hereinafter sometimes referred to collectively as the Shareholders, and each singly as a Shareholder, and **ABC,** a New Jersey corporation hereinafter called the Company.

EXPLANATORY STATEMENT

A. The Shareholders own capital stock (hereinafter referred to as Shares) of the Company as indicated on Exhibit A, and desire that the Shares remain closely held in order to promote harmonious management of the Company's affairs. As of the date of this Agreement, the Company has five thousand (5,000) authorized Shares, and two thousand (2,000) Shares are currently outstanding.

B. The Shareholders desire to set forth the terms and conditions pursuant to which they and the Company will govern their future relationship, as well as to provide for certain matters relating to the Shares.

C. It is the purpose of this Agreement to place certain restrictions on a Shareholder who during his lifetime, desires to sell, assign, pledge, or transfer in any manner any or all of his Shares. Each Shareholder hereby acknowledges the reasonableness of the restrictions on transfers imposed by this Agreement in view of the purposes of the Company and the relationships of the Shareholders.

D. It is the further purpose of this Agreement to provide, in the event of a voluntary withdrawal of a Shareholder from the Company during his lifetime, or in the event of termination of employment of a Shareholder for cause, a method for the purchase of his Shares by the Company or the other Shareholders.

E. It is the further purpose of this Agreement to provide a method whereby the Company or the other Shareholders may purchase the Shares of a Shareholder who dies or becomes disabled.

F. The Shareholders, as identified above, desire that the terms and conditions set forth herein apply to any additional Shareholders who will be required to execute a joinder to this Agreement contemporaneous with the issuance of Shares to such proposed Shareholder.

G. Strict compliance shall be required with each and every provision of this Agreement and particularly with the procedures set forth herein with respect to any transfer of any of the Shares of any Shareholders or restrictions on said Shareholders with respect to noncompetition.

H. It is understood and agreed by the parties hereto that no Shareholder shall have the right or power to transfer any Shares except in strict compliance with the procedures set forth in this Agreement. All Shares of the Company, however acquired, shall be subject to this Agreement and all Shareholders current or future shall be required to join and adhere to this Agreement. The transfer of any Shares by any Shareholder shall be deemed invalid, null and void, and of no force or effect, and the transferee of any such Shares shall not be entitled to vote such Shares, receive dividends on such Shares or have any other rights in and with respect to such Shares, unless such transfer is made in conformance with and pursuant to the terms of this Shareholder Agreement.

NOW THEREFORE, in consideration of the mutual covenants and promises set forth herein, the parties hereto, intending to be legally bound, agree as follows:

1. RESTRICTIONS ON TRANSFER. No Shareholder shall sell, assign, transfer, give, donate, or dispose of any of his or her Shares, or any right or interest in any Shares hereafter acquired by him or her, whether voluntarily, by operation of law, by order of court, or otherwise, to any person or entity other than the Company, the remaining Shareholders in pro rata amounts as defined in Paragraph 2 (below), or pursuant to the consent of all other Shareholders, except in accordance with the terms and conditions hereinafter set forth in this Agreement.

2. PURCHASE OBLIGATIONS UPON DEATH. Upon the death of a Shareholder, his estate shall sell and the surviving Shareholder(s) may or the Company shall purchase for the price and upon the other terms hereinafter provided all (and not less than all) of the Shares which the deceased Shareholder owned at his death. Purchases by Shareholders shall be on a pro rata basis in accordance with the Shares of the Company then owned by them. The Shareholders shall have forty-five (45) days from the date of notice of the death of such Shareholder to exercise their option to purchase such deceased Shareholder's Shares pursuant to this Paragraph 2. The Company will have seventy (70) days from the date of notice of the death of such Shareholder to purchase the deceased Shareholder's Shares pursuant to this Paragraph 2. A pro rata basis shall be defined hereinafter as the percentage of Shares of the Company owned by such Shareholders on the date of the triggering event exclusive of such Shares owned by the disabled, deceased, or otherwise withdrawing Shareholder.

3. OPTION UPON VOLUNTARY TRANSFER.

3.1 Notice of Transfer. If a Shareholder intends to voluntarily transfer any Shares of which he is owner to any person, he shall give forty-five (45) days written notice to the remaining Shareholder(s), with a copy to the Company, of his intention to transfer Shares. The notice, in addition to stating the fact of the intention to transfer Shares, shall state (i) the number of Shares he wishes to transfer, (ii) the name, business, and residence address of the proposed transferee, (iii) whether or not the transfer is for a valuable consideration, and, if so, the amount thereof and the other terms of the sale.

3.2 Primary Option to Purchase. Within forty-five (45) days of the receipt by the remaining Shareholder(s) of the notice, such remaining Shareholder(s) may exercise an option to purchase an amount of such Shares proposed to be transferred equal to their pro rata ownership amount in the Company, as defined in Paragraph 2, or any lesser amount thereof, for the price hereinafter provided in Exhibit A and upon the other terms provided for in this Agreement. The purchase option granted in this paragraph is sometimes hereinafter referred to as the Primary Option. Each remaining Shareholder must notify, in writing, the Shareholders and Company, of his decision, and the amount of Shares he decides to purchase, if not his full pro rata amount.

3.3 <u>Secondary Option to Purchase.</u>   If the remaining Shareholder(s) do not exercise the Primary Option to purchase all of the Shares proposed to be transferred, the Company, within seventy (70) days of the remaining Shareholder(s) receipt of the notice of the proposed transfer, may exercise an option to purchase that portion of the Shares as to which the remaining Shareholders do not exercise their purchase option. The Purchase Option granted by this Paragraph is sometimes hereinafter referred to as the Secondary Option.

3.4 <u>Partial Exercise of Options Prohibited.</u>   The remaining Shareholders and the Company must in the aggregate exercise their options to purchase all of the Shares proposed to be transferred. In the event a Shareholder or the Company elects not to purchase any Shares transferred pursuant to this Agreement, such Shareholder or the Company shall forfeit their options provided herein. Provided, however, that the remaining Shareholders exercising their option or the Company shall be required to purchase all of the Shares proposed to be transferred pursuant to this Agreement.

3.5 <u>Death Prior to Closing.</u>   If a Shareholder who proposes to transfer Shares dies prior to the closing of the sale and purchase contemplated by this Paragraph 3, his Shares shall be the subject of sale and purchase under Paragraph 1.

4. <u>OPTION UPON INVOLUNTARY TRANSFER.</u>   If other than by reason of a Shareholder's death, Shares are transferred by operation of law to any person (such as but not limited to a Shareholder's trustee in bankruptcy, a Shareholder's spouse pursuant to a Decree of Dissolution of Marriage, Marital Settlement Agreement, or other marital transfer or division of property, a purchaser at any creditor's or court sale or the guardian or conservator of an incompetent Shareholder) or upon the conviction of a crime classified as a felony, the remaining Shareholder(s) may, within forty-five (45) days, or the Company, within seventy (70) days of the receipt by the remaining Shareholder(s) of actual notice of the transfer or conviction, shall exercise an option to purchase all, but not less than all, of the Shares so transferred. The purchase of such Shares proposed to be transferred shall be upon the same procedures provided for in Paragraphs 3.2, 3.3 and 3.4, the procedure being the only applicable portion of such paragraphs.

5. <u>PURCHASE UPON TERMINATION OF EMPLOYMENT.</u>
5.1 <u>Purchase Obligation upon Termination of Employment by the Company.</u> Upon the termination of a Shareholder's employment by the Company, for any reason whatsoever, the Shareholder shall sell and the remaining Shareholder(s) may, within forty-five (45) days of the date of termination of employment, or the Company, within seventy (70) days of the date of termination of employment, shall purchase the Shares which the selling Shareholder owned at the time of such termination, on a pro rata basis, as defined in Paragraph 2, in accordance with the Shares of the Company then owned by them. Such purchase shall be upon the

same procedures provided for in Paragraphs 3.2, 3.3 and 3.4, the procedure being the only applicable portion of such paragraphs.

5.2 <u>Purchase Option upon Termination of Employment by Shareholder.</u> Upon the termination of a Shareholder's employment by said Shareholder for any reason whatsoever, the remaining Shareholder(s), within forty-five (45) days may, or the Company, within seventy (70) days of the effective date of such termination, shall exercise an option to purchase all, but not less than all of the terminating Shareholder's Shares by the same procedures provided for in Paragraphs 3.2, 3.3 and 3.4, the procedure being the only applicable portion of such paragraphs

5.3 <u>Purchase Obligation upon Retirement.</u> In the event that a Shareholder (the Retiring Shareholder) retires from employment, the remaining Shareholder(s) may or the Company shall purchase all Shares owned by the Shareholder on the date of such termination of employment (the Retirement Date) by providing written notice to that effect to the Retiring Shareholder within one hundred eighty (180) days of the Retirement Date. Said purchase shall be by the same procedure provided for in Paragraphs 3.2, 3.3, and 3.4, the procedure being the only applicable portion of such paragraphs.

5.4 Anything herein to the contrary notwithstanding, the provisions of this Paragraph 5 shall not apply to a termination of employment as a result of any of the following:

(a) Total disability, as hereinafter defined in Paragraph 6;

(b) Dissolution, liquidation, merger, consolidation, or other reorganization of the Company, or any corporate transaction the result of which is the creation of an employment relationship with a successor or a surviving entity; and

(c) Employment by an affiliate or a subsidiary of the Company, at the written request of the Company.

6. PURCHASE OBLIGATION UPON DISABILITY.

6.1 If a Shareholder shall become totally disabled, the remaining Shareholder(s) may, within forty-five (45) days of the commencement of such total disability, or Company, within seventy (70) days of the date of the commencement of such total disability, shall purchase all (and not less than all) of the Shares owned by the disabled Shareholder at the time of the commencement of his total disability for the price and upon the same procedures provided for in Paragraphs 3.2, 3.3, and 3.4, the procedure being the only applicable portion of such paragraphs and in accordance with their pro rata interest, as defined in Paragraph 2. A Shareholder shall be deemed "totally disabled" within the meaning of this Paragraph 6 if as a result of sickness, accident, injury, or mental disorder, he becomes wholly and continuously unable to perform the duties of his position or any other position of similar responsibility with the Company for a period of twelve (12) months and his disability shall be deemed to have commenced at the end of said twelve (12) month period. Successive periods of disability shall be considered one (1) period of continuing disability unless separated by a return to employment for a period of at least forty-five (45) days.

6.2 In the event the parties fail to agree whether the Shareholder is totally and permanently disabled for the purposes of this Paragraph, the Shareholder, on the one hand, and the remaining Shareholders, on the other hand, shall each designate an Arbitrator, and the two (2) Arbitrators so selected shall designate a third Arbitrator to reach a disability determination which shall be binding upon the Parties. The Arbitrators shall be entitled to receive and rely on any medical evidence or other information which they shall deem required in order to enable them to make a determination as to whether or not a purchase and sale of Shares shall take place.

7. <u>EXERCISE OF OPTIONS AND EFFECTS OF NONEXERCISE OF OPTIONS.</u>

7.1 The remaining Shareholder(s) and/or the Company who exercise the purchase options granted in Paragraphs 2, 3, 4, 5, or 6 shall do so by delivering written notice of their exercise of the options within the times provided in such paragraphs to the executor or representative of a deceased Shareholder's estate in the case of a Paragraph 2 transfer; to the proposed transferor in case of a Paragraph 3 option; to the transferee in the case of a Paragraph 4 option; to the terminated or terminating Shareholder-employee in the case of a Paragraph 5 option; or the disabled Shareholder or his legal representative in the case of a Paragraph 6 option. If the Company is the purchaser, written notice of its exercise of the option shall also be given to the remaining Shareholders in the case of a Paragraph 2, 3, 4, 5, or 6 option.

7.2 If the purchase options are forfeited or are not exercised in compliance with Paragraphs 2, 3, 4, 5, or 6 then, in the case of the death of a Shareholder, the estate may distribute such Shares in accordance with the deceased Shareholder's testamentary intent or, in the absence of same, in accordance with the law. In the case of a proposed transfer under Paragraph 3, the Shares may be transferred, within ten (10) days after the expiration of the seventy (70) day option period provided by Paragraph 3, to the transferee named in the notice required by Paragraph 3, and upon the terms therein stated, such transfer being free of the transfer restrictions set forth in this Agreement but such transferee being subject to the terms and conditions of this Agreement by virtue of Paragraph 22 and also being required to execute a joinder to this Agreement. In the case of a proposed transfer under Paragraph 4, the Shares may be transferred, within ten (10) days after the expiration of the seventy (70) day option period provided by Paragraph 4, to the appropriate transferee by virtue of such involuntary transfer, and upon the terms of such involuntary transfer, such transfer being free of the transfer restrictions set forth in this Agreement but such transferee being subject to the terms and conditions of this Agreement by virtue of Paragraph 22 and also being required to execute a joinder to this Agreement. If the purchase options granted by Paragraph 5 or 6 are forfeited, or not exercised in compliance with said paragraph, the Shares subject thereto shall remain subject to this Agreement.

7.3 If, in the case of a Paragraph 3 transfer, the transfer is not upon the terms or is not to the transferee(s) stated in the notice required of the transferring Shareholder by Paragraph 3, or is not within the aforesaid ten (10) day period, or the transferor, after the transfer, reacquires all or any portion of the transferred Shares, the Shares transferred shall remain subject to this Agreement as if no transfer had been made.

7.4 A proposed transferor of Shares under Paragraph 3, 4, 5, or 6 or a transferee of Shares under Paragraph 6, either or both, as a Shareholder or Director of the Company, shall abstain from voting on the Company's exercise of the Secondary Purchase Options granted to it by this Agreement at any meeting of Shareholder or Directors called for such purpose, unless such participation shall be required (and in such event only to the extent required) for purposes of a quorum in which event the proposed transferor (or transferee as the case may be) shall vote as directed by a majority of the remaining Directors at any meeting of Directors called for such purpose or as directed by a majority of the remaining Shareholders at any meeting called for such purpose.

8. THE PURCHASE PRICE.   The Purchase Price (hereafter the Purchase Price) of Shares shall be determined in accordance with the provisions of Exhibit B annexed hereto by the Company's Certified Public Accountant and shall be binding on all Parties.

9. PLEDGE OF SHARES PROHIBITED.   No Shareholder shall encumber or use any of his Shares as security for any loan, except upon the written consent of the remaining Shareholder(s), or pursuant to the terms of this Agreement, specifically Paragraph 10.

10. PAYMENT OF THE PURCHASE PRICE.
10.1 The Purchase Price for Shares shall be paid in cash or, at the option of the purchasing parties, ninety percent (90%) of the Purchase Price may be deferred and ten percent (10%) paid at the closing.

10.2 NOTE.
10.2.1 The deferred portion of the Purchase Price shall be evidenced by the promissory note of each of the purchasing party(s) made payable to the order of the selling party. The note of a purchasing party shall be in substantially the form of that attached as Exhibit C.

10.2.2 If the maker of the note is the Company, the note shall not be secured by the Company but shall be personally guaranteed by the surviving or remaining Shareholders in substantially the form of that attached as Exhibit D. Such Shares purchased by the surviving or remaining Shareholders shall be pledged by him to the payee of the note to secure the payment of the guarantee. The Parties hereto specifically consent to the pledge of Shares provided for in this Paragraph 10.2.2.

10.2.3 If the maker of the note is a Shareholder, the note shall be secured by the Shareholder's pledge, to the payee of the note, of the Shares purchased, and the form of the note set forth in Exhibit C shall contain, as an additional paragraph immediately preceding the signature line, the supplementary paragraph also set forth in Exhibit C. The Parties hereto specifically consent to the pledge of Shares provided for in this Paragraph 10.2.3.

10.3. <u>INSURANCE.</u>

10.3.1. Notwithstanding Paragraph 10.1, if the purchasing party is the owner and beneficiary of insurance on the life of a deceased Shareholder from whose estate the purchaser is purchasing Shares, an amount equal to the lesser of the full purchase price or the policy proceeds payable to the beneficiary under the policy or policies shall be paid in cash to the estate of the deceased Shareholder on account of the Purchase Price of the Shares, and only the balance, if any, may be deferred as provided in Paragraph 10.1.

10.3.2 In the case of a purchase of Shares from a disabled Shareholder pursuant to Paragraph 6, if said disabled Shareholder dies <u>after</u> the closing of the sale and purchase contemplated by said Paragraph 6 but <u>prior</u> to full payment on the note contemplated by this Paragraph 10, then the policy proceeds payable to the purchasing party/beneficiary under the policy or policies shall be applied toward the unpaid balance of principal due on said note.

10.3.3 If the purchasing party is the owner of disability buyout insurance on a disabled Shareholder from whom the purchaser is purchasing Shares, any installment or periodic payments paid to said disabled Shareholder (whether paid by the insurance company directly to the disabled Shareholder or paid to the owner of the policy and subsequently paid to such disabled Shareholder) on account of such disability insurance shall be applied as a credit against the then current installment of principal and interest on the Note. Any excess of such payment (either installment or lump sum payment) over the amount of such installment payment on the Note shall be applied as a credit against principal.

10.3.4 If the Company is prohibited by law from using all or any portion of the proceeds of the insurance policy or policies it owns on the deceased Shareholder's life, Paragraph 10.3.1 shall apply only to insurance proceeds which the Company may, by law, use to apply on the purchase price of the Shares. All Shareholders are required to take any and all action allowed by law to effectuate the use of such insurance proceeds in the manner intended for funding any purchase of Shares pursuant to this Agreement.

10.3.5 The term *policy proceeds* shall include the face value of the policy and any additions, dividends, or accumulations paid with the claim, less any loans and unpaid interest outstanding against the policy.

11. <u>THE CLOSING.</u>

11.1 Unless otherwise agreed by the Parties, the closing of the sale and purchase of Shares, as provided in this Agreement, shall take place at the general offices of the Company. In the case of a purchase of Shares from a deceased Shareholder's estate under Paragraph 2, the closing shall take place thirty (30) days after the appointment of a personal representative for the deceased Shareholder's estate. In the case of a purchase of Shares from a disabled Shareholder under Paragraph 6, the closing shall take place thirty (30) days after the date upon which total disability is deemed to have occurred (or if a determination of total disability by arbitration is required pursuant to Paragraph 6.2, within thirty days after the date on which the arbitrators file with the Parties a notice of determination). In the case of a purchase of Shares under Paragraph 5.1, the closing shall take place thirty (30) days after the date of termination of the selling Shareholder's employ-ment. In the case of a purchase of Shares under Paragraphs 3, 4, or 5.2, the clos-ing of the sale and purchase shall take place thirty (30) days after the delivery to the selling Shareholder of written notice by the last of the purchasing party or par-ties to deliver such notice of its, his, or their exercise of the option or options to pur-chase the selling Shareholder's Shares.

11.2 Upon the closing of the sale and purchase, the selling and purchasing Parties shall execute and deliver to each other the various documents which shall be required to carry out their undertakings hereunder, including, but not limited to, the payment of cash, the execution and delivery of notes, and the pledge or assign-ment and delivery of stock certificates. At the same time the Purchasing Share-holder (or the remaining Shareholder if the Company is the Purchaser) shall execute and deliver to the Selling Shareholder (or his successors and assigns) an agreement indemnifying the Selling Shareholder (or his successors and assigns) or the spouse of such Selling Shareholder (to the extent such Spouse may have provided a personal guarantee for any corporate debt or obligation) against any lia-bility imposed upon such Shareholder (or Spouse) by reason of any personal guar-antee given by such Selling Shareholder (or Spouse) for any such corporate debt or obligation. In addition, the Company and the remaining Shareholder shall utilize their best efforts to obtain a full release of the Selling Shareholder (or Spouse) from said guarantees. At closing the selling Shareholder shall deliver to the Com-pany his resignation and that of his nominees, if any, as officers and directors of the Company and any of its subsidiaries.

12. NONCOMPETITION.

12.1 The Company engages in the business of production services and the event production business for corporate, political, theatrical, entertainment, and other special events throughout the United States. As a material inducement to the execution of this Agreement, each of the Shareholders voluntarily agrees to the fol-lowing additional restrictions:

(a) Each of the Shareholders agree that as long as he is a Shareholder and, further, during a five (5) year period beginning on the closing date for the sale of his Shares under this Agreement that, without the prior written consent of the remain-ing Shareholders of ABC, he will not disclose or use for his direct or indirect bene-fit or the direct or indirect benefit of a third party, and he will use his best efforts to maintain, both during and after his employment, the confidentiality of any and all proprietary or confidential information of ABC or its subsidiary(s) that he acquires because of his equity interest in ABC. In general, *confidential information* means any information that ABC treats as confidential, including, but not limited to, any information relating to business procedures, business studies, clients lists, data bases, employee lists (both permanent and part-time), sales, marketing, public relations and advertising campaigns, strategies or plans, financial information, either prepared by or for ABC, in-house manuals, and any information relating to research processes, inventions, products, methods, software, and documentation, and any other materials that have not been made available to the general public. Failure to mark any of the confidential information as confidential or proprietary will not affect its status as confidential information under the terms of this Agreement. The Shareholders' exposure to any of the aforementioned shall not be constructed as granting him a license or any other right with respect to such information.

(b) Each of the Shareholders agrees that, as long as he is a Shareholder and, further, during a five (5) year period beginning on the closing date for the sale of his Shares under this Agreement (or as may be limited by a court of competent jurisdiction), without the express written consent of the remaining Shareholders of ABC, he will not, directly or indirectly, contact, solicit, call on, or otherwise deal in any way with any client or prospective client with whom ABC shall have dealt with at any time during or prior to the Shareholder's ownership of ABC Shares for a purpose which is competitive with the business of ABC, or influence or attempt to influence any client, prospective client, vendor, or contractor of ABC to terminate or modify any written or oral agreement or course of dealing with ABC.

(c) Each of the Shareholders agrees that as long as he is a Shareholder and, further, during a five (5) year period beginning on the closing date for the sale of his Shares under this Agreement (or as may be limited by a court of competent jurisdiction) without the express written consent of the remaining Shareholders of ABC, directly or indirectly, anywhere in the United States, engage in any activity which is, or participate or invest in, or provide or facilitate the provision of financing to, or assist (whether as owner, part-owner, shareholder, partner, director, officer, trustee, employee, agent or consultant, or in any other capacity), any business, organization or person other than ABC or its subsidiary(s) whose business, activities, products, or services are competitive with any of the business, activities, products, or services conducted or offered by ABC or its subsidiaries during any period in which the selling Shareholder owed Shares of ABC, which business, activities, products, and services shall include in any event the provision of providing event production services and field sales force logistics services, or providing other services currently provided by ABC or its subsidiaries or contemplated to be provided by ABC or its subsidiaries in such general areas of service. Without implied limitation, the forgoing covenant shall include hiring or engaging or attempting to hire or engage for or on behalf of themselves or any such competitor any officer or employee of ABC or any of its direct and/or indirect subsidiaries, encouraging for or on behalf of themselves or any such competitor any such officer or employee to terminate his or her relationship or employment with ABC or any of its direct or indirect subsidiaries, soliciting for or on behalf of themselves or any such competitor any client of ABC or any of its direct or indirect subsidiaries and diverting to any person (as hereinafter defined) any client or business opportunity of ABC or any of any of its direct or indirect subsidiaries.

(d) Each of the Shareholders agrees that as long as he is a Shareholder and, further, for an unlimited period subsequent to the closing date for the sale of his Shares under this Agreement, such Shareholder will not disparage ABC or any of its direct or indirect subsidiaries, the business, or the products or services conducted or offered by ABC and its subsidiaries during any period in which such Shareholder owned Shares of ABC.

(e) Each Shareholder to this Agreement, or who joins this Agreement, has represented, and now warrants to each other and ABC that they are not subject to any other agreement that such Shareholder will violate by signing this Agreement or which prevents such Shareholder from disclosing confidential information. Each Shareholder agrees to disclose the terms of this Agreement to any employer or potential employer that may seek to employ or does employ him or any other Company or other business entity in which the Shareholder is invested or intends to invest during the effective period of this Paragraph 12.

12.3 Each Shareholder acknowledges that his right to compete has been limited only to the extent necessary to protect the Company from unfair competition. The parties recognize, however, that reasonable people may differ in making this determination. Therefore, if this restrictive covenant's scope or enforceability is disputed, a court or other trier of fact may modify and enforce the covenant to the extent that it believes to be reasonable under the circumstances existing at that time.

12.4 Each Shareholder acknowledges that compliance with these restrictions is necessary to protect the Company's business and goodwill and that a breach shall irreparably and continually damage the Company, for which money damages will not be adequate. Consequently, if a Shareholder breaches or threatens to breach any of these covenants, the Company shall be entitled to a preliminary or permanent injunction to prevent the continuation of this harm and money damages. Money damages shall include the Company's right to recover fees, compensation, or other remuneration earned by said Shareholder as a result of any breach. Nothing in this Agreement shall be construed to prohibit the Company from also pursuing any other remedy.

13. REPRESENTATIONS AND WARRANTIES.

13.1 Each Shareholder represents and warrants, severally and not jointly, to the Company and to each other as follows:

(a) The execution, delivery, and performance of this Shareholder Agreement will not violate any provision of law, any order of any court or other agency of government, or any provision of any indenture, agreement, or other instrument to which such Shareholder or any of his properties or assets is bound, or conflict with, result in a breach of, or constitute (with due notice or lapse of time or both) a default under any such indenture, agreement, or other instrument, or result in the creation or imposition of any lien, charge, or encumbrance of any nature whatsoever upon any of the properties or assets of such Shareholder.

(b) This Agreement has been duly executed and delivered by such Shareholder and constitutes the legal, valid, and binding obligation of such Shareholder, enforceable in accordance with its terms.

14. LEGEND ON CERTIFICATES.

14.1 All Shares now or hereafter owned by the Shareholders shall be subject to the provisions of this Agreement, and the certificates representing same shall bear the following legend:

The sale, transfer, or encumbrance of this certificate is subject to an agreement dated September 1, 1998, among the Company and all of the Shareholders of the Company. A copy of the agreement is on file in the office of the Secretary of the Company. The agreement provides, among other things, for certain prior rights to purchase and certain obligations to sell and to purchase the Shares evidenced by this certificate for a designated purchase price. By accepting the Shares of stock evidenced by this certificate, the holder agrees to be bound by said agreement.

14.2 Certificates of Shares which are pledged by a purchasing Shareholder, as provided in Paragraph 10, shall, in the hands of the pledgee, be subject to the terms of this Agreement and the certificates evidencing the same shall bear the above legend, and upon return to the pledgor such Shares shall continue to be subject to the provisions hereof, and certificates therefore shall bear the above legend.

15. TERMINATION.

15.1 This Agreement and all restrictions on stock transfer created thereby shall terminate on the occurrence of any of the following events:

(a) The bankruptcy or dissolution of the Company.

(b) A single Shareholder's becoming the owner of all of the Shares which are then subject to this Agreement.

(c) The execution of a written instrument by all of the parties who then own Shares subject to this Agreement which terminates the same.

15.2 Upon termination of this Agreement, by reason of the occurrence of any of the foregoing events, either Shareholder shall have the right to purchase within thirty (30) days after termination from the other Shareholder (including the personal representative of a deceased Shareholder's estate) or from the Company who owns any insurance policy or policies, on his life or disability, such policy or policies, for cash in the amount of the cash surrender value thereof and the amount of unearned premiums thereon both amounts as of the date of the termination of the Agreement.

15.3 This Agreement shall also terminate upon the death of all of the Shareholders within a period of thirty (30) days of each other, in which case the termination shall be effective as of the day preceding the day of the death of the first Shareholder to die, and the Shares and any insurance policies owned by either deceased Shareholder's estate shall be owned free of the terms of this Agreement.

15.4 The termination of this Agreement for any reason shall not affect any right or remedy existing hereunder prior to the effective date of termination hereof, except as provided in Paragraph 15.3.

15.5 If, under Paragraph 7, all of a Shareholder's Shares are transferred free of the terms hereof, but the transfer does not terminate this Agreement, then, within thirty (30) days from the date of transfer, the transferor of the Shares shall have the right to purchase, for cash, policies of insurance on his life from the Company or the other Shareholder owning such policies, and the latter shall within such thirty (30) days have the right to purchase, for cash, policies of insurance on his life or disability from the transfer or of Shares owning such policies. The purchase price of each policy shall be the cash surrender value thereof plus the net unearned premiums thereon, both amounts as of the date the transferor's Shares become free of the terms of this Agreement.

16. INSURANCE ON SHAREHOLDERS' LIVES.

16.1 The Shareholders may desire to insure or partially insure their promises in this Agreement made to purchase from a deceased Shareholder's estate Shares that he owned prior to his death. In the event the Shareholders obtain such insurance, they agree as set forth in this Paragraph 16. Each Shareholder agrees to continue in force, by the payment of the premiums due from time to time thereon, any of the insurance policies purchased on the other's life of which each purchaser is the owner and beneficiary, as may be set forth as an Exhibit to this Agreement.

16.2 The Shareholders may desire to insure or partially insure their promises in this Agreement to purchase from a disabled Shareholder the Shares which he owned prior to his Total Disability. Therefore, each Shareholder may purchase disability insurance policies of which the purchaser is the owner, as may be set forth as an Exhibit to this Agreement. In the event the Shareholders obtain such insurance, they agree to maintain such insurance as set forth in this Paragraph 16. Each Shareholder agrees to continue in force by the payment of the premiums as may be due from time to time on such insurance.

16.3 If either Shareholder fails to pay any premiums due from him on any of the policies, the other Shareholder may, but need not, pay the premium and, if he does, shall have an enforceable claim against the nonpaying Shareholder for the amount of the premium plus interest (at the then current prime rate) from the date of payment of the premium to the date of payment of the claim. *Prime rate* shall be defined as the rate charged by the Company's lead Commercial Bank, adjusted annually from the date of payment of the premium.

16.4 Each Shareholder by signing this Agreement agrees that at the request of the other Shareholders he will cause the insurance company which is the issuer of any policy scheduled in an Exhibit to this Agreement of which the Shareholder is owner and beneficiary to send the other Shareholder premium-due notices and premium-paid receipts with respect to such policy.

16.5 The terms of this Paragraph 16 shall automatically apply to any policies not scheduled as an Exhibit to this Agreement but which are acquired by any of the parties hereby subsequent to the date hereof on the life or disability of the other Shareholder party to this Agreement and of which the Shareholder is owner and beneficiary. The terms of this Paragraph shall not apply to a certain company-provided group disability insurance policy (currently with Standard Select Insurance Company), the proceeds or benefits of which, when received by the recipient disabled shareholder, shall not be applied as a credit against the Note given by the purchasing party to the disabled Shareholder.

17. GENERAL PROVISIONS.

17.1 Governing Law Consent to Jurisdiction and Service of Process. This Agreement shall be construed pursuant to the laws of the State of New Jersey, without regard to conflicts of laws provisions. Therefore, the Shareholders and

Company expressly consent to jurisdiction in the State of New Jersey and service of process by certified mail, return receipt requested.

17.2 <u>Remedies for Breach.</u>   The Shares are unique chattels, and each party to this Agreement shall have the remedies that are available to him for the violation of any of the terms of this Agreement, including, but not limited to, the equitable remedy of specific performance. The parties hereby declare that it is impossible to measure in money the damages that will accrue to a party hereto or to the personal representatives of a decedent by reason of a failure to perform any of the obligations under this Agreement. Therefore, if any party hereto or the personal representatives of a decedent shall institute any action or proceeding to enforce the provisions hereof, any person (including the Company) against whom such action or proceeding is brought hereby waives the claim or defense therein that such party or such personal representatives has or have an adequate remedy at law, and such person shall not allege in any such action or proceeding the claim or defense that such remedy at law exists.

17.3 <u>Notices.</u>   All notices provided for by this Agreement shall be made in writing, (1) by actual delivery of the notice into the hands of the parties thereunto entitled or (2) by the mailing of the notice in the U.S. mails to the last known address of the party entitled thereto, registered mail, return receipt requested. The notice shall be deemed to be received in case 1 on the date of its actual receipt by the party entitled thereto and in case 2 on the date of its mailing.

17.4 <u>Descriptive Headings.</u>   Titles to paragraphs hereof are for information purposes only.

17.5 <u>Binding Effect.</u>   This Agreement is binding upon and inures to the benefit of the Company, its successors and assigns, and to the Shareholders and their respective heirs, personal representatives, successors, and assigns, and the Shareholders by the signing hereof direct their personal representatives to open their estates promptly in the courts of proper jurisdiction and to procure, execute, and deliver all documents, including, but not limited to, appropriate orders of the Probate Court (or court of comparable jurisdiction) and estate and inheritance tax waivers as shall be required to effectuate the purposes of this Agreement. The estate of the deceased Shareholder shall bear, and shall hold the purchasing party harmless from, all costs and expenses required for securing any court orders, court decrees, court approvals, inheritance tax clearances, and estate tax clearances required to enable the estate of the deceased Shareholder to transfer to the purchasing party full legal and equitable tax-free title to the Shares of the deceased Shareholder in the Company.

17.6 <u>Estate of Deceased Shareholder Defined.</u>   The term *estate of the deceased Shareholder* as used in this Agreement, shall include as those terms are understood under the laws of the State of New Jersey.

(a) The duly appointed and qualified executor, administrator, or personal representative with the will annexed of the estate of the deceased Shareholder.

(b) The surviving joint tenant of the deceased Shareholder when Shares of the Company are owned by the deceased Shareholder and another person as joint tenants.

(c) Any other person who may, because of the community property or other law of any jurisdiction, acquire without formal probate proceedings any right, title, or interest in or to the Shares of the deceased Shareholder in the Company because of the death of the Shareholder.

17.7 <u>Severability.</u> Should any part or provision of this Agreement be, at any time, not enforceable or not capable of legal performance, the remaining parts and provisions of this Agreement shall, nonetheless, be enforceable as though the unenforceable or illegal part or provision did not appear in this Agreement at all. It is the express intent and agreement of all of the parties hereto that such unenforceable or illegal part or provision be severed from the balance of this Agreement and that the balance of this Agreement be enforceable.

17.8 <u>Further Instruments.</u> The parties hereto do hereby agree to make, execute, and deliver any documents necessary to carry out this Agreement.

17.9 <u>Attorneys' Fees.</u> In the event of a dispute between the parties hereto or their personal representatives arising out of the terms, conditions, and obligations imposed by this Agreement, the prevailing party shall be entitled to recover reasonable attorneys' fees incurred in connection therewith from any one or any combination of the opposing parties, whether or not actual litigation ensues.

17.10 <u>Prior Agreements.</u> This Agreement supersedes any prior or contemporaneous understanding or agreement among the parties respecting the subject matter hereof. There are no arrangements, understandings, or agreements, oral or written, among the parties hereto relating to the subject matter of this Agreement, except those fully expressed herein or in documents executed contemporaneously herewith. No change or modification of this Agreement shall be valid or binding upon the parties hereto unless such change or modification or waiver shall be in writing and signed by the parties hereto.

17.11 <u>Counterparts.</u> This Agreement may be executed in any number of counterparts, each of which so executed shall be deemed to be an original, and such counterparts shall together constitute but one in the same Agreement.

17.12 <u>Consents and Waivers.</u> No consent or waiver, express or implied, by any party hereto of the breach, default, or violation by any other party hereto of his obligations hereunder shall be deemed or construed to be a consent or waiver to, or of any other breach, default, or violation of, the same or any other obligations of such party hereunder. Failure on the part of any party hereto to complain of any act of any of the other parties or to declare any of the other parties hereto in default, irrespective or how long such failure continues, shall not constitute a waiver by such party of his rights hereunder.

18. AGREEMENT OF COMPANY.

18.1 In consideration of these premises, the Company agrees for itself and its successors and assigns as follows:

(a) Insofar as it is proper or required, it is bound by this Agreement;

(b) It will not transfer or reissue any of its capital stock in violation of this Agreement or without requiring proof of compliance with this Agreement; and

(c) All stock certificates issued to a Shareholder by the Company during the life of this Agreement shall be endorsed as stated herein.

19. <u>COUNTING OF DAYS.</u>   In computing the number of days for purposes of this Agreement, all days shall be counted, including Saturdays, Sundays, and holidays; provided, however, that if the final day of any time period falls on a Saturday, Sunday, or holiday, then the final day shall be deemed to be the next day which is not a Saturday, Sunday, or holiday.

20. <u>CONFIDENTIALITY.</u>   Each Shareholder recognizes and acknow-ledges that the Proprietary Information (as hereinafter defined) is a valuable, special, and unique asset of the business of the Company. As a result, both while such Shareholder owns Shares and thereafter, and in addition to any additional covenants to which such Shareholder may be bound by the terms of this Agreement, or otherwise, such Shareholder shall not, without the prior written consent of the Company, for any reason either directly or indirectly divulge to any third party or use for his own benefit, or for any purpose other than the exclusive benefit of the Company, any and all confidential proprietary, business, and technical information or trade secrets of the Company or of any subsidiary or affiliate of the Company (Proprietary Information) revealed, obtained, or developed from or on behalf of the Company while such Shareholder owned Stock. Such Proprietary Information shall include, but shall not be limited to, cost information, pricing information, marketing methods and plans, identities of customers and suppliers, the Company's relationship with actual or potential customers and the needs and requirements of any such actual or potential customers, and any other confidential information relating to the business of the Company; provided that nothing herein contained shall restrict a Shareholder's ability to make such disclosures as may be necessary or appropriate to the effective and efficient discharge of his duties as an executive and/or director of the Company or as such disclosures may be required by law; and further provided that nothing herein contained shall restrict a Shareholder from divulging information which is readily available to the general public so long as such information did not become available to the general public as a direct or indirect result of such Shareholder's breach of this Paragraph 20.

21. <u>PRESERVING S COMPANY ELECTION.</u>   The Shareholders acknowledge that the Company has elected to be taxed as a small business Company under Subchapter S of the Code, or such provisions of law as may now or hereafter be applicable to such election. The Shareholders further acknowledge their intention to continue such election, if made, unless all Shareholders agree that the Company shall terminate such election without delay and the Shareholders shall take necessary action to this end. The Company and each Shareholder agree to execute any documents and consents necessary and to cause them to be delivered in a timely manner to the Internal Revenue Service in order to allow the Company to continue to be taxed as an S Company under Internal Revenue Code, Sections 1361–1379, on an ongoing basis as may be required from year to year. Despite any provision of this Agreement to the contrary, no transfer of the Company's Shares shall be made by any Shareholder to any Company, partnership, or trust, or to any other transferee, whether voluntarily, involuntarily, or by operation of

law, if the effect of the transfer would be to cause the election to be terminated. In accordance with the foregoing, it shall be a condition of any transfer of shares by a Shareholder that the transferee agree in writing with the Company and the other Shareholders, prior to such transfer, to be bound by the provisions of this paragraph. In addition, the personal representative of a deceased Shareholder or transferee, or, if such Shareholder or transferee dies intestate, then his or her heirs, shall, immediately following the death of such Shareholder or transferee, file the appropriate document with the appropriate district director to continue such election, if made.

22. <u>ADDITIONAL STOCK, ADDITIONAL SHAREHOLDERS.</u> Each Shareholder agrees that any Shares acquired by him or her after the date hereof shall be subject to all the terms and conditions of this Agreement. The Company and each Shareholder agree to take appropriate action to require each person who, after the date hereof, purchases or otherwise acquires any Shares to agree to be bound by and comply with all the terms and conditions of this Agreement, such agreement to be evidenced by the execution by such person of a counterpart of this Agreement. A copy of this Agreement executed by any new Shareholder shall be delivered to the Secretary of the Company. Each person who becomes a Shareholder shall have his or her name and address and the number of Shares owned by him or her set forth on Schedule 1 attached hereto and made part hereof.

IN WITNESS WHEREOF, the Company has caused this Agreement to be signed by its duly authorized officers, and the Shareholders have executed this Agreement on the date set forth on page 1.

_____
William Williams, Shareholder

_____
John Johnson, Shareholder

Attest: ABC, INC.

_____   _____
John Johnson, Secretary   William Williams, President

EXHIBIT A

SHARES OWNED BY THE SHAREHOLDERS

Name of Shareholder	Number of Shares Owned
WILLIAM WILLIAMS	1,600 (80%)
JOHN JOHNSON	400 (20%)

EXHIBIT B

For purposes of this Agreement, *purchase price* shall be defined as the sum of the Earnings Before Interest, Taxes, Depreciation, and Amortization (EBITDA) for the last three (3) years most recent to the subject stock transaction, within the scope of this Agreement, as reported in the Company's financial statements, divided by three (3), to arrive at the average EBITDA. The average EBITDA is increased by a multiple of six (6) reduced by total interest-bearing debt as of the most recent financial statements.

EXHIBIT C

(Form of Installment Promissory Note)

INSTALLMENT PROMISSORY NOTE

_____ (Date)

FOR VALUE RECEIVED, the undersigned promises to pay, to the order of

_____

_____

(the transferring Shareholder, the transferee, or estate of the deceased Share-holder) _____ the principal sum of $_____
(deferred portion of the purchase price) with interest at a rate equal to the prime rate of interest charged to ABC, Inc., (the Company) by its lead commercial bank adjusted annually (on January 1 of each year) from the date hereof on any principal sum balance from time to time unpaid. The principal sum of this Note shall be paid in forty (40) equal quarterly installments, the first installment to be payable at the end of three (3) months from the date hereof and the remaining installments at the end of each succeeding three-month period (quarter) thereafter until the principal sum of this Note shall have been paid. Interest accruing from time to time of the principal sum shall be paid at the times above provided for payments of installments of the principal sum. Payments of principal sum and interest shall be made at the place which the holder of this Note from time to time shall direct in writing. Upon a default by the undersigned to make any payment of principal or interest due hereunder and continuing for thirty (30) days after written notice is given by the holder hereof to cure the same, then at the option of the holder of this Note, all unpaid installments of principal and accrued interest due shall become immediately due and payable.

At the option of the undersigned, all or any portion of the unpaid principal sum and accrued interest on this Note may be prepaid without premium or penalty, the amount of the prepayment to be applied first to accrued interest and the remainder to such unpaid principal installments as the undersigned shall designate in a written prepayment notice delivered to the holder of this note concurrently with the making of the prepayment.

In the event that the Company sells or otherwise disposes of all or substantially all of its assets; is merged into, consolidated, or otherwise acquired by another Company; ceases doing business as a going concern; makes an assignment for the benefit of creditors; files a voluntary petition in bankruptcy or a petition seeking for itself any reorganization, arrangement, composition, liquidation, dissolution, or similar arrangement under any present or future state or federal law or regulation or has filed against it a petition for any such proceeding; or there is appointed a trustee, receiver, or a liquidator of the Company or all or any substantial part of its assets or properties; or the Shareholders of the Company take action to dissolve or liquidate the Company, then the principal balance of this Note and any interest accrued thereon may at the option of the holder be accelerated and made immediately due and payable upon delivery to the maker or written notice of acceleration.

[Form of supplementary paragraph to be inserted if the maker is a Shareholder]

The undersigned hereby transfers, pledges, and delivers to the payee the following Shares of stock of the Company, subject to the terms of the Shareholders Agreement dated _____, as collateral security for the payment of this Note.

[Insert description of certificates which are to be pledged by the maker of the note]

And the undersigned hereby gives the payee, or the holder hereof, authority to sell, assign, and deliver said certificates, or any part thereof, or any substitutes thereof, and all additions thereto, on the default of this Note, or any time thereafter, at public or private sale without advertising the same, or demanding payment or giving notice to the undersigned, and, at such sale or sales, the payee or any holder hereof may become the purchaser, free from any right of redemption when public sale is made or when sale is made at any broker's board. After deducting all costs and expenses, including reasonable attorney's fees, from the proceeds of any such sale, the residue shall be applied to the payment of the principal and interest due on this Note, returning the overplus to the undersigned; and in case the proceeds of such sale or sales do not cover the principal sum, interest, and expenses, the undersigned engages to pay the deficiency forthwith after such sale or sales, with legal interest.

So long as the undersigned is not in default in the payment of any sums due under this Promissory Note, the undersigned shall have the right to vote all certificates of stock pledged to the payee hereunder.

EXHIBIT D

GUARANTEE

The undersigned, _____, does hereby guarantee payment when due by _____ (the Company) of each installment of principal and interest due on its Promissory Note, dated _____, which is payable to the order of _____ in the principal sum of $_____. Upon default by the Company to make any of the principal or interest payments due on said Note for a period of thirty (30) days or more, the undersigned agrees that the holder of said Note may, without seeking to collect any such due amounts from the Company, demand and receive payment of all principal and interest due under the Note from the undersigned.

The undersigned hereby transfers, pledges, and delivers to _____ hereinafter referred to as the Payee, the following Shares of Stock of the Company, subject to the terms of the Shareholders Agreement dated _____, as collateral security for the discharge of the guarantee herein made:

[Insert description of Shares, which are to be pledged by guarantor]

And the undersigned hereby gives the Payee authority to sell, assign, and deliver all certificates, or any part thereof, or any substitutes therefore, and all additions thereto, upon this guarantee becoming effective, or at any time thereafter, at public or private sale without advertising the same, or demanding payment under this guarantee or giving notice to the undersigned, and at such sale or sales the Payee may become the purchaser, free from any right of redemption when public sale is made or when sale is made at any broker's board and after deducting all costs and expenses, including attorney's fees, from the proceeds of any such sale, the residue shall be applied to the payment of the amount due on this guarantee, returning the overplus to the undersigned, and, in case the proceeds of such sale or sales shall not cover the amount of this guarantee and the aforesaid costs and expenses, the undersigned engages to pay the deficiency forthwith after such sale or sales with legal interest.

If the Note which is the subject of this guarantee lawfully passes to a holder other than the Payee, the terms of this guarantee shall accrue to the benefit of such other holder without the necessity of the Payee's rights under this guarantee being formally assigned to such holder.

So long as the Company is not in default in the performance of its obligations under said Promissory Note, or so long as the undersigned is not in default in the performance of his or her obligations under this guarantee, the undersigned shall have the right to vote the stock pledged as security for the discharge of this guarantee.

DATED _____

_____
Guaranteeing Shareholder

CONSENT OF SPOUSE OF WILLIAM WILLIAMS

I, WANDA WILLIAMS, acknowledge that I have read the foregoing Stock Purchase Agreement and that I know of its contents. I am aware that by its provisions my spouse agrees to sell all his Shares of the Company, including my equitable property interest in them, on the occurrence of certain events. I hereby consent to the sale, approve of the provisions of the Agreement, and agree that those Shares and my interest in them are subject to the provisions of the Agreement and that I will take no action at any time to hinder operation of the Stock Purchase Agreement on those Shares or my interest in them.

_____

Effective: _____ (date)

CONSENT OF SPOUSE OF JOHN JOHNSON

I, Johanna Johnson, acknowledge that I have read the foregoing Stock Purchase Agreement and that I know of its contents. I am aware that by its provisions my spouse agrees to sell all his Shares of the Company, including my equitable property interest in them, on the occurrence of certain events. I hereby consent to the sale, approve of the provisions of the Agreement, and agree that those Shares and my interest in them are subject to the provisions of the Agreement and that I will take no action at any time to hinder operation of the Stock Purchase Agreement on those Shares or my interest in them.

_____

Effective: _____ (date)

MISSION STATEMENT OF ABC PRODUCTIONS

The mission of ABC Productions is to provide valuable consulting services to event companies that cannot be obtained elsewhere. With a mix of event and legal knowledge, we provide a unique viewpoint and knowledge base that works to the benefit of the clients. Our services will include legal checkups in numerous areas, sales, and sales management reviews; business planning; marketing plans and strategic thought processes.

Our goal is to market to a limited number of companies and to take on as clients a manageable number that can afford the services and have the need for them, thus deriving benefit and value for their expenditure.

A book, magazine articles, speaking engagements, and direct marketing will support this goal.

SUBCONTRACTOR AGREEMENT

Dear _____ :

This letter will serve as an agreement between <u>EVENTCO</u> and you, VENDOR, INC., with regard to work that we are requesting you to perform on our behalf. We ask that you sign and return a copy to us (by mail or fax) indicating your acceptance of the terms contained herein. These terms will be incorporated into the actual contract for services between our companies. The signing of this agreement is a requirement of our doing business together.

Each and every term of this agreement is important to EVENTCO and should be considered as substantial.

It is our desire to maintain our personal relationship with our client, and accordingly we wish to maintain total and strict control of any and all contact with our client, our client's client, or representatives of either who may appear on-site or at meetings which you might be asked to attend as a representative of EVENTCO.

Without the specific approval of an EVENTCO officer, manager, or salesperson/producer on-site:

1. You and your employees will have no direct contact with our client, and if approached or questioned on the event site by the client or the client's representative, you will defer all inquiries to the EVENTCO person in charge at the site.

2. You and your employees will carry no business cards with your company name, and will, if requested, carry ours. Any inquiries or discussions of future business shall be referred to the EVENTCO person on-site.

3. You and your employees will wear no clothing (T-shirts, hats, etc.) identifying your company, and, if requested by us, will wear EVENTCO clothing.

4. You will not discuss your charges for services rendered on this event with any other party on the event site.

5. Unless you receive a specific written release from EVENTCO, you will not submit a bid directly to our client or our client's client for work on this event or any other event which EVENTCO would have a reasonable likelihood of producing within the next two years.

6. You will not identify yourself as a representative of any company other than EVENTCO.

7. You will not offer yourself or your services or those of any other party to any entity with whom you come in contact while working for EVENTCO.

8. While working for EVENTCO, you will be held to the same safety, health, dress, controlled substance, ethical, and moral standards as EVENTCO employees, and will be subject to all applicable EVENTCO policies and procedures, as well as those of the client or the venue in which you will be working. Attached are the relevant pages of the EVENTCO manual to which you must abide, as well as the rules of the facility.

9. With reference to Section 8 above, it is forbidden for any individual provided by you for an EVENTCO project to use or be under the influence of alcohol or controlled substances at any time while working for EVENTCO on the clock. Any person found to be in violation of this shall be banned from the job site and denied compensation. Further, any individual driving on behalf of EVENTCO must meet the NHSA standards with regard to drugs and alcohol in their systems.

10. Appropriate dress will be required on-site. During installation, rehearsal, and strike, all workers shall wear polo shirts or T-shirts. T-shirts must not have any language, pictures, or symbols which could be deemed offensive, politically controversial, sexist, or racist. For show call, any technicians should be dressed, as requested by EVENTCO, in theater blacks, suit, or tuxedo.

Last, you must maintain on file with us a current Certificate of Insurance showing the existence of liability and workers' compensation insurance.

All of the above terms are material to this agreement, and as such are not waivable. The parties recognize that breach of these terms could cause substantial monetary damage to EVENTCO. EVENTCO may enforce this agreement in either law or equity.

EVENTCO takes the work it does for its clients very seriously and expects its vendors to do so as well. Thank you for your cooperation, and we look forward to working with you on this event and others in the future.

Sincerely,

EVENTCO   Vendor

By: _____   By: _____

Date: _____   Date: _____

HIRE LETTER

_____ (date)

Mr. John Employee
100 Main Street
Philadelphia, PA
Dear John:

We are pleased to offer you a position with EVENTCO as an event producer and salesperson. A complete written job description of your position is attached to your copy of this agreement so that your duties will be clear to you.

As was made clear to you during your interview period, we are a small company in which it is imperative that everyone be able to function together as a team. Mutual respect and cooperation are required of our employees. We anticipate that this will be no problem for you.

We will treat the first sixty (60) days of your employment as a probationary period in order to determine whether there is a good fit between your skills and personality and those that are needed by EVENTCO. We have every hope that you can fulfill the responsibilities of the position, but the 60-day period will give you and us an opportunity to evaluate how well the relationship is working. It is crucial that you be punctual and that your attendance be exemplary during this period.

You are being hired at a salary of $75,000 per year. For this salary, you are expected to produce sales of $750,000. A commission structure has been established for all producers and salespeople in the company, and a copy of that, setting forth commission on several increased levels of sales, is attached to your copy of this letter.

In addition to the job description, we are providing you with the office policy and procedures manual. We request that you sign the form in the manual, indicating that you have received it, and return it to us immediately for inclusion in your personnel file. We will also, in the near future, entrust you with a key and alarm code. It would be our desire to reward good work by you, but there have been no specific promises made with regard to promotion or future duties. Advancement within the company will be a function of several factors, including performance on your part.

We ask that you sign the company's Confidentiality Agreement with regard to those matters that we deem to be trade secrets or of crucial importance to us, and your agreement to do so should be considered a condition of being hired.

I would like to make a few priorities clear from the outset to avoid later misunderstandings. It is important to us that there be no excessive absenteeism. We need someone we can count on day in and day out, and while we try to be sympathetic to any unusual personal situations, we cannot tolerate irregular attendance at work. As you will see in the Policy Manual, tardiness is unacceptable as well. This includes office days, as well as meetings with clients, vendors, and others. In our company, being on time is a value we treat as important.

We are a **NONSMOKING** office. No smoking is allowed throughout the office space. If you smoke, you may do so only outside and only at intervals deemed reasonable so as not to adversely affect productivity. We also have a strict policy against the use of drugs (other than those legally prescribed) or alcohol on the job or in a manner that job performance is affected. Breach of this rule is cause for immediate dismissal.

While we are a somewhat casual office in a casual industry, there should be no mistake about the fact that we are a business doing business at all times. Your dress and your manner should at all times reflect this and should be appropriate for all occasions.

In your position, you will be dealing firsthand with our clients, and it is important that at all times this experience be a pleasant one for them.

Kindly sign both copies of this letter. By so doing, you are indicating that you have read it, that you understand it, and that you agree to all contained herein. This letter should not be viewed as an employment contract, but rather as a letter of understanding.

We look forward to working with you. Welcome aboard!

Sincerely,

President

_____

Employee

INDEPENDENT CONTRACTOR AGREEMENT

This Agreement is made this _____ day of August, 2003, between EVENTCO (Client) and VENDOR, INC. (Independent Contractor).

For good and valuable consideration, the receipt and sufficiency of which is hereby acknowledged, and intending to be legally bound hereby, Client and Independent Contractor agree as follows:

1. Independent Contractor is in fact an independent contractor and not an employee, agent, or legal representative of Client. At no time shall Independent Contractor represent, either directly or indirectly an employee, agent, partner, or joint venture relationship with Client, nor shall any employee or agent of Independent Contractor do so.

2. Independent Contractor shall be solely responsible for the payment of withholding taxes, FICA, state or local taxes, social security, and unemployment taxes for Independent Contractor and its employees. Independent Contractor agrees that none of its employees are entitled to unemployment benefits in the event this Agreement terminates in any manner, or to workers' compensation benefits in the event of injury during the performance of this contract. Independent Contractor agrees to provide Workers' Compensation insurance for its employees and to hold harmless and indemnify Client for any and all claims arising out of any injury, disability, or death of Independent Contractor employees while performing obligations under this Agreement, including travel to and from the workplace. Client will not withhold any taxes or prepare W-2 forms for Independent Contractor's employees, but will provide Independent Contractor with a Form 1099, if required by law.

3. Independent Contractor may, at Independent Contractor's own expense, employ such employees or agents as are necessary to fulfill the obligations under this Agreement. They will remain solely and exclusively the employees and agents of Independent Contractor, subject to its direction, control, and supervision.

4. Independent Contractor acknowledges that its employees are not entitled to any employee benefits of any kind from Client.

5. Independent Contractor will provide the services of [here the services should be spelled out.]

6. Independent Contractor acknowledges that it has received full information showing the areas where the work is to be performed and that, from prior

working arrangements with Client, it has complete familiarity with the nature and style of work to be performed. Independent Contractor acknowledges working on assignments such as this in the past and has experience with this type of work. Independent Contractor acknowledges that small design changes may take place on-site, and so long as they do not involve redoing work already completed, they shall be done within the contract price.

7. The fee to be paid by Client to Independent Contractor is $_____. Payments will be made as follows: A 50 percent deposit in the amount of $_____ will be paid upon the signing of the Agreement. The balance will be paid within 30 days of the completion of all work.

8. Independent Contractor will be financially responsible, within its fee, for the van(s) transporting its workers the 500 miles to the event site and for paying for all hotel rooms and related charges, as well as per diems for its employees during the stay out of town. Client is not responsible for any expenses other than those set forth in this Agreement and will not reimburse Independent Contractor for supplies, equipment, or operating costs, nor will these expenses be defrayed in any way by Client. Independent Contractor has set its fee, and Client does not guarantee to Independent Contractor that the fee derived from this event will exceed Independent Contractor's costs.

9. Independent Contractor shall indemnify and hold harmless Client, its officers, directors, agents, and employees from and against any and all claims, actions, losses, damages, expenses, and all other liabilities arising out of or resulting from the acts or omissions of Independent Contractor, its agents, employees, or subcontractors.

10. Client wishes to maintain its direct relationship with its clients on this event, and Independent Contractor understands and accepts the importance of this and accordingly agrees to the following:
    a. Independent Contractor will have limited direct contact with Client's clients and, if approached or questioned on-site, will refer all inquiries to Client.
    b. Independent Contractor and its employees will neither carry nor distribute business cards other than Client's on the event site.
    c. Independent Contractor will not discuss the charges for services rendered on this job site with any party.
    d. Independent Contractor will not smoke or drink any alcoholic beverages or use or allow any illegal drug use on this event site at any time prior to, during, or after this event.
    e. Independent Contractor will direct its employees that foul language, cursing, racial, ethnic, religious, and sexual slurs of any kind are strictly

forbidden, as is any clothing bearing slogans which might be inter-preted as such.

f. Client shall have the right to instruct Independent Contractor to remove any employee or agent from the job site if in violation of items a through e above, with Independent Contractor's fee being adjusted accordingly.

IN WITNESS WHEREOF, the parties hereto have executed this Agreement by their authorized representatives and are bound hereby, this _____day of August, 2003.

(CLIENT)   **(INDEPENDENT CONTRACTOR)**

By:_____   By:_____

CONFIDENTIALITY AGREEMENT

This Agreement is made this 4th day of August, 2003, by and between **EVENTCO, INC.** (the Company) and **JOHN Q. EMPLOYEE** (the Undersigned).

The Company is engaged in the business of providing event production services, including, but not limited to, lighting and electrical services, special effects, audio services, decor, and special events consulting to a wide variety of clients within the private social, charity and cause, corporate, and sports markets. The Company has expended substantial dollars and time developing marketing and sales programs to attract said clients, as well as special equipment, designs, and production processes to use in the performance of its work for these clients.

The Company desires to protect that which it has developed and will continue to develop in order to maintain and enhance its competitive position in the marketplace. It can best do so by keeping all information it deems important secret and confidential.

Recognizing that the success of the Company depends, in part, on the protection of trade secrets, trademarks, copyrights, innovations, processes, products, programs, and information held or utilized by the Company, and recognizing that during the Undersigned's employment he may have access or contribute to such matters, and in consideration of his employment by the Company, and intending to be legally bound by the Agreement, the Undersigned agrees to the following:

1. Without the prior written consent of an officer of the Company, he will not disclose or use for his direct or indirect benefit or the direct or indirect benefit of a third party, and he will use his best efforts to maintain, both during and after his employment, the confidentiality of all confidential information that he acquires because of his employment with the Company. In general, *confidential information* means any information that the Company treats as confidential, including, but not limited to, any information relating to business procedures, business studies, client lists, databases, employee lists (both permanent and part-time), sales, marketing, public relations and advertising campaigns, strategies or plans, financial information, either prepared by or for the Company, in-house manuals, any information relating to research, processes, inventions, products, methods, software, and documentation, and any other materials that have not been made available to the general public. Failure to mark any of the confidential information as confidential or proprietary will not affect its status as confidential information under the terms of this Agreement.

2. During and after his employment, the Undersigned will not remove from the Company's offices or premises any documents, records, notebooks, files, corre-

spondence, reports, memoranda, computer tapes, computer disks, or similar materials of or containing information of the type identified in the preceding paragraph, or other materials or property of the Company of any other kind, unless necessary in accordance with his duties and responsibilities of employment by the Company. In the event that he removes such materials or property, he will return such property to their proper files or places of safekeeping as promptly as possible after the removal will have served its specific purpose. Except as may be necessary in the discharge of his assigned duties, the Undersigned will not make, retain, remove, or distribute any copies of any of the foregoing for any reason whatsoever, and he will not divulge to any third person the nature or contents of any of the foregoing or of any other oral or written information.

Upon the termination of his employment with the Company, he will leave with or return to the Company all originals and copies of the foregoing then in his possession, whether prepared by him or others. This includes all photographs, videotapes, photodiscs, CDs, DVDs, and computer storage and enhancement of same, prepared by and for the Company.

3. The Undersigned's exposure to any of the aforementioned shall not be constructed as granting him a license or any other such right with respect to such information. Further, any work in which the Undersigned is or will be involved during his employment with the Company, including any and all writings, documents, inventions, discoveries, plans, client lists, memoranda, designs, specifications, models, diagrams, light plots, renderings, CAD layouts, budgets, spreadsheets, financial statements, and/or projections (whether reduced to written form or not) that he makes, conceives, develops, or designs, either solely or jointly with any other person, at any time during the term of his employment and whether upon the suggestion of the Company or otherwise, that relate to or are useful in any way in connection with any business now or hereafter carried on by the Company (collectively, "Intellectual Work Product") will be the sole and exclusive property of the Company. He acknowledges that all Intellectual Work Product that is copyrightable will be considered a work made for hire under United States Copyright Law.

4. During the period of his employment by the Company, the Undersigned will not, directly or indirectly, perform any services within the scope of or similar to the services performed by him on behalf of the Company, for or on behalf of any other party, without the express written consent of an officer of the Company.

5. For the two (2) year period immediately following the termination of the Undersigned's employment with the Company, the Undersigned will not directly or indirectly, contact, solicit, call on, or otherwise deal in any way with any client with whom the Company shall have dealt at any time during or prior to the performance

of his services to the Company, for a purpose which is competitive with the business of the Company, or influence or attempt to influence any client, vendor, or contractor of the Company to terminate or modify any written or oral agreement or course of dealing with the Company.

6. For the two (2) year period immediately following the termination of his employment with the Company, the Undersigned will not, directly or indirectly, employ, engage, or retain, or arrange to have any other person or entity employ, engage, or retain any person who is an employee, contractor, consultant, or agent of the Company or shall have been employed, engaged, or retained by the Company as an employee, contractor, consultant, or agent at any time during the one (1) year period preceding the date upon which his employment with the Company is terminated. Additionally, the Undersigned will not, directly or indirectly, influence or attempt to influence any such person to terminate or modify his or her employment arrangement or engagement with the Company.

7. The Undersigned is not subject to any other agreement that he will violate by signing this Agreement or which prevents him from disclosing confidential information. The Undersigned agrees to disclose the terms of this Agreement to any employer or potential employer that may seek to employ or does employ him during the effective period of this Agreement.

8. This Agreement constitutes the complete agreement on the subject matter contained herein between the Undersigned and the Company, and supersedes any and all prior written or oral agreements relating to the subject matter of this Agreement. This Agreement may not be amended or modified except in writing and will be governed by the laws of the Commonwealth of Pennsylvania without regard to conflicts of law principles. If any provision or portion of any provision of this Agreement shall be determined to be void, invalid, or unenforceable for any reason, the validity and enforceability of the remaining provisions or portions of provisions will not be affected. The Company may assign this Agreement to, and this Agreement will bind and inure to the benefit of, any parent, subsidiary, affiliate, or successor of the Company. The Undersigned acknowledges that this Agreement is not assignable by him.

9. The Undersigned agrees that any suit, action, or other legal proceeding arising out of or relating to this Agreement, including but not limited to, any action commenced by the Company for preliminary or permanent injunctive or other equitable relief, will be instituted in the United States District Court for the Eastern District of Pennsylvania, or if such court does not have or will not accept jurisdiction, in any court of general jurisdiction in Montgomery County, Pennsylvania, and the Undersigned consents and submits to the personal and exclusive jurisdiction of such courts in any such suit, action, or proceeding. This provision shall not prevent the Company from seeking to enforce this Agreement in any other court of competent

jurisdiction. The Undersigned agrees that service of process upon him may be effected by certified mail or by any other means permitted by law, and he waives any objection which he may have to the laying of venue of any such suit, action, or proceeding in any such court and any claim or defense of inconvenient forum. If an action at law or in equity is necessary to enforce or interpret the terms of this Agreement, the prevailing party shall be entitled to recover, in addition to any other relief, reasonable attorneys' fees, costs, and disbursements.

10. The Undersigned acknowledges that it is impossible to measure fully, in money, the injury that will be caused to the Company in the event of a breach or threatened breach of this Agreement, and he waives the claim or defense that the Company has an adequate remedy at law. The Undersigned will not, in any action or proceeding to enforce the provisions of this Agreement, assert the claim or defense that such a remedy at law exists. The Company will be entitled to injunctive relief to enforce the provisions of this Agreement, without prejudice to any other remedy the Company may have at law or in equity.

11. The Undersigned acknowledges that this Agreement does not constitute a right to continued employment, and his employment by the Company may be terminated by the Company at any time, with or without cause.

COMPANY

BY_____   _____
                President

_____   _____
Date   Date

PROPRIETARY COVER LETTER

August 1, 2003

Ms. Jane Smith
Event Planners of America
500 Main Street
Anycity, USA

Dear Ms. Smith:

Enclosed please find our creative proposal for the production of the Technology Corporation's annual employee awards program to take place at the Metropolis Hotel on December 1, 2004. The proposal includes an overall thematic treatment that includes room decor, table decor, stage sets, video, lighting design, entertainment, and scripting of the event. We have included computer-generated floor plans and elevations, lighting plots, and a rough script for the evening. We have also attached a production schedule for your perusal. It is our practice to break down the overall design into meaningful segments so that you can look at them individually and see what they cost to produce. We hope that this meets with your approval. If the design we presented exceeds your budget, we would suggest that we have further discussions to determine where your priorities lie, so that we can then allocate the available dollars in the most meaningful manner.

This event is a most unique one and the creative designs that we have prepared for you are totally custom and individual in nature. We have spent a significant amount of time and creative effort preparing this plan in order to make the event space look as much like your vision of it as possible. We do feel that it provides you with all that you have requested.

In that we are one of several companies that are submitting proposals for this event, we recognize that there is a possibility that you will choose to work with someone other than us. We are desirous of protecting the creative effort that has gone into the preparation of our proposal. You have come to us because of our design abilities and creativity and, accordingly, we ask that you recognize our rights in our ideas. Thus, please take note of the following paragraph which sets forth our respective rights to those ideas.

This proposal is not deemed to be "work for hire," and all rights in each creative idea presented therein are reserved by EVENTCO, Inc. Should you accept the proposal, you will be licensed to use the ideas contained in it on this particular event only. Should you, for any reason, decide not to accept this proposal, ownership of the ideas remains with EVENTCO, Inc., and they cannot be used by you or any other supplier without our express written permission and without compensation to EVENTCO, Inc., for the creative effort involved. Under no circumstances may the creative ideas contained herein be used as the basis for a bid package or set of specs to be submitted to other suppliers to bid on this or other events. Further, EVENTCO, Inc., confers no authority to you to give any other party any rights in these ideas.

The above merely offers reasonable protection to us and is presented solely for the purpose of ascertaining that we receive fair compensation for the designs we have devised. We are sure that you can understand that.

By opening the proposal package and reviewing it, you signify your acceptance of the terms set forth in this letter. We hope that you find our proposal to be to your satisfaction and that we will have the opportunity to work with you on this project. If you have any questions or comments, please feel free to call us and we will make every effort to provide you with the information you need. Thank you for the opportunity to provide you with a proposal.

Sincerely,

EVENTCO, Inc.

AGREEMENT FOR PHOTOGRAPHIC SERVICES

This Agreement, this _____ day of _____, 2003, shall be the basis for the ongoing legal relationship between EVENTCO, Inc. (hereinafter referred to as Client), and _____ (hereinafter referred to as Photographer). Both parties recognize this as a blanket Agreement, which shall apply to all engagements of Photographer by Client, unless otherwise specified in writing, and both parties agree to be legally bound by the terms set forth below.

1. When Client hires Photographer to shoot an event on its behalf, it does so with the understanding that Photographer has been engaged to shoot solely for Client. Photographer may not solicit other participants in the event without the express written consent of Jim Johnson, President. Further, if Client has brought Photographer into the event, Photographer may not accept a request by other participants in the event to shoot it for them without the express consent of Jim Johnson, President. Further, Client will, upon granting any such requests, receive a financial benefit for doing so, equal to the Photographer's shooting fee as charged to Client. Further, if Client does give consent to Photographer to shoot for others, those others shall receive prints of their work only, and not all of the photographs commissioned by Client.

2. When the Photographer is shooting for Client, the negatives or any prints, slides, photodiscs, or other images created therefrom can be used for the purposes of Client only. Neither the facility in which the event is shot nor any of the event participants can have access to negatives or prints without Jim Johnson's express written permission. Further, the Photographer cannot use the images for Photographer's own marketing purposes, or for the benefit of any other clients, without Client's express written permission. If Photographer receives any such permission, all prints shall have stamped on them "Courtesy of EVENTCO, Inc." Under no circumstances shall Photographer grant any party the right to use the images commissioned by Client for any purpose without the express written permission of EVENTCO, Inc.

3. When Photographer is commissioned jointly by Client and one or more other parties, Photographer must still abide by all conditions set forth in Paragraphs 1 and 2 above.

4. On Client's job site, Photographer may not pass out cards or solicit business from anyone there without Client's express permission. If asked for a card, Photographer will refer to Client's representative on site.

5. All negatives are the property of Client, even if, by Client's choice, they remain in the possession of Photographer. Photographer will remit them to Client

immediately, if requested to do so, or will create a duplicate set of negatives for Client, immediately upon request by Client.

6. Photographer will be hired by Purchase Order, with all terms of the engagement being included on the Purchase Order. As Purchase Orders are matched to Photographer's invoices before payment, any difference between the Purchase Order and invoice will delay payment. Unless changes are made with prior written approval of EVENTCO, Inc., Client will be responsible for payment of the amount in the Purchase Order only.

7. Photographer will create a rate sheet to which Client can refer to figure the cost of photography for any given event. The rate sheet will enumerate shooting fees for each photographer and/or assistant; film cost; travel cost; print cost; enlargement cost; custom printing expense; color copy expense; the cost of making slides from negatives; and any other relevant expenses.

8. Photographer will submit an invoice with the prints/proofs, which will be payable within 30 days from its receipt.

9. Client and Photographer desire a mutually amicable and profitable relationship. Photographer desires to provide client with a high level of service for a fair price; Client desires to have its work documented by Photographer and to develop a library of images that it can use to sell and market its services. Further, Client hopes to provide Photographer with orders for enlargements, reprints, etc., and to receive same in a timely manner and at a fair price.

10. Should Photographer's film be lost, damaged, or have anything happen to it that keeps Photographer from providing Client with the images contracted for, Client shall have no liability to Photographer for any film, shooting, or travel expense.

11. At all times, Photographer is acting as an independent contractor, and under no circumstances is Photographer to be deemed an employee of Client for any purpose. Photographer acknowledges full responsibility for maintaining liability, workers' compensation, and any other insurance appropriate for Photographer's business. Should Photographer or one of Photographer's employees or agents be injured or injure others while on-site shooting for Client, Photographer assumes all responsibility for said damages and agrees to indemnify and hold Client harmless.

12. Photographer is at all times responsible for any equipment and supplies brought onto Client's site. Client will have no responsibility for any equipment that is damaged, stolen, or lost.

13. Should the relationship between Client and Photographer terminate for any reason, Photographer shall immediately forward to Client all negatives, slides, proofs, and prints of events that Photographer has shot on Client's behalf, at no charge. While Photographer has an artistic interest in the photographic images, it does not have an ownership interest, and they remain at all times the property of Client.

14. The terms set forth above shall be legally binding on Client and Photographer for any work that Photographer performs for Client. Failure to attach these terms to any individual contract or Purchase Order shall in no way constitute a waiver of any of these terms.

_____   _____

Photographer   EVENTCO

_____   _____

Date   Date

RENTAL AGREEMENT

TERMS AND CONDITIONS

ABC, Inc., doing business as ABC (Lessor) hereby agrees to provide to Client (Lessee) the equipment described on the face of this Rental Agreement, in accordance with the following terms and conditions.

1. The equipment rented under this Agreement is intended to be operated by professionals trained and experienced in the use of such equipment and shall be used in a manner consistent with the purpose for which it was designed. The equipment shall at all times be and remain the sole exclusive property of Lessor. Lessee shall have the right to use the equipment only in accordance with the terms of this Agreement. Lessor shall have the right to display notice of its ownership of the equipment by display of an identifying stencil, plate, or other marking, and Lessee agrees that it will not remove or cover such markings without the written permission of Lessor. It is expressly intended and agreed that the equipment shall be personal property even though it might be affixed or attached to real estate.

2. Equipment shall be returned within the rental period set forth on the face of this Agreement. Any equipment not returned within the specified period in the condition in which it was rented shall be subject to additional rental charges until such equipment is returned.

3. All equipment shall be returned in the condition in which it was rented, meaning that all cables should be coiled in an orderly fashion, all fixtures returned in road cases, etc. Any additional time required by Lessor to return equipment to this condition shall be billable to Lessee, and Lessee agrees to pay such additional charges.

4. Lessee assumes all responsibility for loss or damage to the equipment during the period from the delivery of the equipment to its subsequent return (the *use period*). Lessee will pay for all equipment lost and/or damaged in an amount equal to the replacement cost of the equipment. Lessee assumes all risks and liability for the use and operation of the equipment for personal injuries and property damage arising from or incidental thereto. Lessee shall protect, defend, and indemnify Lessor and hold Lessor harmless, from and against all losses, damages, injuries, claims, demands, and expenses, including legal expenses, of whatsoever nature, arising out of the use, condition, or operation of the equipment during the term of this Agreement. Lessee shall assume defense of any suits or other legal proceedings brought to enforce all such losses, damages, injuries, claims, demands, and expenses, and shall pay

judgments entered in any such suit or suits or other legal proceedings. The indemnities and assumptions of liabilities and obligations herein provided for shall continue with full force and effect, notwithstanding the termination of this Agreement, whether by expiration of time, by operation of law, or otherwise.

5. Lessee represents and warrants that Lessee has insurance against liability for injury to persons and property in amounts equal to or in excess of a combined single limit of $1,000,000 and that Lessee maintains insurance against loss or damage to the equipment in an amount equal to or in excess of $1,000,000.

6. Lessor shall at all times, after prompt and responsible notice to Lessee have the right to enter any premises where the equipment may be located for purposes of inspecting it. Lessee shall make no alterations whatsoever in the equipment without having obtained the prior written permission of Lessor.

7. In the event that the Lessee or Lessor changes any of the arrangements relating to the services to be performed or to equipment to be provided, Lessor shall have the right to add or subtract such equipment, service, or servicemen as in its sole discretion may be necessary to maintain the safety and quality of the work to be performed. Lessee shall pay for any additional equipment, service, or servicemen (or shall receive credit for any reduction thereof) at Lessor's customary charge therefor. No such modification may occur without the written approval of Lessor. Lessor shall not be responsible for any damages or for disruption of Lessee's event should any other party tamper with, abuse, or damage Lessor's equipment, plug into any of the Lessor's circuits, or in any way affect electrical distribution, causing overload, blown fuses, or tripped circuit breakers, causing lights and other electrically operated equipment to cease functioning.

8. Lessee shall pay the contract price, plus such additions thereto as may be agreed upon or chargeable pursuant to the terms hereof within the period specified herein. If the balance due is not paid at that time, an amount equal to 1.5 percent (18 percent annually) of the outstanding balance due shall be charged every month thereafter until final payment is made by Lessee. In the event that Lessee has directed that Lessor's charges hereunder be billed to another person or organization, and payment is not made by such person or organization within the terms specified, Lessee shall, promptly upon receiving notice of nonpayment, pay such additional charges as may be added to the outstanding balance pursuant to the terms hereof.

9. The occurrence of any of the following events shall, at the option of Lessor, terminate this Agreement and Lessee's right to possession of the equipment provided: (a) the nonpayment by Lessee (b) the noncompliance by Lessee with any other term, covenant, or condition of this Agreement which is not cured

within reasonable time after notice thereof from Lessor (c) should any execution or other writ or process of law be issued in any action against the Lessee, whereby the said equipment might be taken or distrained, or if a proceeding in a bankruptcy, receivership, or insolvency shall be instituted by or against Lessee shall enter into any agreement or composition with creditors or if Lessor shall deem itself insecure.

10. Any person executing this Agreement on behalf of Lessee Corporation or organization warrants in his or her individual capacity that he or she is acting within the scope of his or her authority and that the Lessee Corporation, organization, or entity shall be bound thereby.

11. This Agreement shall be governed by and the construction and enforceability thereof shall be interpreted under the laws of the State of New York. For all purposes relevant hereto, the place of signing of this Agreement shall be New York, New York. The terms of this Agreement shall be binding upon the executors, administrators, successors, and assigns of the parties hereto. Lessee shall not assign this Agreement without the prior consent of Lessor.

12. Read the product instructions and labels and follow them. If you do not have a copy of the instructions request a copy from ABC.

13. Lessee warrants that he or she is trained in the proper use of the equipment and in the appropriate techniques for its installation, rigging, use, packing, and transportation. Proper training includes knowledge of all appropriate safety procedures, limitations of the equipment, inspection of the equipment, and risk management. If you are not competent in the use of a product, do not use it.

14. Lessee will use good judgment and will not exceed the limitations of the Lessee's skills or the equipment's capabilities.

15. Lessee will use adequate safety precautions and backup systems. Lessee will practice risk management at all times.

16. Acceptance of the rental signifies understanding and acceptance of all of the Rental Terms and Conditions.

_____   _____

Lessee   Date

JOB DESCRIPTION

Job Title: Account Executive
Reports To: General Manager
Prepared By: CEO
Prepared Date:

A. Summary

An Account Executive (AE) of the Company is primarily responsible for locating, cultivating, and bringing new business into the company, while at the same time nourishing and maintaining existing clients.

B. Essential duties and responsibilities

The primary duties and responsibilities of the position include:

1. Maintaining an understanding of current conditions in the special events market in which the AE is working, including but not limited to the conventions, trade shows, and special events coming into the AE's geographical area; the potential corporate, association, political, sports, and social prospects in the marketplace; and a strong knowledge of other special event vendors, including facilities, caterers, decor companies, florists, audiovisual companies, electrical services companies, meeting, event, and party planners, producers, lighting designers, technical directors, destination management companies, incentive travel companies, and any other individuals who might represent a source of business for the Company.
2. Developing relationships with the above individuals, and maintaining these relationships by calling on them on a regular basis.
3. Understanding the production needs of the above individuals and relating how our services can fulfill those needs.
4. Creating an interest in working with us.
5. Creating the opportunity for us to propose on the client's work.
6. Closing the sale.
7. Completing all internal paperwork responsibilities, including job costings, proposals, purchase orders, and any others.
8. Working with the client through preproduction and production.
9. Speaking with the client postproduction to make certain the client was happy with our services.
10. Approving the file for invoicing.
11. Following all procedures set forth in the *Sales Procedure Manual*.
12. Understanding the importance of building new business relationships as well as strengthening existing relationships.
13. Being on-site during an event load in (and show if the event merits it) to ensure that the client, our production staff, and other suppliers have the information, direction, and support from the Company that they should reasonably expect.

14. Serve as technical on-site manager/project manager on large projects as necessary.

C. Qualifications

The qualifications for this position include:

1. The ability to speak clearly and concisely in English using correct grammar and pronunciation.
2. The ability to read and write in English.
3. The ability to write correspondence, proposals, memoranda, and other written communications in a literate, understandable manner.
4. The ability to understand pricing, job costing, and other mathematical calculations that must be made on a regular basis.
5. An understanding of lighting, audio, electricity, and event production concepts.
6. An ability to relate to people, make them feel comfortable, and develop strong business relationships.
7. Organizational skills.
8. The ability to make quick decisions.
9. The ability to multitask.
10. Perseverance, follow-up.
11. A valid driver's license and the ability and willingness to drive to and from appointments and event sites.
12. Appropriate dress and grooming when meeting with clients and others, when attending events, and on other public occasions.
13. The ability to keep good records and files, to track expenses according to procedure, and to follow all Company policies and procedures.
14. The knowledge of and ability to use Microsoft Office programs.

D. Physical demands

The primary physical demands to perform essential job functions include:

1. The ability to drive a vehicle.
2. The ability to perform site inspections, many of which take place outside, in large public or private facilities

I acknowledge that I have received, read, and understand the job description of Account Executive as stated above. I further understand that the Company may alter, amend, or depart from any such job responsibility or procedure at any time and at its sole discretion.

_____

Name (Print)

_____

Signature/Date

**SALES PROCEDURE MANUAL
ABC PRODUCTIONS, EFFECTIVE SEPTEMBER 1, 2003**

**TO: ALL ACCOUNT EXECUTIVES
DATE:
FROM: VP SALES AND CEO
RE: SALES PROCEDURE MANUAL**

Attached is a copy of the Company *Sales Procedure Manual,* effective September 1, 2003. This copy supersedes all previous sales procedure manuals.

We encourage you to read this information and become familiar with the following policies and procedures. If you have any questions concerning this manual, please contact VP Sales or CEO.

To ensure that all Account Executives receive a complete copy of our sales procedure manual, we request that you print and sign your name and date a duplicate copy of the last page of this manual. THE SIGNED COPY MUST BE RETURNED TO CEO. There are thirty-two (32) pages to this manual.

CONTENTS

COMPANY DISCLAIMER

IT IS OUR HOPE THAT EACH EMPLOYEE WILL FIND THE COMPANY TO BE A FULFILLING PLACE TO WORK AND THAT THESE POLICIES AND PROCEDURES WILL ASSIST YOU. NEVERTHELESS, NOTHING CONTAINED IN THIS OR ANY OTHER MANUAL, OR ANY POLICY, WORK RULE, OR ORAL OR WRITTEN STATEMENT OF THE COMPANY REPRESENTS PROMISES OR CONSTITUTES A CONTRACT OF EMPLOYMENT. THE EMPLOYMENT RELATIONSHIP OF EACH ASSOCIATE REMAINS, AS IT ALWAYS HAS BEEN, *AT WILL,* WHICH MEANS IT MAY BE TERMINATED AT THE COMPANY'S OPTION OR THE ASSOCIATE'S OPTION AT ANY TIME FOR ANY REASON OR NO REASON, WITH OR WITHOUT PRIOR NOTICE.

THESE POLICIES AND PROCEDURES SET FORTH GUIDELINES WHICH ARE SUBJECT TO CHANGE BY THE COMPANY AT ITS DISCRETION WITHOUT PRIOR NOTICE AND WITHOUT APPROVAL OR CONSENT BY ASSOCIATES.

THIS POLICY STATEMENT SUPERSEDES AND REPLACES ALL PREVIOUS STATEMENTS AND OTHER RULES, PROCEDURES, AND POLICIES.

NO ONE HAS THE AUTHORITY TO MODIFY THIS POLICY EXCEPT THE COMPANY'S PRESIDENT WHEN DONE IN WRITING AND SIGNED.

INTRODUCTION

The Company is represented in the marketplace by our sales force. We put a face on the Company and establish the contacts that we hope will lead to long-standing client relationships. We at all times must distinguish ourselves from the other companies attempting to sell to the same pool of potential clients. We do that by establishing strategic partnerships with our clients, meaning that we base the relationship on a win-win proposition. From us they get a vendor that understands the entire event process, with particular emphasis on the client's goals and objectives for the event and how we can help achieve them. From us they get a vendor that cares about what they care about, that comes to their aid and assistance wherever they need us to make the event go well. From us they get a partner that holds up the technical end of the event, and beyond, if necessary. In return, we will get loyalty, trust, and more business. Customer retention is critical at the Company. "If we do not take care of the customer . . . someone else will!" Not only must Account Executives retain existing clients, but we must also **grow** the business that comes from them.

Account Executives at the Company are not simply order takers. While a certain amount of business will come to Account Executives via clients coming to us by word of mouth or referral, it is expected that the majority of business will come from going out and looking for it. We should always be searching for bigger and better business. Being aware of what is happening in the marketplace, networking, cold calling, working with marketing to cultivate leads, and other techniques are all part of being in sales. We provide high-quality services at premium fair prices. We offer value to our clients. We need to match our capabilities to our clients' needs, and we can only do that once we know what their needs are. The following represent the policies and procedures for Account Executives at the Company. They must be followed on all occasions, and by doing so we present ourselves in the best possible light.

I. PRESENTATION

A. Dress

1. On sales calls, at client meetings and during any other public appearances, our Account Executives are required to wear clothing consistent with the expectation of the client. Meetings involving corporate planners or executives should require dress equivalent to what they will wear

(e.g., suit or khakis and button-down shirts). **Under no circumstances should an Account Executive wear blue jeans, shorts, T-shirts, or overly casual clothes.**

2. All Account Executives are required to dress in a professional manner. Associates must wear slacks or skirts and a button-down or collared shirt when on a site inspection. When meeting with clients, all production associates must consult with the Account Executives in regard to attire.

3. On job sites, Account Executives should be dressed in a Company or appropriate shirt and appropriate pants or skirt.

4. While the Company has a casual atmosphere, there should be no mistake about the fact that we are a business conducting business at all times. At all times your attire should reflect this. If in the office and no appointments are scheduled, Account Executives may dress casually.

5. On all occasions, the Account Executive is a representative of the Company and must recognize that vendors, potential clients, and the public may form their opinion of the Company based on what they see.

B. Manner

1. Account Executives should at all times act in a polite, respectful manner to all with whom they come in contact.

2. Account Executives should be careful of their language at all times, and not speak obscenely or disrespectfully of clients or others in the presence of others.

3. Account Executives should at all times sell by speaking positively of the Company, not negatively of the competition.

4. Account Executives should always exhibit a high degree of ethical behavior, even when faced with a lack of ethics on the part of competitors or others.

5. Account Executives should always ascertain the rules of any facility in which we work, distribute them to the appropriate production managers for distribution to the crews, and make certain that we are obeying them on-site.

II. REQUIRED KNOWLEDGE

A. Technical

Our Account Executives are responsible for selling technical services such as lighting, audio, video, staging, power generation and distribution, and technical event management. Accordingly, they have to be knowledgeable enough to discuss these services with clients in a competent and confidence-building manner. If a scheduled meeting would seem to involve a need for technical knowledge beyond the Account Executive's knowledge, a production expert or another Account Executive must accompany the individual. This is an opportunity to show the depth and breadth of our expertise and our ability to service clients. We have the human resources at our fingertips, and we should use them to our best advantage. While having experience with event elements beyond technical services offered by the Company is helpful, Account Executives should avoid providing pipe and drape, decor, entertainment, and other such services under the Company moniker, as our event planner/producer clients may view this practice as competition.

1. <u>Lighting.</u> Our Account Executives must have a working knowledge of the qualities and capabilities of the fixtures that we maintain in inventory, an understanding of rigging and ground support systems, an understanding of basic electrical power; a basic understanding of generators, and an understanding of what effects can and cannot be accomplished within a given event space.

2. <u>Audio.</u> Our Account Executives must have a working knowledge of the qualities and capabilities of the audio components we maintain in our inventory and should exhibit an understanding of basic audio configurations, including what would be required for spoken word, entertainment, and major act.

3. <u>Video.</u> Our Account Executives should have a basic working knowledge of video production, including front projection, rear projection, image mag, projectors, and video lighting.

4. <u>Staging.</u> Our Account Executives should understand staging in terms of the size needed for a given event, the sizes available from subcontractors, and the need for skirting, steps, and railing.

5. <u>Power.</u> Our Account Executives need to understand single-phase and three-phase power, need to be able to understand situations in which generators are required, and should be able to determine proper placement of generators.

B. The Event Process

Our Account Executives should exhibit a big-picture understanding of the event process and where our company fits into it on any given event. In looking at the big picture, we must consider the client's objective in holding the event and what we can do to help achieve it. We must work closely with other vendors and our subcontractors to be focused on the client's objectives. We need to be cooperative and helpful in scheduling, from load in, through installation, to load out.

C. Market

Our Account Executives must exhibit an understanding of the event and entertainment markets within the geographic region in which they work. This includes an in depth knowledge of:

1. Special event planners/producers
2. Meeting planners
3. Corporations headquartered there
4. Facilities and their key personnel
5. Public events within the area
6. Municipality events people
7. Convention and visitors bureau
8. Convention centers
9. Other special event suppliers
10. Industry organizations (e.g., ISES)
11. Competitors and their respective sales pitches
12. Lighting designers
13. Concert/festival promoters (promoter's reps)

Our Account Executives must also keep up with the local news from newspapers, magazines, business journals, etc., and make themselves aware of local and regional news (groundbreakings, promotions, etc.) that should be followed up for new business.

D. Sales Techniques

Our Account Executives should understand the basic concepts of selling, including getting your foot in the door, listening to the client to understand their perceived needs, overcoming objections, pricing, value, and closing a sale. The Company will support Account Executives interested in attending sales courses. They are expected to develop their own careers as well, through reading relevant articles, books, and networking wherever possible. The Company will support Account Executive's memberships in appropriate networking organizations. In return, the Account Executives are expected to actively work the organization, spending time within it, developing contacts, and making a name as a serious, creative, valuable individual.

E. Computer

The computer is our primary tool for written communications of all types. It is important to have a working knowledge of the computer operation, an understanding of our networks, our e-mail system, and the manner in which we use templates and in which we save different types of files.

1. <u>Microsoft Word.</u> The word processing program in which we write all proposals, correspondence, and memos.
2. <u>Job costing on Microsoft Excel.</u> Our spreadsheet program in which we prepare a job costing for each event.
3. <u>Access.</u> The database in which we prepare purchase orders and manage our marketing leads.
4. <u>PowerPoint.</u> Our presentation software.

F. Grammar and Letter Writing

All Account Executives are expected to have the ability to write proposals and correspondence in a grammatically correct and correctly spelled form. The use of spell check and grammar check in Microsoft Word is mandatory. Remember that we are judged on every communication we send out.

III. SALES CALLS

Account Executives should spend much of their time on sales calls. It is important to set up meetings as far in advance as possible, and to confirm them the day before or morning of. Some sales calls serve as an opportunity to introduce our company to a potential new client. This will be the first real impression that this person/company will have of the Company. On such sales calls, Account Executives should:

A. Always be on time, but if late due to circumstances beyond your control, you must call ahead and advise of the tardiness. Ask if the meeting is still convenient or whether it should be rescheduled. Upon your arrival, apologize for being late and thank your contact for holding the appointment.
B. Be prepared. Do homework on the person and company on whom you are calling (e.g., web site and Internet research), and prepare to listen to his or her needs and know what questions you would like to ask after listening. Asking questions about the individual and company projects your interest in him or her. Discussing a person's employment history can lead to additional conversations.
C. Once you have obtained from the client all of the information you need, give your pitch based on how our capabilities can service their needs.
D. Make sure that there is an action plan before leaving, either a follow-up telephone call, a second meeting, a proposal, etc. Make sure that you and the client are both clear on any deadlines.
E. Make sure you take business cards and appropriate Company promotional materials.
F. Take Company photo albums, photo CDs and portfolios as part of your presentation to show clients examples of our work.
G. Be prepared with reference letters.

H. Do not promise anything to a client you cannot deliver. Do not break the cardinal rule of Sales: "Never overpromise and/or underdeliver." Do not promise proposals too quickly.

I. Do not chew gum or smoke during a meeting.

J. Prior to the conclusion of your meeting, establish a meeting to discuss promotional material.

On second sales calls or on follow-up calls for specific events, be prepared to discuss whatever the client has as an agenda. Much of the above applies.

Once an individual or corporation becomes a client, our work is not done. Each Account Executive should have a call schedule for existing clients. It is important to maintain our client relationships by staying in touch. Each Account Executive needs to have a sense of how each client needs to be related to. Some need to be seen in person weekly, others monthly, or even quarterly. Telephone calls between visits should be scheduled as well. As each client is added, it should be placed on the Account Executive's call schedule. Sales management should be able to obtain a copy of any Account Executive's call schedule upon request.

If an Account Executive lands a meeting with a client that may be too advanced for them or a client that would be impressed if management were part of the sales call, he or she should ask the Vice President of Business Development to team-sell on that call. It is a sign of strength to attend meetings with multiple Account Executives and/or production team members. Fortune 500 companies make a practice of team selling. President and Vice President of Business Development are happy to comply and indeed expect such requests.

At some point, the Account Executive has to ask for the business. It is a critical step. **Do not omit it.**

IV. WORKING WITH MARKETING

Account Executives should work with their local Administrative Assistant (AA) to send marketing packages out to prospects. AA will simultaneously make record of the prospect in the local database.

Giving the Company the edge: When Account Executives are in a bid situation or when working on a large project, marketing tools such as plots, renderings, photo CDs, PowerPoint presentations, and proposals printed on marketing material should be used to delineate differences between the Company and the competition to the client. Since some of these tools require expenditures by the Company, said costs should be included in costing.

V. CLIENT SERVICE

A. Return of Telephone Calls

Account Executives should be diligent in returning calls in a timely fashion. This is a key element of customer service. If we do not return their calls, they will find someone who will. We must make it as easy as possible for clients to get to us. Clients should have our pager numbers and cellular telephone numbers. If you give clients your cell phone numbers, establish protocol with them. Explain that there will be times when you are in meetings and you cannot respond, but that you will call back as soon as possible.

B. Timely Paperwork

Paperwork should be delivered when promised. This is particularly important when it comes to proposals. If we are in a bidding situation, being late probably means automatic elimination of our bid automatically and losing the business.

C. Voice-Mail Messages

Record either a generic message with all your contact information or a custom voice-mail message, and make sure you keep it up-to-date. You should be checking your voice mail several times per day, returning calls and forwarding messages that are more relevant to other associates. If you go out of town or on vacation, you must put a message to that effect on your voice mail, with a return date and with an alternative number for callers who are unable to wait until you return. It is important that your voice-mail message includes your cellular telephone number.

D. Keeping the Office Posted of Your Schedule

The administrative assistant in your respective location should be advised of each Account Executive's schedule. You should not leave the office without first advising him or her of where you are going and when you will be back. The administrative assistant will be advising clients of your return time based on what you told him or her. If you are running late, call in.

VI. PROPOSAL AND JOB COSTING PROCEDURE

A. Our proposals should be uniform in containing relevant information for internal purposes and to make them appropriate for our clients.

B. Upon receipt by an Account Executive of the prospective event from a client, the Account Executive should determine the date and place of the event. This information should be entered into the revenue track at once, a job number should be assigned, and the sales and production folders set up.

Upon completion of the job costing and proposal, as described below, revenue track should be completed, with information on scope of services, pricing, subcontractors, and days of use of equipment.

If proposals are later amended, all changes should be reflected in revenue track as well. Revenue track *must* be accurate and remain accurate, as it is used by Accounting as a cash forecasting tool.

The status of every event should be updated immediately upon receipt of information, from "pending" to either "confirmed" or "canceled."

C. The proposal should include:
    1. Date of the proposal.
    2. Proper form of address of the client, including billing address if different.
    3. The job number.
    4. The date, time, and location (city and state) of the event.
    5. Description of the services we are providing.
    6. Complete Production Schedule detailing beginning and end times for Load In, Rehearsal, Programming, Focus, Sound Checks, Show Call, and Strike/Removal.
    7. Clearly stating when technicians will remain for the event.
    8. Setting forth the price for the services in the body of the proposal,and any options. Illustrating the Retail Value (top-line price) and the Discounted Price (actual price charged).
    9. Requesting a signed contract and deposit in a fixed amount based on the Company's payment policy as well as the new contract clause verbiage.
    10. Requesting the check box be initialed by client, indicating they have read and understand their union labor payment options (when applicable).
    11. Including the Terms and Conditions pages and requesting signing of it. Oftentimes a client's legal department will reject certain sections of our Terms and Conditions. Account Executives should feel free to consult with the Vice President of Business Development or CEO regarding these sections. Account Executives *must* receive approval from the Vice President of Sales or CEO prior to striking or amending *any* sections of Terms and Conditions.

D. Before a proposal is actually sent out to a client, the Account Executive must produce a costing for that job, which must be reviewed and authorized via signature by a Production Manager or General Manager. The production review of the costing is to ascertain that all costs of production are included (labor, rental gear, materials to be purchased, trucking, travel, etc.). The costing must be accurate. Discounts on jobs must occur on a percentage of the total job cost amount. This review is not to provide the final price given to the client, as pricing is only a Sales issue and remains in the Sales Department. The General Manager should be involved in pricing of any multiple-discipline events. Any disagreements over costing parameters will be settled by the National Production Manager. General Manager has right of final approval of costings and may request the opportunity to compare costings to contracts prior to submission to clients. General Managers are authorized to provide input with regard to pricing and thus may approve discounts below 20 percent net profit if they deem it necessary. Any disagreements between Account Executive and General Manager regarding pricing should be referred to Vice President of Sales for final arbitration.

If an Account Executive anticipates the desirability of photography of an event, the cost should, where possible, be included in the costing. If the photography takes place, the appropriate forms (Request for Photography and Purchase Order) must be completed according to procedure prior to confirming Photographer (see vendor agreement procedure).

E. Price to be charged is determined by the profit percentage on the costing. We prefer to price at the top-line price. Sometimes, in a competitive situation, we will have to deviate from this. If there is any doubt about the appropriateness of a price, the Account Executive should check with the General Manager before issuing a price in a proposal. If the Account Executive desires to price an event at below 20 percent profit, the Account Executive **must** get approval of the General Manager or Vice President of Business Development.

F. There are times when we can price lower than normal. During slow times, if there is a strategic reason, if it is an important client, or for other good reasons, pricing may be flexible, but the Account Executive must be able to vocalize the rationale and must get written approval of the General Manager or Vice President of Sales.

G. We should always make a special note of power charges, union labor, facility charges, and other such costs that may come up as part of a production, making it clear whether they are included within our proposal or not.

H. If the client requires changes to the original proposal or contract, the costing must be reevaluated and redone. If necessary, a revised proposal needs to be generated and a Production Manager's approval received prior to submitting revised proposal to client.

If the client requests significant changes be made to scope of work on-site after the contract has been executed, AE must secure the signature of client on a change order form that clearly states the changes and the associated costs. AE must also secure the verbal commitment of appropriate Production Manager or General Manager prior to committing to Company's ability to produce the requested changes.

I. We must communicate whether the Account Executive is going to be there for installation, staying until the start of the event, remaining through the event, etc. This will eliminate confusion on the job site.

J. We cannot issue deposits to subcontractors unless we receive a deposit from the client. It is important to get as big a deposit as possible from the client prior to the event. If there are doubts about the client or if the client is a first-time client, we must receive payment in full in advance. Terms other than our existing payment policy for existing clientele must be approved by General Manager. Terms for new clients may be approved only by Vice President of Finance, Vice President of Sales, or the CEO.

K. The Company's payment policy is 50 percent deposit prior to the event and the balance payable on the day of event. For new clients, send the client profile with the initial proposal to avoid unnecessary delays in booking the event. Upon receipt of the completed client profile, the Accounting Department will research bank and trade references. The Accounting Department will make a decision on the creditworthiness of the client. The respective Account Executive will be notified of the findings. All invoices relating to new clients will be cross-referenced to the client profile file. Accounting will not process an invoice for a new client without the profile.

L. Once the proposal is sent, the Administrative Assistant should place a follow-up call to determine whether the client received it and whether they have any questions. Proposals may be faxed for speed, but originals must be sent unless otherwise advised by the client.

M. Proposal revisions must be done in writing, with copies going to production, in order to keep everyone current on what is actually being produced. The client must sign these revisions. **This is a crucial step.** Revisions *must* be numbered (Revision I, Revision II, etc.).

VII. JOB FILE PAPERWORK

A. To open a job file, an Account Executive must assign a job number to the event. It should be entered into the revenue track and job calendar form in Outlook on the appropriate date. Then an Account Executive should e-mail the job number, date, client name, and venue in order for the Administrative Assistant to create a folder for both Sales and Production.

The Administrative Assistant will create labels for the sales folder, the production folder, and the production calendar. The label will contain the date of the job, the job number, the client name, and the event site.

B. Every job must have an updated and complete Job Information Form submission that details venue address, dress for technicians, and other such details, which must be completed in full for the sales-production meetings on this event.

All client correspondence should be in the sales file.

C. Copies of any layouts, renderings, production schedules, etc., must be in both files.

D. Any contracts with subcontractors must be in both files.

Memos of discussions with the client, facility, or other vendors must be in the sales file, with relevant information highlighted.

E. Copies of deposit checks and signed contracts must be in the sales file.

Meeting notes must be included and reviewed to make sure all details are covered.

F. Original sales folder must remain in the office at all times. Copies should be made for documents required on the job site or at meetings.

VIII. VENDOR AGREEMENT

Account Executives are authorized to seek the services of only those companies that provide services that the Company does not list as its core competencies (video, pyro, etc.). Any time an AE is required to hire a subcontractor, the following procedure should be followed: Upon initial contact with any vendor(s), the Account Executive must provide vendor(s) with a purchase order (PO) number for referencing and billing purposes. Once the AE has settled upon a vendor to provide the necessary services, AE must submit the completed PO and proposal/contract from vendor to General Manager (GM) for approval. AEs may *not,* under any circumstances enter any agreements, verbal or otherwise, on behalf of Company. After GM approval, AE should submit GM-executed contract, PO, and vendor agreement to vendor. The vendor must sign a vendor agreement before the Company's services are implemented. The vendor agreement addresses all Company policies and procedures governing subcontractors and serves as a noncompete contract.

IX. PRESENCE ON EVENT SITES

It is the responsibility of Account Executives to know the degree to which the client depends on their presence on the job site. The Account Executive should communicate with the Production Manager and/or General Manager regarding when he or she will be present. The following factors should be considered in a determination of whether, when, or for how long an Account Executive should be on the event site:

A. Complexity of the event
B. Involvement of the Account Executive in the entire event process
C. Degree to which the client depends on the Account Executive
D. Degree to which production depends on the Account Executive for design, production, or client assistance
E. Networking opportunities that exist on the job site
F. Relative importance of the event and/or the client to the Company (e.g., political events *require* AE attendance)
G. Relationship we have with the facility in which the event is taking place
H. Whether we have hired subcontractors, and what our level of trust is with them
I. Presence of a Production Manager

If the Account Executive has multiple events on the same date, assistance in covering them must be requested of the General Manager. If the Account Executive has a previously scheduled personal day on the date of an event, the client should be notified and coverage arranged. If the Account Executive requests a personal day on the date of a previously scheduled event, the granting of that personal day is at the total discretion of the General Manager. The busiest months, such as April, May, June, September, and October, are normally full of our largest events, and the Account Executives should attempt to schedule their vacations and other personal business at slower times whenever possible.

X. EVENT SITE RULES

If the Account Executive is on the event site, that person will be responsible for all communication with the client. Should the need arise for technical discussions with the client, the Account Executive shall involve the appropriate production personnel in the discussion. Discussions about pricing, feasibility of creating certain effects, and anything that might be deemed to be an internal Company discussion must be held out of the presence of the client.

If the Account Executive is not present on the event site, the highest-ranking Company production person shall have the sole responsibility and authority for discussions with the client. Pricing must not be discussed. If questions arise that require the Account Executive's involvement, the appropriate Account Executive must be contacted immediately.

Company personnel, when on an event site, are representatives of the Company. The impression they make is the main impression that the client will have of our Company. As stated previously, we should always dress in a clean, neat manner, in a Company or appropriate shirt. We should always be polite and respectful to the client. Account Executives should always be aware that the client might have representatives on the site that you do not know and will not recognize, and, accordingly, you should never speak about the client or others involved in the event in a disparaging manner. Be smart about what you talk about on an event site. **Profanity on the event site is strictly prohibited.**

Always assume that we want to try to service all of the client's needs, but first we must be sure to complete those services for which the client has contracted. We can worry about additions, time permitting. Be as flexible as possible with changes that come up on an event site. Flexibility is one of the things that separate the Company from its competitors. Any additions or changes should be set forth in writing on a change order form with the client signing where indicated.

We want to convey that we take pride in our work and being a part of the Company team; in working with the client and being a part of what the client is producing.

A. Smoking

There should be *no* smoking on the event sites unless cleared with the facility or clients. If smoking is permitted, it should be done in the designated areas only and out of the presence of clients.

B. Facility Rules

All facility rules should be followed at all times while on the property.

C. Property Damage

All effort should be made to avoid any damage to the event facilities. Any damage inadvertently caused should be reported to the supervisor on-site. The supervisor shall use the disposable camera maintained in each company vehicle to photograph the damage and attach the developed pictures to the incident report and forward it all to Human Resources.

D. Event Site Injuries

If any injury occurs to any associate on the event site, the supervisor shall use the first-aid materials and procedures set forth in the packet in each of the company vehicles. Then the supervisor would follow the Accident Notification procedure outlined in this handbook.

If any injury occurs to a bystander on the event site, first aid should be immediately applied. The supervisor should be immediately informed and shall get full information from the individual (name, address, telephone number, etc.), then complete an accident report as outlined in the Accident Notification section and immediately submit it to HR.

E. Parking Tickets

The Company will pay an associate's parking tickets for expired meters or being parked in a space beyond the legally allowed hours.

The Company will not pay parking tickets for parking in a No Parking or loading zone. The Company will not pay for any moving violations.

XI. SALES REPORTS

Each Account Executive has the responsibility of documenting his or her activities in e-mail form on a weekly basis. The purpose of sales reports is to allow the General Manager and Vice President of Sales understand how the Account Executives are spending their time so as to offer them guidance on the appropriate directions to follow; to monitor progress with regard to monthly quotas and quarterly goals; to assist with potential clients contacted; and in other ways to act in an advisory capacity. A further purpose is to ascertain how the Account Executive's activities relate to the goals of the sales department and the Account Executive's individual goals.

The reports should be done day by day, and it is recommended that Account Executives make entries as they go along rather than trying to reconstruct an entire week at the end of the week. The entries should document telephone calls, both incoming and outgoing, with the substance of the call noted; meetings, indicating who was present and what was discussed; sales calls; proposals worked on; correspondence sent; and marketing packages sent. Those activities that directly correspond to the quarterly sales plan should be in bold type.

Account Executives will generate a monthly report (job profitability report) to their General Manager, indicating job date, job number, client, location, status (pending, confirmed, canceled), proposed fee total, confirmed fee total,

total job cost of each job, total subcontractors, payment status (50 percent, 100 percent, etc.) net profit percentage, net profit amount for each job in that month, running total at bottom of form, and the Account Executive's monthly quota. Net Profits to be defined as those dollar amounts that are in excess of total job cost.

Account Executives should submit these reports to their General Manager by e-mail on a weekly basis.

XII. PRODUCTION-SALES MEETINGS

Account Executives have the responsibility to be present and prepared for a weekly sales-production meeting. **These meetings are mandatory.** Whatever day and time of the week is designated and agreed upon by sales and production shall be kept available each week for this meeting. At the meeting, the Account Executive must prepared to discuss events from the previous week. Also discussed will be events for the upcoming three weeks. The Account Executive will have all or as much paperwork as possible prepared for production. It is the responsibility of the Account Executive to maintain the appropriate paperwork and get it to the Production Manager(s) in a timely manner. The Account Executive must recognize the need of production to have the paperwork for scheduling of labor and equipment as soon as possible. Attendees will include all Account Executives, Production Managers, and the General Manager.

XIII. SALES QUOTAS

As part of the budgeting process and for the purpose of commission payments, each Account Executive will be given a monthly sales quota. These quotas are an integral part of the budgeting process and thus *must* be taken very seriously.

Monthly quotas will replace the former base sales figure as a salary justification and will truly be the infrastructure upon which all sales compensation will be based. The following procedures and policies have been constructed to ensure that monthly quotas are achieved.

Account Executives must meet their Monthly Quota (within a 10 percent margin) in a given month or the following actions will be taken:

First Month
Meeting held between Account Executive, responsible GM, and Vice President of Sales in order to identify why quota was not achieved, formulation of plan to ensure that this does not happen again, and reminder of steps to be taken if a monthly quota is missed again.

Second Consecutive Month

Account Executive put on probation, meeting held between Account Executive, responsible GM, and Vice President of Sales to readdress why quota was again not achieved, formulation of plan to ensure that this does not happen again, and reminder of steps to be taken if a third monthly quota is missed. Need for meeting made part of Account Executive's personnel record and taken into consideration during salary review.

Second Nonconsecutive Month

Meeting held between Account Executive, responsible GM, and Vice President of Sales to readdress why quota was again not achieved, formulation of plan to ensure that this does not happen again, and reminder of steps to be taken if a third monthly quota is missed. Need for meeting made part of Account Executive's personnel record and taken into consideration during salary review.

Third Month (Consecutive or Nonconsecutive)

Missed monthly quota by Account Executive for a third month may result in immediate dismissal or reduction in salary. This decision to be made at the sole discretion of the Vice President of Sales or President of the Company.

The abovementioned stringent measures are necessary to ensure that each Account Executive achieves the compensation level he or she anticipates and that we as a company do not experience any significant cash flow shortfalls.

XIV.   COMMISSIONS

Each Account Executive will have a yearly sales base figure that will consist of 12 monthly quotas, which he or she must achieve to justify his or her salary. Upon achieving the monthly quota, each month, the Account Executive may be awarded 5 percent commission of the net profits from the Account Executive's jobs in that particular month, based upon certain criteria. The following illustrates the steps taken to determine what, if any, commission will be paid to the Account Executive:

Step 1. At the end of each month, gross revenue and net profit are totaled, verified by GM, submitted to Vice President of Sales for authorization, and then submitted to Accounting.

Step 2. Potential commission is calculated by Accounting, based upon criteria listed below.

Step 3. Accounting to review receivables compared to potential commissions and make payments to Account Executive via payroll, as appropriate. This step to be repeated on a weekly basis, up until 90 days after a given month.

A. Commission Calculations

Commission calculated on a monthly basis as 5 percent multiplied by the net profit (amounts beyond total job cost and equipment charge) of each job sold by the Account Executive in that month. Account Executives are eligible for full 5 percent commission in given month *only* if they have hit their monthly quota.

If Account Executives do *not* hit their monthly quota, then the commission rate will be reduced as follows:

- If the Account Executive's gross revenue is within 5 percent of his or her monthly quota, commission is reduced to 4 percent.
- If the Account Executive's gross revenue is within 10 percent of his or her monthly quota, commission is reduced to 2 percent.
- Anything less than 10 percent would make the Account Executive ineligible for commission from that month.

If the Account Executive is within the 10 percent margin, but that gross revenue that is allowing him or her to be within that margin is not paid within 90 days, Account Executive becomes ineligible for any commissions for that month.

B. Subcontractors

The following scenarios shall serve to clarify any questions regarding the use of subcontractors and how they relate to quotas and commissions.

1. If a subcontractor is outside of Company's core competencies of lighting equipment, audio equipment, and labor, then its cost is *not* includable in gross revenue quotas or commissionable sales.
2. If the subcontractor is within our core competencies and we are booked and cannot produce the job in-house, or if it is cost-prohibitive for us to handle a particular job in-house, the cost of the subcontractor *is* includable in gross revenue quotas and commissionable sales.
3. If the subcontract is for union labor, our first step is to attempt to get the client to pick up the cost directly. A section of form language in our proposals will address this issue and will require initialing by the client, indicating they understand they have considered paying union labor direct. If the client pays the union subcontract directly, it will not enter into quota or commissionable sales calculations at all.

4. IF the subcontract is for union labor and the client does *not* want to handle it directly, then it will become part of our contract and *is* includable in gross revenue quota and commissionable sales numbers. A union labor estimate is to be provided in the proposal, as a separate line item, as language shall be included in the proposal that will allow us to back-bill for *any* union overages. Our line item estimate should include the cost of payrolling unions, plus our markup on that cost.

C. Payment of Commissions

Vice President of Finance will review all calculations, track late payments, make appropriate adjustments as stated above, and then pay commissions to Account Executives via payroll—again, depending upon when actual monies are collected. Account Executives will receive a commission statement with each paycheck, reviewing their earned and paid commissions on an ongoing basis.

D. Receivables

While commissions will be calculated and paid on an ongoing basis, they will not be paid until payment is received in full from client. Any receivable outstanding over 60 days will result in commission for that particular job being reduced by 50 percent. Any receivable over 90 days will result in the particular job becoming noncommissionable, and no commission payments will be made to the Account Executive for that job. Again, if a particular job is the only revenue causing an Account Executive to come within 10 percent of his or her monthly quota and that revenue is not paid within 90 days, the entire month will be deemed noncommissionable.

With regard to payment terms, as mentioned later in this handbook, the extension of terms beyond our usual policy (50 percent down, balance on-site) may be approved only at the GM level or higher.

XV. REIMBURSEMENT OF EXPENSES

Account Executives are reimbursed for out-of-pocket, work-related expenses. Associate Expense Reports are available from the administrative assistant in each facility. All expense reports submitted to the Company for reimbursement must include appropriate receipts and documentation. No reimbursable expenses will be paid unless the original receipt is attached.

All expense items must have a job name and job number. Please record "NJR" (not job related) in the job name column for expenses not related to a specific job. Include a complete expense description to ensure proper financial statement classification. If reimbursement is sought for meal expense, a copy of the restaurant receipt should accompany the credit card receipt. The face of the receipts must state the client's name, the name of the persons who were present at the meal, and the purpose of the expense. The restaurant bills must provide a breakdown of food and beverage items. Alcohol is not a reimbursable expense.

The Company reimburses associates $.30 per mile to cover the cost of fuel and vehicle wear and tear. The mileage log submitted to the Company must include the date the vehicle was driven, the place of departure, the destination, and total business miles. For all other expenses, a receipt from the business establishment is sufficient. The Company reimburses only those miles in excess of commuter miles. *Commuter miles* are defined as those miles to and from the Company's facilities. If an associate travels to a job directly from his or her residence, then the number of business miles is computed as total miles driven less commuter miles.

The Company does not pay or reimburse associates for the following expense:

- In-room movies.
- Room service. Room Service may be submitted only *after* subtracting the 18 percent hotel charge and the tip. Only the cost of the meal may be submitted.
- Hotel services (valet, dry cleaning, etc.).
- Long-distance telephone calls.

These costs are the responsibility of the associate and must be paid by the associates from their personal funds. The Company does not pay for or reimburse associates for telephone calls on airplanes and/or phone service on trains.

XVI. ACCOUNT EXECUTIVE'S PERFORMANCE EVALUATIONS

Supervisors and associates are strongly encouraged to dis-cuss job performance and goals on an informal, day-to-day basis. Additional formal performance evaluations are conducted on an annual basis to provide both supervisors and associates with the opportunity to discuss job tasks, identify and correct weaknesses, encourage and recognize strengths, and discuss positive, purposeful approaches for meeting goals. The Account Executive will be asked to sign the evaluation form and will be given a copy for his or her own files. The company copy will go into the Account.

XVII. TRAVEL PROCEDURES

Account Executives are to use their own personal vehicles for all local travel. A rental vehicle shall be obtained when it becomes more cost-effective to the Company than the mileage reimbursement would be. Normally, a rental vehicle can be obtained for under $40 per day with no additional mileage charge. Thus, on any trip in excess of 150 miles per day, it is more cost-effective to use a rental vehicle.

When traveling by air on company business, Account Executives must book coach tickets, and must look for the best available price within the time constraints available. The boarding pass and/or other supporting documentation serve as a receipt. An Account Executive may obviously use frequent-flier miles to upgrade on his or her own. If a client is buying the tickets directly, an Account Executive may fly in whatever class the client pays for.

All taxi expenses should be submitted via receipt. When on the road, Account Executives are expected to keep reimbursable meal expense within $35 per day, not including alcohol, which is not reimbursable. Account Executives may opt for a $35 per diem in lieu of submitting their expenses. If the Account Executive wishes to receive per diem or float money for expenses, a Petty cash/Per diem form must be filled out properly with the General Manager's approval. However, Associate will receive a 1099 for all per diems received in a calendar year unless balance of unused per diem is returned and accompanied by receipts for all legitimate expenses (not including alcohol, cigarettes, etc.).

All out-of-town travel *must* be approved in writing by General Manager prior to purchasing any travel arrangements (airline tickets, rail tickets, etc.). Request-for-travel forms must be filled out by the Account Executive and approved by the General Manager.

XVIII.   INVOICING PROCEDURE

At the conclusion of an event, the Account Executive should ascertain from our production staff and our client how the event went, whether there were additions, whether any adjustments need to be made for problems, and so on. Thereafter, the file should be submitted to Accounting for invoicing. The file should contain all the information that follows (for both productions *and* rentals):

- Company/Client name
- Contact person
- Shipping *and* billing addresses, if different
- Phone number
- Fax number
- Job number
- Date(s) of event/rental

- Description of items rented/provided
- Quantity, selling price, and extended amounts
- Copy of purchase order if client requires one to process payment
- Proper terms for payment (e.g., Net Due, Net 10, Net 30)

The information on contract must be accurately reflected on the revenue track. If any discrepancies exist or any of the information listed above is missing, the contract *will not* be processed for invoicing but returned to the Account Executive or Rental Manager to make the necessary corrections. Once all information is verified as accurate, an invoice will be produced from the accounting system. Once produced, it will be sent to the Account Executive or Rental Manager for a signature/initials, approving the amount and billing information. Only after this is returned to Accounting approved will an original invoice be mailed to the client. If discrepancies are found on the invoice, such as an unapplied deposit or payment, the Account Executive must forward the invoice with a copy of the missed payment(s) in order for a new invoice to be produced.

XIX. COLLECTIONS

Account Executives or Rental Managers have 30 days to obtain payment before collection efforts are taken over by the Accounting Department. The 30-day period begins from the date of the invoice, which is equivalent to the date of the event or rental. For example, a production invoice dated March 1, 2003, will be for an event that occurred (or ended if event was more than one day) on March 1, 2003. The Account Executive has until March 31, 2003, to collect payment before Accounting will begin the collection process. Even if a finalized invoice is not sent out until March 10, 2003, this does not affect the 30-day period, since the signed contract price was to be collected on the date of the job. Any discrepancies which need to be corrected cut into the time the Account Executive has to collect the outstanding balance before the client is charged interest and the Account Executive's commission is reduced. For those clients that have preapproved terms, the AE will have 30 days from the day the final balance was actually due. For example, if the final balance for the March 1, 2003, event date listed above was actually due on March 31, 2003, the AE would have until April 30, 2003, to collect the balance.

Any client who is listed on the aged receivables report is immediately put on cash-on-delivery (COD) status until the account is paid in full.

With regard to payment terms, the extension of terms beyond our usual policy (50 percent down, balance on-site) may be approved only at the GM level or higher.

XX. CELLULAR PHONE

The Company offers a digital cellular phone arrangement that may be taken advantage of by the Account Executive. The Company purchases and retains ownership of the phone, as well as paying the monthly fee, less $16.15, which will be deducted from the associate's paycheck, and which covers personal use of the telephone. If the Account Executive loses or damages the telphone, he or she is liable for the replacement cost.

XXI. PHOTO ALBUMS AND PHOTO CDs

The Company will provide photo albums and photo CDs for use by the Account Executive as a marketing and selling tool. Each album represents a substantial investment by the Company. The Account Executive is responsible for maintaining them in good condition.

XXII. PROFESSIONALISM AND ACCOUNTABILITY

Each Account Executive is accountable for his or her own behavior. Account Executives should remember that they represent the Company, and as company representatives should not act in any manner detrimental to the Company.

Account Executives will be held accountable for careless errors that lead to losses for the Company.

XXIII. OFFICE HOURS/ATTENDANCE

The Company's facilities are open from 9:00 A.M. to 5:30 P.M. Monday through Friday unless otherwise noted.

Regular attendance is essential for the success of the Company, because each associate plays a specific and important role in the operation of the Company. Excessive absenteeism on the part of any associate hinders the Company's operations. Accordingly, all associates are required to make every effort to report to work regularly. Obviously, appointments and events will keep the Account Executive out of the office for a significant amount of time.

If you are unable to report to work due to illness or for another reason beyond your control, you must notify your General Manager prior to the beginning of the workday. Failure to do so may result in disciplinary action.

Repeated absenteeism or tardiness, whether you notify the Company that you expect to be absent or not, may result in disciplinary action up to and including discharge without prior notice.

XXIV. PURCHASE ORDERS

Account Executives must generate purchase orders for all their subcontractors. As soon as Account Executives negotiate a price with a subcontractor, they should complete a purchase order and seek out the General Manager for approval, in writing. Purchase orders *must* be complete with the job number, cost code, and be approved *prior* to entering into *any* agreements (verbal or otherwise) with subcontractors. Approved POs can then be submitted to the subcontractor, and the General Manager should forward them to Accounts Payable. *Only* **General Managers, the National Production Manager, the Vice President of Sales, or the CEO are empowered to sign any agreements or contracts on behalf of the Company.** Account Executives are *not* under *any* circumstances permitted to sign agreements or contracts. Any agreements or contracts of subcontractors that require a payment in advance, whether a deposit or payment in full, must have a deposit collected from our client before such payment is made.

XXV. RECEIVING CHECKS ON THE JOB SITE

The Company should be receiving checks on the job site, as we do request final payment the day of the event. If the Account Executive cannot be present on the job site, he or she must instruct the production supervisor of the job to receive the check. Whoever receives the check should follow these guidelines:

- Make sure the check is made out directly to Current Events and that the check is signed.
- The check must be made out for the proper amount. If the production supervisor is to receive the check, he or she must be made aware by the Account Executive of the correct amount.
- The check must be dated the same day as the event. Do not accept any postdated checks (checks dated in the future).
- The check should not have "payment in full," "full payment," or any statement to that effect written on it. This can be individualized on a job-to-job basis. If there are no additions to the job, the check is acceptable as is. Any additions to a job are determined when the respective Account Executive reviews the job the following business day.

It will be up to the discretion of the Account Executive, if he or she is on the job site, regarding what to do if there is a problem with the check. If the production supervisor has a problem, he or she should contact the Account Executive or Vice President of Sales regarding the matter to find out how to proceed.

ACKNOWLEDGMENT

These policies may be supplemented, amended, or eliminated, in whole or in part, from time to time at the discretion of the Company.

I acknowledge that I have received, read, and understood ABC Productions' *Sales Procedures Manual* effective September 1, 2003. I further understand that it does not constitute a contract of employment, and that the Company may alter, amend, or depart from any of the policies or procedures contained therein at any time at its sole discretion.

_____

Name (Print)

_____

Signature

_____

Date

References

Engel, Peter H. *What's Your Exit Strategy: 7 Ways to Maximize the Value of the Business You've Built.* Roseville, CA. Prima Publishing, 1999.

Gerber, Michael E. *The E Myth: Why Most Small Businesses Don't Work and What to Do About It.* New York: HarperBusiness, 1986.

Hamel, Gary, and C. K. Pralahad. *Competing for the Future.* Boston: Harvard Business School Press, 1994.

Kriegel, Robert, and David Brandt. *Sacred Cows Make the Best Burgers.* New York: Warner Books, 1996.

Pine, B. Joseph II, and James H. Gilmore. *The Experience Economy: Work Is Theater & Every Business a Stage.* Boston: Harvard Business School Press, 1999.

Wolf, Michael J. *The Entertainment Economy: How Mega-media Forces Are Transforming Our Lives.* New York: Times Books, 1999.

Zemke, Ron, and Dick Schaaf. *The Service Edge.* New York: New American Library, 1989.

Index

About the Author

David Sorin is an attorney, businessman, and consultant to companies in the special events industry. He has been in the special events industry for more than 15 years, most recently as president of Current Events International, a lighting, audio, and technical production company.

Sorin has been involved in number of major projects, among them the 1993 opening of the Pennsylvania Convention Center, 1996 Olympic Games, the 1992 and 1996 Clinton/Gore campaigns and inaugurals, and the 1996 Dole/Kemp campaign. He spearheaded his company's handling of more than 70 events for the 2000 Republican National Convention in Philadelphia and the technical production for the 2001 Bush/Cheney inauguration ceremony. Political and corporate events for clients have taken him to more than 25 states in the United States and to Canada, Europe, and the Middle East.

In 1994, Sorin completed a term as president of the International Special Events Society (ISES). He has served on the ISES Executive Committee, the Board of Governors, and as founding president of the Philadelphia Chapter of ISES. In 1993, he achieved the Certified Special Events Professional (CSEP) designation, one of the first 24 individuals to attain it.

Sorin has been an active speaker in the special events industry, previously speaking at The Special Event, The Event Solutions Expo, American Rental Association meetings, Industrial Fabric Association and Tent Rental Division meetings, ISES Conferences for Professional Development, and before numerous local associations in several cities. His speeches have covered diverse topics: "Turning Leads into Sales," "Creating a Marketing Plan for Your Business," "Direct Mail Marketing," "Special Events as a Marketing Tool," "Ethics in Special Events," "Running Your Events Business as a Business," "Working with Labor Unions," "What Makes a Site Event Friendly," in addition to lighting and technical areas. He has been a guest lecturer on various aspects of entrepreneurialism at the University of Pennsylvania's Wharton School. He has also taught review classes for the CSEP exam in the areas of risk management and law.

Before getting into special events, Sorin practiced law full time in Philadelphia from 1975 to 1984 and ran several small companies that he started. He and his wife Linda reside in Valley Forge, Pennsylvania. They have two children and four grandchildren.